Football Quiz Book

Nick Holt

Collins

Published in 2007 by HarperCollins*Publishers*

HarperCollins*Publishers*
77-85 Fulham Palace Road
London
W6 8JB

www.collins.co.uk

© 2007 HarperCollins

Reprint 10 9 8 7 6 5 4 3 2 1

The Sun and *Sun* are registered trademarks of News Group Newspapers Ltd

ISBN-13 978-0-00-725975-5
ISBN-10 0-00-725975-1

A catalogue record for this book is available from the British Library.

Collins uses papers that are natural, renewable and recyclable products made from wood grown in sustainable forests. The manufacturing processes conform to the environmental regulations of the country of origin.

Created by SP Creative Design
Edited by Michael Munro
Designer Rolando Ugolini

Typeset by MATS Typesetters, Southend-on-Sea, Essex
Printed and bound in Great Britain by Clays Ltd, St Ives plc.

Contents

Introduction

The Sun Football Quiz Book is easy to use. We have divided the book into sections according to preference or area of knowledge, or, for those who like a more general approach, there is a large Mixed Bag section with questions across assorted topics.

Most of the sections are set out in an identical manner; ten straightforward questions with a single answer, followed by five two-part or harder questions for 2 points each. Thus each quiz can be marked out of 20.

The True or False quizzes have – obviously! – a simple answer. If you want these to be more interesting, ask for some detail on why they have given the answer True or False and allocate marks for accurate detail.

The Name the Team quizzes are a tough test. After each question target figures are given in brackets: we recommend that 1, 2 or 3 marks be allocated if those three target figures are reached. If eleven names are required, the first eleven names given should be taken as the answer. This avoids 'grape-shot' answers with forty names on a list.

Obviously the book can be used either with friends and family, or for organising a pub quiz – so go out there and astound everyone with your knowledge!

League

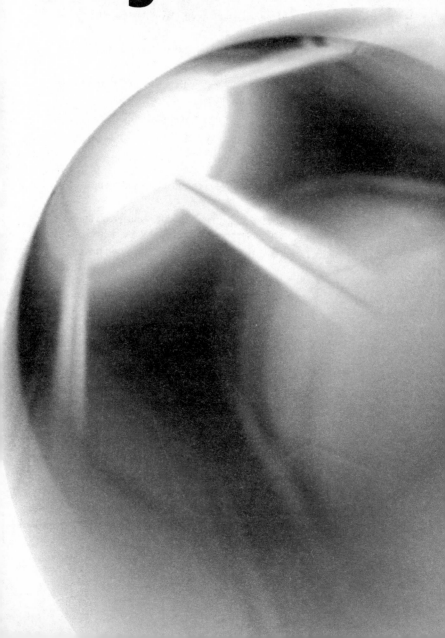

Questions 1-10, for 1 point each

1 In his younger days at Manchester United, David Beckham had a brief spell on loan at which Lancashire club?

2 Which team are known as 'The Cobblers', after the town's history of shoemaking?

3 Bobby Zamora scored 76 goals in 125 matches for which lower-division club before finding the Premiership a lot tougher?

4 Who returned to management after a 3-year gap in 2006 at QPR, but found it a bit of a struggle?

5 Which league club are known as 'The Iron'?

6 David Platt, Danny Murphy and Neil Lennon all started their careers with which club?

7 Jimmy Walker played over 400 games in goal for which club before leaving in 2004 to become reserve goalkeeper at West Ham?

8 Gary Mabbutt, Larry Lloyd and Nathan Ellington all started their careers with which club?

9 The purchase of which Stoke City forward for £1.7m in 2001 was Cardiff's biggest transfer outlay?

10 Who won the league in 1936-37 but were relegated the following season?

And some harder or two-part questions for 2 points

11 With which club did Osvaldo Ardiles win promotion as manager, and why did it end badly?

12 Where was Clinton Morrison in between his 2 spells at Crystal Palace? For which country has he played international football?

13 In which season were play-offs first used to decide promotion and relegation issues? (1 pt for a year either way)

14 In 1996, for which club did Peter Shilton make his 1000th appearance in a home fixture against Brighton? For which club did he make his first league appearance?

15 Which 2 sides have been champions of all 4 divisions of the league?

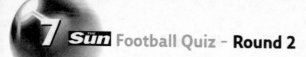

Questions 1-10, for 1 point each

1 With which club was Frank Lampard Snr a stalwart in the 1970s and early 80s?

2 Which goalkeeper retired in 1999, aged 42, after 15 years as first choice at Coventry City?

3 Whose move from Burnley to Sheffield United in January 2006 meant he was joining his 11th club (inc loans – 9th without)?

4 Which striker, scorer of over 100 goals for the club, returned to Millwall after a 2-year gap in January 2007?

5 1974-75 was a solitary season in the top division for which league club?

6 Which league side are known as 'The Bantams'?

7 Who regained league status in 2006 after a gap of 9 years?

8 Who did Leicester buy from Cambridge United for £1.5m in 2000, a record sale for the smaller club?

9 Manchester City won promotion to the Premiership in 2000 and 2002. Who was their top scorer in the league in both promotion seasons?

10 Who was the 4th tier's top scorer in 1987-88, as Wolves won the first of 2 successive promotions?

And some harder or two-part questions for 2 points

11 Name 2 of the Aston Villa midfield who all played every game in their 1981 title-winning season?

12 What nationality is Leicester City striker Iain Hume, and from which club did they buy him?

13 Which 2 players were joint top scorers for Blackburn when they were promoted via the play-offs in 1991-92?

14 The talent of young goalkeeper Peter Shilton allowed Leicester the luxury of cashing in which star in 1966? To which club did they sell him?

15 Who took over as manager of West Bromwich Albion during the 2006-07 season? Who did he replace?

8 The Sun Football Quiz – **Round 3**

Questions 1–10, for 1 point each

1 With which club did Alan Ball begin his career?

2 Which was Nat Lofthouse's only club?

3 Reading signed Leroy Lita in 2005 after he had a good season at which lower-division club?

4 Who replaced Mike Newell when he was sacked as Luton manager late in the 2006–07 season?

5 With which club do you associate Harry Cripps, Barry Kitchener and Eamon Dunphy?

6 Peter Beardsley, Matt Jansen and Rory Delap all started at which lower-division club?

7 Who took Hartlepool (as Hartlepools) into the 3rd tier for the first time in their history in 1967–68?

8 Who was manager of Notts County when they won promotion from the 4th tier by mid-March in 1998 and won the division by 17 points?

9 Which goalscorer moved from Newcastle to Arsenal for £330,000 in 1975?

10 Who scored 5 times in Middlesbrough's record league victory, 9–0 against Brighton in 1958?

And some harder or two-part questions for 2 points

11 Who were the 2 main goalkeepers in Don Revie's durable Leeds side of the late 1960s/early 70s?

12 Which 37-year-old rejoined his original club, Hull, in January 2007, 12 years after he left for Aberdeen? For which club did he score nearly 100 goals in all competitions?

13 In 1994–95, who finished 2nd in the 2nd tier but missed out on automatic promotion because the FA were reducing the number of clubs in the Premier League? Who beat them 4–3 in the play-off final?

14 In 2003–04, which Bournemouth striker scored the fastest hat-trick in league history? Who were on the receiving end of a 6–0 thrashing that day?

15 With which Midlands club did Robbie Keane make his first league appearance? And who brought him back after an unhappy year in Italy with Internazionale?

Answers on page 193

Questions 1-10, for 1 point each

1 Who was the gifted, if portly, Liverpool star of the 1980s who played for Denmark and was convicted for drink-driving?

2 What is Luton Town's nickname, a reflection of the town's history of millinery?

3 With which other Championship side was Billy Davies the manager before joining Derby County in summer 2006?

4 Which club went from the 4th tier to the 2nd in 2004-05 and 2005-06?

5 Who were relegated to the bottom tier in 1982, their 3rd successive relegation?

6 Which club are managed by their former striker Martin Foyle?

7 Which former England player's tenure as Walsall manager ended in 2006 as it had begun in 2004 – with a 5-0 defeat?

8 Which manager earned Grimsby Town promotion to the 2nd tier twice in the 1990s, in different spells at the club?

9 Which club received £2,250 for Lomana LuaLua when Newcastle bought him in 2000?

10 Who won the league in 1951 having only been promoted the previous season?

And some harder or two-part questions for 2 points

11 Which Queens Park Rangers striking partnership of the 1980s shared their surnames with a famous music-hall act?

12 Three players named Holt played in League One in 2006-07; 2 of them played for which club? What are their first names?

13 Who hold the record for the highest number of points won in a league season (106)? Whose record of 105 did they beat?

14 Dave Jones became manager of Premiership Southampton after a successful spell at which lower league club? Where was he manager in 2006-07?

15 Malky Mackay was promoted from the Championship with which 3 different sides in 2004, 2005 and 2006?

Questions 1-10, for 1 point each

1 Which was Tom Finney's only club?

2 Who played 808 games for Southampton over 18 seasons?

3 Who is the promising winger Wolves signed from non-league Grays Athletic during the 2006-07 season?

4 Which former Oldham Athletic player was appointed manager of the club in 2006?

5 Who scored 174 goals in 294 games for Tranmere Rovers, despite joining them when he was over 30?

6 Who spent their only spell as high as the 2nd tier of the league between 2000 and 2005?

7 England manager Steve McLaren made nearly 200 appearances for which league club between 1979 and 1985?

8 Who took over as manager of Macclesfield Town in December and improved results after a disastrous start to the season?

9 Who scored 41 league goals as Liverpool won promotion from Division 2 in 1961-62?

10 Who finished runners-up in the league in 1969-70, 1970-71 and 1971-72?

And some harder or two-part questions for 2 points

11 Name 2 of Alan Hansen's regular centre-half partners in his 13 years at Liverpool.

12 Which 2 strikers led the line in Millwall's 1988-89 season, which saw them achieve their highest-ever position of 10th in the top division?

13 From which club did Liverpool acquire the ruthless Graeme Souness? With which London club did his career start, but never take off?

14 Who notched up a record 9 consecutive clean sheets (all victories) when they beat Swindon 3-0 in March, 2007? From which club was their young goalkeeper Wayne Hennessy on loan?

15 Which striker failed to make it at Newcastle but was an instant hit at Cardiff in 2006-07? And where did he have a successful loan season in 2004-05?

Questions 1-10, for 1 point each

1 From which club did Leeds buy Johnny Giles, converting him from a winger into a midfield general?

2 Which Newcastle and, even more famously, Sunderland legend of the post-war years was known as 'The Clown Prince'?

3 Bradley Wright-Phillips followed brother Shaun down South to which 2nd-flight club in 2006?

4 Which club did Ronnie Moore manage from 1997 to 2004, taking them on a rare excursion into the 2nd tier of the league?

5 Which England international scored a hat-trick on his debut for Swansea as they beat Leeds 5-1 in their first game back in the top flight in 1981?

6 What was the old, more familiar name of Bournemouth's Fitness First Stadium?

7 Which divine-sounding forward had a nightmare in the Premiership with Everton, but was a consistent scorer in 2 spells at Stockport County?

8 Which former Welsh international took over as Wrexham manager in 1989 and stayed for 12 years?

9 Which international of the post-war years remains Middlesbrough's most-capped player for England?

10 Who was top scorer in the top flight in 1978-79, even though his Bolton side finished in the bottom 6?

And some harder or two-part questions for 2 points

11 Which 2 Liverpool stars won 8 league titles each in the 1970s and 80s?

12 Millwall had 4 managers in the calendar year 2005. Name any 2.

13 Which elegant midfield playmaker was known as 'Stroller' in his Arsenal days in the late 1960s/early 70s? To which club did he move when he left the Gunners?

14 In 2002-03, who were docked 4 points at the start of their first-ever season in the league, but avoided relegation back to the Conference? Which other Conference side protested that the points deduction should have meant they joined the league instead?

15 Who was Bolton's top scorer in their promotion season of 2000-01? Which club signed him for £3m in January 2003?

Questions 1–10, for 1 point each

1 Who won the league title in his first season as player-manager of Liverpool?

2 With which side did Alf Ramsey win the league title as manager before being appointed to the England job?

3 Success at which lower-league club got Paul Simpson the Preston manager's job in 2006?

4 Bristol City manager Gary Johnson was previously with which other West Country club?

5 With which club do you associate Johnny Quigley, Ian Storey-Moore and John McGovern?

6 Mark Lawrenson was promoted into the top flight with which club in 1979, 2 years before his transfer to Liverpool?

7 Who was appointed manager of Wimbledon in 1992?

8 Colin Bell, Neville Southall and Dean Kiely all started their league careers with which North-West club?

9 Which side in the 1970s could have included South African Colin Viljoen and Northern Ireland stopper Allan Hunter?

10 Who joined Manchester City from Bolton in October 1967 and won a league title winner's medal at the end of the season?

And some harder or two-part questions for 2 points

11 Who holds the record as Liverpool's all-time top scorer in all competitions? Who has scored the most league goals for the club?

12 Who played their last game at Vetch Field in 2005, and which stadium replaced it?

13 Who led Manchester City to their only league title in 1969? Who was his flamboyant assistant?

14 Who did West Bromwich Albion buy from Kidderminster Harriers in July 1997 for £380,000? With which other West Midlands club did he have a brief, unsuccessful spell?

15 Who lost 6-0 at home to their 2nd-tier play-off rivals in March 2007? Who were the opponents?

Questions 1-10, for 1 point each

1 Which Scottish striker commanded a then-record fee of almost £1.5m when he moved from Wolves to Aston Villa in 1979?

2 Who scored 10 goals for Luton Town in a 12-0 rout of Bristol Rovers in 1936?

3 Who joined Plymouth on loan from QPR in 2007, with over 100 goals for the London club to his name?

4 Who play at Bloomfield Road?

5 Which legendary side of the 1950s played their last season of top-flight football in 1970-71?

6 Who netted their record transfer receipts when they sold Kevin Davies to Southampton for £750,000 in 1997?

7 When Peterborough joined the league in 1960, which North-East club did they replace?

8 Who sold Lee Sharpe to Manchester United for £180,000 in 1988, then the club's record sale?

9 Who was manager of Preston North End when they lost the 2nd-flight play-off Final in 2001?

10 Which of these sides has never dropped into the 3rd tier of the league: Manchester City, Middlesbrough, Newcastle United, Sheffield Wednesday?

And some harder or two-part questions for 2 points

11 Either side of his first spell with FC Cologne, for which 2 sides did England striker Tony Woodcock play?

12 Which striking partnership paired up at York City, Bournemouth, Norwich and Southampton between 1968 and 1978?

13 Which future England manager started in a low-key job as player-manager of Lincoln City? With which club did he return to club management after losing the England job?

14 Who won the first of many league titles in 1930-31? Which inside-forward, bought for a record fee from Bolton, was their top scorer?

15 Which former Scottish international was manager of Nottingham Forest in 2006-07? With which club had he achieved promotion from the 3rd tier in 2005-06?

Questions 1–10, for 1 point each

1 Who scored all 7 goals when Arsenal beat Aston Villa 7–1 in 1935?

2 Derek Fazackerley was a great servant to which club as a defender in the 1970s and 80s and later as a coach?

3 With which club was David Nugent earning rave notices in 2006–07, with a move to the Premiership anticipated in the summer?

4 Which Bristol City striker was bought from Port Vale in 2003–04 and formed a prolific partnership with Leroy Lita?

5 With which club do you associate Ian Wood, Earl Barrett and Frankie Bunn?

6 With which club do you associate Jimmy Glazzard, Clem Stephenson and George Brown?

7 Which Swindon Town defender holds the English league record for first-team league appearances with one club (770)?

8 What was ironic about the relegation of Oxford United from the league in 2006, and the promotion of Accrington Stanley as one of the teams entering the 4th tier in their place?

9 Who were – briefly – the league's only Harriers?

10 Frank Worthington won promotion from the 2nd tier with which Yorkshire club in 1969–70?

And some harder or two-part questions for 2 points

11 Who scored the goal that relegated Manchester United in 1974? For which team was he playing?

12 Who was sacked as manager of Bradford City in February 2007, and which long-serving member of the squad took temporary charge of the team?

13 Who, along with Alan Ball, formed Everton's midfield 'Holy Trinity' in their title-winning side of 1970?

14 Which lanky Southampton striker was top scorer in the top division in 1966–67? He was joint top scorer the following season with which Manchester United legend?

15 Who left Swansea City after nearly 3 years as manager in February 2007? Which former player took over after 3 more games?

Questions 1-10, for 1 point each

1 Whose long-standing Arsenal goalscoring record did Ian Wright break?

2 Frank Cuggy, Charlie Buchan and Jackie Mordue were key players in the success of which club in the years before the First World War?

3 It was during a loan spell with which lower-division club that a young Jermaine Defoe emerged as a natural goalscorer?

4 Which 3rd-tier club did former England international Nick Barmby join in 2004?

5 Who was Millwall's record sale when he left to join Liverpool in March 1994 for £2.3m?

6 Who took over as manager of Crewe Alexandra in June 1983?

7 In the 2005 play-offs, who lost in extra time to Sheffield Wednesday and so missed their chance to join the 2nd tier of the league for the first time?

8 Which lower-division side are known as 'The Stags'?

9 Which former Bury, Ipswich Town and Nottingham Forest striker was forced to retire in 2006 after a succession of injuries?

10 Who won successive league titles in 1924, 1925 and 1926?

And some harder or two-part questions for 2 points

11 Who, in 1977, was the only manager to have got Tottenham relegated since they were promoted to the top flight in 1950? How many years did they stay down?

12 With which club is long-serving Steve Perryman most readily associated? And with which other club did he see out his career as player-manager?

13 Where did Newcastle's Kieron Dyer and Jermaine Jenas start their careers?

14 Which year was the first league season played? (1 pt for within 3 years)

15 Former Director-General of the BBC, Greg Dyke, is chairman of which league club? Who was the club's controversial former owner?

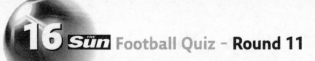

Questions 1-10, for 1 point each

1 Which England striker made an extraordinary move in 1948, moving from Chelsea to Notts County of the 3rd Division for a then-record fee of £20,000?

2 Who scored 31 goals for Leeds in the top flight in 1991?

3 Who play at Oakwell?

4 Who are the only league club in Gloucestershire?

5 With which club do you associate comedian Charlie Williams, Alick Jeffrey and the Snodin brothers, Ian and Glyn?

6 Chris Kamara, Marcus Gayle and Dean Holdsworth all made over 100 appearances for which club?

7 Who was the manager who took Notts County from the bottom tier in 1969 back to the top flight in 1981, after a gap of 55 years?

8 Who scored a phenomenal 42 league goals for Portsmouth in the 2nd tier in 1992-93, more than half the side's tally?

9 Who scored 4 times in Southampton's record league victory, 9-3 against Wolves in 1965?

10 Who was the 4th tier's top scorer whilst a Darlington player in 1998-99 and again the following season?

And some harder or two-part questions for 2 points

11 Which 2 managers, in 1974 and 1978 respectively, managed Leeds United for 44 days each?

12 Allen Batsford managed Wimbledon when they joined the league. Which 2 well-known names then took them through the divisions to the top flight?

13 Who were Arsenal's long-serving full-backs from the 1970s, who won 100 caps between them, and for which country?

14 Who was the amazingly successful penalty taker with Don Revie's Leeds? How many of his 78 penalties did he miss?

15 Who were promoted to the top flight for the first time in their history in 1988? How many seasons did they last?

Questions 1-10, for 1 point each

1 Who scored the injury-time goal against Liverpool that clinched a dramatic league title win for Arsenal in 1989?

2 Charlie Aitken holds the appearance record for which current Premiership club?

3 Which Championship side did former Newcastle defender Steve Caldwell join in the 2007 January transfer window?

4 Which brother of a much-capped former England international was manager of Brighton & Hove Albion in 2006-07?

5 On-loan goalkeeper Jimmy Glass scored an injury-time goal to prevent which club dropping out of the league in 1999?

6 Between 1996 and 2006, which team were promoted 4 times, relegated only once, but remain in the 3rd tier of the league?

7 Who swapped Gay Meadow for a New Meadow in the summer of 2007?

8 Which 'bad-boy' Blackburn striker has scored the most league goals for the club?

9 Who is Southampton's all-time top scorer in the league?

10 Which portly jailbird was the 2nd flight's top scorer with 32 league goals for Newcastle in 1989-90?

And some harder or two-part questions for 2 points

11 Who were the two Dutch internationals imported by Bobby Robson in 1978 to add guile to his Ipswich Town side?

12 Which experienced manager has been in charge of Hereford United since 1995, and what other post has he held since 1997?

13 Hull City manager Phil Brown had a tough managerial baptism at which club? Where was he assistant manager for many years before that?

14 Which Wolves striker was known as 'The Tipton Terror'? For which club did he make his league debut?

15 Which 2 stars of the Liverpool side of the 1970s started their careers at Scunthorpe?

Answers on page 194

Questions 1-10, for 1 point each

1 Leeds have won 7 major trophies. Who captained the side for 6 of those wins?

2 Which former Scottish international did Stoke City take on a free transfer from Blackburn in January 2007?

3 Where did West Brom's Jason Koumas have a successful 2005-06 on loan before returning to the Hawthorns?

4 Who was strangely sacked after guiding Leeds to the play-offs in 2005-06 despite having to sell players to cover debts?

5 Alan Dicks managed which club from 1967-1980, a spell that included a rare sally into the top division?

6 With which club do you associate Roy Sproson, Ray Walker and Dean Glover?

7 Which midfield player was top scorer for Walsall in 2004-05 and 2005-06 before moving to Leicester City?

8 Who were promoted to the League from the Conference in 1991, and lost their first league match 7-3 to Crewe Alexandra?

9 Jim Cannon made nearly 600 appearances in the league between 1973 and 1988 for which London club?

10 Which striker with newly promoted Leeds United was top scorer in the top division in 1956-57?

And some harder or two-part questions for 2 points

11 Which England centre forward scored 138 goals for Everton in the 1970s? From which club did they buy him in 1973?

12 Who beat Brighton 3-1 in the 1991 play-off final to win their 2nd successive promotion, this time to the top flight? Which 2006-07 Premiership manager was in charge?

13 Who hit a rich vein of goalscoring form for Southampton after joining on loan from Troyes in 2006-07? Who is his compatriot who was the club's leading scorer that season?

14 Who took over as Wolves' manager in 1948, aged 31, and led them to 3 league titles in the 1950s? Who was the captain of that great side?

15 With which club did John Aldridge play his first game in the top division? And which side presented him with his first foray into management?

Questions 1-10, for 1 point each

1 With which other London club did George Graham cut his management teeth before taking the helm at Arsenal?

2 Which flame-haired striker was Liverpool's 'supersub' in their glory days of the 1970s?

3 Which side, then in the 2nd tier of the league, first brought Finland's Shefki Kuqi to England?

4 For which side has the talented but seemingly unambitious Lee Trundle been a regular scorer in recent seasons?

5 With which club do you associate Roger Freestone, Alan Curtis and Robbie James?

6 Nigel Spackman, Matt Holland and Jamie Redknapp all made their professional debuts for which club?

7 Which team dropped into the bottom tier of the league at the end of 2006–07, only 6 years after being in the Premiership?

8 In 2006–07, which manager promised to buy a drink for every fan who made the 800-mile round trip to see their side at Sunderland?

9 Jon Macken cost Manchester City £5m from which club in March 2002?

10 Trevor Senior was a prolific scorer as which club rose from bottom tier to 2nd in the 1980s?

And some harder or two-part questions for 2 points

11 With which London club did Alex Stepney start his career? And for which other London side did he play a mere 9 games before being snapped up by Manchester United?

12 Who scored a hat-trick for Charlton in the 1998 play-off final against Sunderland? With which club had he made his name before joining Charlton the previous summer?

13 Which 2 sides' battle to be the top team in the 4th tier lasted until the very last game of the 2006–07 season?

14 Who was the manager of the Tottenham double-winning side of 1961? And who was the inspirational captain?

15 Wimbledon paid Port Vale their record sales fee of £2m for which winger in 1998? For which club was he playing in 2006–07?

Questions 1-10, for 1 point each

1 Which Championship club did Ray Parlour join on loan in February 2007?

2 Mick Channon spent most of his career with Southampton; with which club did he spend a brief spell in the North-West?

3 Which club did Mick McCarthy join as manager after leaving Sunderland in 2006?

4 Which veteran defender played the 500th league match of his career with Oldham in 2006-07 following his move from Norwich the previous summer?

5 With which club do you associate Harold Bell, Ian Muir and Steve Yates?

6 With which club do you associate Tom Johnston, Peter Allen and Tunji Banjo?

7 Lincoln City received what was at the time their record fee (£400,000 from Newcastle) for which exceptionally quick forward in 1995?

8 In 1977-78, who hit dizzy heights when they won the 3rd Division and the Welsh Cup, and won through to the QF of both domestic cups in England?

9 Who won 58 of his 91 caps for Northern Ireland playing for Luton Town in their 1980s heyday?

10 Who was top scorer for Manchester United as they won promotion back to the top flight at the first attempt in 1974-75?

And some harder or two-part questions for 2 points

11 Which 2 players made their 700th appearances for Chelsea on the same day in March 1978?

12 Which 2 Wigan Athletic strikers were the top 2 scorers in the 2nd tier in their promotion season of 2004-05?

13 Who sold his son to Ipswich Town in 2006? For which country has he won Under-21 caps?

14 Who overcame Sunderland on penalties in the 1998 Division 1 play-off final, after a thrilling 4-4 draw? Who missed the crucial penalty?

15 Which 2 clubs bounced back into the top flight at the first attempt in 2006-07?

Questions 1–10, for 1 point each

1 Who played up front alongside Tony Cottee in the West Ham side that finished 3rd in the league in 1986–87?

2 Who were the last side to win the top division in English football in the first season they were promoted?

3 Brett Ormerod was a regular scorer with which North-West club before moving to Southampton in 2002?

4 Nathan Tyson joined Nottingham Forest in 2005 after an impressive scoring record for which side?

5 Who was manager of Oldham Athletic from 1982 to 1994?

6 When were Huddersfield Town last in the top flight: was it 1954, 1965 or 1972?

7 Who became the first club to notch up 100 points when they won promotion from the 4th tier in 1986?

8 Which former Northern Ireland international was manager of Macclesfield Town when they won promotion to the league in 1997?

9 Steve Whitworth and Dennis Rofe were a consistent full-back pairing for a number of years with which club?

10 Who finished runners-up to Manchester City the year they won the title, in 1967–68?

And some harder or two-part questions for 2 points

11 Which two West Brom strikers were top scorers in the top flight in 1970 and 1971?

12 Which Hull City player was top scorer in the 3rd tier in 2004–05? He has over 30 caps for which country?

13 Which Championship manager from which club earned a reproof from the FA after making offensive remarks about women officials in November 2006?

14 From which lower-division club did Liverpool snap up the young Ian Rush? And for which side did he play his last English league game?

15 Jorge Leitao joined which unfashionable Midlands club in 2000? What nationality is Leitao?

Questions 1-10, for 1 point each

1 Which Northern Ireland international led the Wolves forward line from 1967 until 1976?

2 How many league titles did Bill Shankly win as Liverpool manager: was it 3, 5 or 7?

3 Who won promotion to the 2nd tier of the league for the first time in 2005-06?

4 Which Tranmere Rovers player (2006-07) has over 50 caps for Ireland?

5 Who were promoted to the 3rd tier in 1978, and went all the way to the top division before ending up back in the bottom tier in 1986?

6 In the 1980s, who became the only manager to guide Bournemouth into the 2nd tier of the league?

7 After Darlington were relegated into the Conference in 1989, which manager took them straight back out and immediately won promotion into the 3rd tier?

8 Ian Holloway played over 400 games for which club?

9 Alan Cork made over 400 league appearances for which side in 15 years from 1977?

10 Which striker was 3rd-tier top scorer with Reading in 1982-83, and 2nd-tier top scorer with Chelsea in 1983-84?

And some harder or two-part questions for 2 points

11 Which 2 strikers were Reading's joint-top scorers in the league in their 2005-06 promotion season?

12 Who was sacked as manager of Leicester City in 2005? Which Scottish manager replaced him and was sacked in turn a year later?

13 Marcus Stewart first made his name with which lower-division club? With which club from the same region was he playing in 2006-07?

14 With which club did Bill Shankly start his playing career? And with which club did he start his management career?

15 Which 2 former Premiership strikers played alongside Rob Earnshaw for Norwich City in 2006-07?

Questions 1–10, for 1 point each

1 Former England manager Ron Greenwood built his reputation with which club side?

2 Who played 663 games for West Ham between 1967 and 1987, but was never picked for England?

3 Which veteran, once with Fulham in the Premiership, was still scoring regularly for Plymouth in 2006–07?

4 For which side did Blackpool manager Simon Grayson make over 200 appearances, many of them in the Premiership?

5 With which club do you associate Jimmy Hampson, Mickey Walsh and Jimmy Armfield?

6 With which club do you associate Ian Breckin, Steve Blatherwick and Ernie Moss?

7 With which club do you associate Jim Hall, Terry Bly and Mark Tyler?

8 In 2004–05, who finished 3rd, 12 points clear of 6th-placed West Ham in the 2nd tier, but saw the Londoners promoted through the play-offs?

9 Rochdale's record fee was the £400,000 West Ham paid for Stephen Bywater. In which position does he play?

10 Which is the only one of these sides to have dropped into the 4th tier of the league: Aston Villa, Blackburn Rovers, Middlesbrough, Sheffield Wednesday?

And some harder or two-part questions for 2 points

11 Which manager took Andy Johnson to Crystal Palace, and from which club, the manager's former employers?

12 Name Gareth Southgate's 3 clubs in his playing career.

13 With which club does Paul, the brother of England captain, John Terry, play league football? Is he older or younger than John?

14 After a few games for Watford, with which team did Tony Currie establish himself as a top-flight player? Who paid £250,000 for his services in 1976?

15 Which 2 former Premiership clubs found themselves in the 4th tier in 2006–07?

Answers on page 195

Questions 1-10, for 1 point each

1 With which club did Denis Law start his professional career?

2 Who achieved their highest league finish (3rd) in 1990-91?

3 Who were promoted from the 2nd tier in 2000 via the play-offs having lost in the play-offs for the 3 previous seasons?

4 Who play at the Sixfields Stadium?

5 Who returned to the league at the first time of asking in 2005 after winning the Conference play-off?

6 Who have played at Griffin Park since 1904?

7 With which club do you associate Mickey Brown, David Moyes and Arthur Rowley?

8 Who were managed by former Liverpool star Steve McMahon from 2000 to 2004?

9 Who scored 4 times in Watford's record league victory, 8-0 against Sunderland in 1982?

10 Who finished 12 points behind Plymouth and Stockport but beat both in the play-offs to win promotion to the 2nd tier in 1993-94?

And some harder or two-part questions for 2 points

11 Which 2 Welsh international defenders did West Ham buy from Cardiff in 2005?

12 Which 2 players scored over 20 goals apiece (in all competitions) in West Ham's 2004-05 promotion season?

13 Which much-travelled former Manchester United striker was appointed manager of Rotherham in 2006-07? For which club was he top scorer in 2000-01?

14 Who was the manager of Everton when they won the league title in 1985 and 1987? Who was the team's captain?

15 Who scored 6 times in West Ham's record league victory, 8-0 against Sunderland in 1968? Which promising youngster scored 1 of the other 2 goals?

25 **sun** Football Quiz - **Round 20**

Questions 1-10, for 1 point each

1 Which club did Terry Butcher join after leaving Ipswich, where he started his career?

2 With which lower-division club did Martin O'Neill make his initial mark as a manager?

3 Who was tempted back from Australia to continue his career in England with Sunderland in September 2006?

4 Whose goals propelled Scunthorpe to the top of the 3rd tier after his move from Sheffield United in 2005?

5 With which club do you associate John Atyeo, Tom Ritchie and Brian Tinnion?

6 Which long-serving manager took Port Vale into the 2nd tier and kept them there for most of the 1990s?

7 With which club do you associate Gilbert Alsop, Colin Taylor and Alan Buckley?

8 Who started the 2006-07 season 10 points adrift in the 3rd tier after a points deduction for going into administration?

9 The evergreen John McDermott has played over 600 matches for which lower-league side?

10 Which side fell from the top division to the bottom tier between 1984 and 1986?

And some harder or two-part questions for 2 points

11 Which Irish international and former Leeds midfielder was at the heart of Cardiff's promotion challenge in 2006-07? Which other cast-off joined him from Aston Villa in the January 2007 transfer window?

12 Which goalkeeper did Wigan sell for £3m in July 2001, and to which other North-West club did they sell him?

13 Who was named caretaker-manager of Blackpool in November 2005, before earning the post full-time? Which former Scottish international did he replace?

14 Which 2 sides were deducted points after an unseemly brawl during a league match in 1990-91?

15 Which veteran clocked up 931 league appearances (an outfield record) before retiring in 2001? With which club did he play the first 355 games of his career?

Premiership

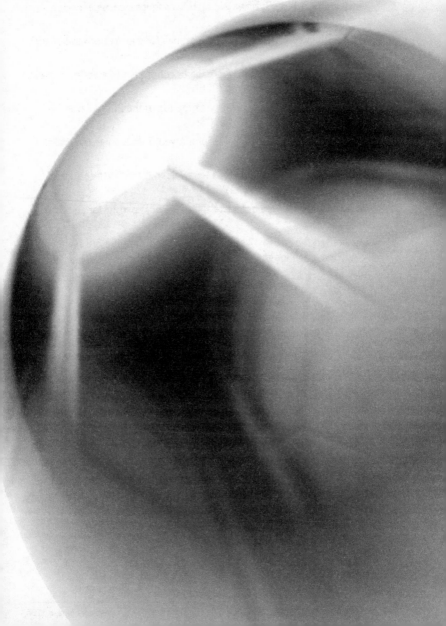

Questions 1-10, for 1 point each

1 Who, as of May 2007, is the Premiership's most expensive player?

2 Ashley Cole joined Chelsea from Arsenal in the summer of 2006; which Chelsea defender went the other way as part of the deal?

3 Who took over the captaincy of Arsenal with great success when Thierry Henry was injured in 2006-07?

4 Which Chelsea striker was Premiership top scorer in 2001?

5 Which Portsmouth defender scored the first 2 goals of his Premiership career against West Ham in a 2-1 win on Boxing Day, 2006?

6 Which club brought Jimmy Floyd Hasselbaink to the Premiership in 1997?

7 Which English midfielder attracted attention with his long-range shooting, including a stunning volley from the half-way line, during 2006-07?

8 Who is the only player to score more than half his side's goals in a Premiership season?

9 Who is the only German player to have been voted PFA Player of the Year?

10 Who were the first team to field a side in the league with no British players?

And some harder or two-part questions for 2 points

11 For which country did Chelsea's Gus Poyet win 25 caps? And which other London team did he leave Chelsea to join?

12 Which 2 former Premiership sides became the first to drop into the bottom tier of the league in 2006?

13 How many seasons have Leicester City spent in the Premiership? (1 pt for one either side)

14 Name the 7 ever-present members of the Premiership. (5-6 for 1 pt, all 7 for 2 pts)

15 Who took over as Liverpool manager after the departure of Graeme Souness? Why did he leave in November 1998?

Questions 1-10, for 1 point each

1 From which club did Manchester United buy Louis Saha?

2 Who was the only player to hit a double-figures goal tally for West Brom when they narrowly avoided relegation in 2004-05?

3 Which overseas star often heard his name chanted by adoring Newcastle fans to the tune of 'Rupert The Bear'?

4 Which £8m striker scored just 4 goals for Arsenal, and was eventually loaned back to the club they bought him from?

5 Which Liverpool player had won the most international caps, as of February 2007?

6 From which league club did Everton buy Australian international Tim Cahill?

7 Who was Wimbledon's record signing in 1999, costing £7.5m from West Ham?

8 Before Steve Coppell in 2006-07, who was the only manager to win the Premiership's Manager of the Year award without winning the title?

9 Which young Southampton star moved to Tottenham at the end of the 2006-07 season?

10 Which West Ham star made his debut for Peterborough aged only 15?

And some harder or two-part questions for 2 points

11 Who were Arsenal's main 2 strikers during their double-winning season of 1997-98?

12 Which 3 members of England's WCFT squad from 2002 were with Manchester City in 2006-07?

13 Who replaced who at Charlton in summer 2006? And who replaced him later in the season on a short-term basis? And then who was brought in to try and escape relegation? And who took his old job?

14 Henning Berg won 100 caps for which country, and won League titles with which two clubs?

15 Who assumed joint control of Bolton Wanderers at the start of their first Premiership season in 1995-96?

Questions 1–10, for 1 point each

1 In 1999–2000 who avoided relegation from the Premiership on the last day with a 1–0 win over Liverpool?

2 Who was Arsenal manager for a solitary season between George Graham and Arsène Wenger?

3 Who was the maverick Colombian star who had Newcastle fans torn between adulation and despair in the late 1990s?

4 Who was regarded as a cert for England's regular No1 spot whilst at Ipswich, but has since become an Arsenal and Everton reserve?

5 Who was the only Irish international on Liverpool's books in 2006–07?

6 Which defender recovered from fitness and discipline problems in 2003 to become Manchester City's most consistent performer over recent seasons?

7 What unenviable record did Swindon achieve when they were relegated after their only season in the top flight in 1993–94?

8 Who beat Arsenal in October 2006 to prevent them recording a 50-match unbeaten run in the Premiership?

9 Who moved from Rangers to Arsenal for £8.5m in 2001?

10 Which frequently injured player cost Tottenham £4.5m from Crystal Palace in 1995?

And some harder or two-part questions for 2 points

11 Which 2 sides played out 4–3 thrillers in consecutive seasons (1995–96 and 1996–97)?

12 Which two members of the 2006–07 Wigan squad have amassed over 150 caps between them?

13 Which Norway international was involved in an Aston Villa and Lyons swap deal which saw Milan Baros join the French club? Which other striker arrived at Villa in the 2007 January transfer window?

14 Name the 4 Bolton players who played in the African Nations Cup in Jan/Feb 2006.

15 'You'll never win anything with kids.' Whose assessment of Manchester United at the start of the 1995–96 season? Whose 10-point lead did they overhaul to win the Premiership?

Questions 1-10, for 1 point each

1 Who kicked off the 1995-96 season with a hat-trick for Southampton, but ended up losing as Nottingham Forest beat the Saints 4-3?

2 Which team were relegated from the Premiership with 42 points, the highest total by a relegated club?

3 Who did Manchester United buy from Tottenham in 2006 as a long-term replacement for Roy Keane?

4 For which country does West Ham goalkeeper Roy Carroll play international football?

5 Which long-serving Scot had an outstanding first Premiership season as captain of Reading?

6 Arjan De Zeeuw had 3 seasons with which club in between his 2 spells at Wigan?

7 Who was the Norwegian striker who played for Swindon in the Premiership, known for his aeroplane goal celebration?

8 Which Leeds United debutant from August 2003 remains the Premiership's youngest player?

9 Who was the Premiership's only representative in the 2006 Ghana World Cup squad?

10 Who swapped Shakhtor Donetsk for Manchester United in 1991, and proved a great success?

And some harder or two-part questions for 2 points

11 Since Wayne Rooney became the Premiership's youngest scorer, the record has been broken twice; by which 2 players?

12 Which 3 managers failed to stop Nottingham Forest being relegated in 1997?

13 From which other Premiership side did Manchester United buy Edwin Van Der Sar? Who proved an effective understudy in 2006-07?

14 Who was the first Premiership manager to be dismissed in the 2005-06 season? And in 2006-07?

15 When Steve Coppell resigned as Crystal Palace manager in 1998, which Italian player took over as temporary coach? Who moved in as manager at the end of that season?

31 *Sun* Football Quiz - **Round 5**

Questions 1-10, for 1 point each

1 What nationality is Arsenal's Philippe Senderos?

2 Who were Manchester United playing when Eric Cantona launched his infamous kung-fu attack on an abusive spectator?

3 In 1995, who did Alex Ferguson allow to leave Manchester United, believing there was no room at the club for both him and Roy Keane?

4 An injury to which promising striker, which kept him out most of the season, hampered West Ham's progress in 2006-07?

5 From which club did Everton buy defender Joleon Lescott in 2006?

6 Morocco defender Talal el-Karkouri played for which Premiership club in 2006-07?

7 Who finished runners-up to Chelsea when they won their first league title for fifty years in 2005?

8 What was Charlton's highest Premiership finish, in 2004?

9 Which was the first season of the newly formed Premier League?

10 For which country has Shaka Hislop made his international appearances?

And some harder or two-part questions for 2 points

11 Name the 3 American goalkeepers who were first choice for their Premiership clubs in 2006-07?

12 Name the 3 Premiership managers from 2006-07 who played BEFORE 1990 for the clubs they manage.

13 Which defender started his career in the North West and returned there in January 2007 via Rangers and PSV Eindhoven? And to which club did he return?

14 Name the 6 sides for whom Les Ferdinand has scored in the Premiership. (Name 4-5 for 1 pt, all 6 for 2 pts)

15 Who was the Arsenal captain when they won the double in 1997-98? Which of their players was PFA and the Football Writers' Player of the Year?

Answers on page 197

Questions 1–10, for 1 point each

1 Which player has twice set a new Premiership transfer record when he has moved clubs?

2 Who completed a controversial move to West Ham from Blackburn in January 2007, having turned down an offer from Liverpool?

3 Which centre-back scored on his debut for Spurs against Manchester United in 2001, but saw his side surrender a 3-goal lead to lose 5–3?

4 Who is the only player to have scored 30 goals in 3 successive Premiership seasons?

5 Who scored 21 premiership goals in 2003–04 only to see his side relegated?

6 Charlton's Darren Ambrose started his career with which club?

7 In 2004–05 3 from 4 teams had to be relegated on the last day; which of the 4 survived?

8 Which Crystal Palace striker cost £4.5m when he moved to Tottenham in 1995?

9 Which Brazilian international signed for Middlesbrough in 1995?

10 Whose goalscoring record did Alan Shearer overhaul with his 201st Newcastle goal, against Portsmouth in February, 2006?

And some harder or two-part questions for 2 points

11 Apart from Alan Shearer, which 3 players have managed 30 goals in a Premiership season (excl 2006–07)?

12 Which Chesterfield striker moved to Premiership Wigan Athletic in the 2007 January transfer window? Which other Premiership side did his goal eliminate from that season's Carling Cup?

13 What was Derby County's best Premiership finish, in 1999? (1 pt for one either way)

14 Name the 3 Premiership managers from 2006–07 who were under 40 years old at the start of the season.

15 Which club gave George Graham his first job back in the game after he served his one-year ban for accepting illegal payments? Where did he cause a stir by taking over in 1998?

Questions 1–10, for 1 point each

1 Who managed Norwich City to their highest-ever finish of 3rd in the Premiership in 1992–93?

2 Gregorz Rasiak has scored prolifically for Derby and Southampton. With which Premiership side did he have a brief and unsuccessful spell?

3 Who did Ruud Gullit succeed as manager of Chelsea?

4 Which club first brought Sergei Rebrov to London for an unsuccessful spell?

5 From which debt-ridden club did Tottenham sign Aaron Lennon as a youngster?

6 Who played for Tottenham against Newcastle in January 2007, and played against the same opposition for West Ham the following week?

7 Who set a landmark by keeping his 142nd clean sheet in the Premiership, against Aston Villa in April 2007?

8 Which player did Middlesbrough buy from Empoli for over £8m in July 2002?

9 Who incensed Tottenham fans by moving to Arsenal on a free transfer in 2001?

10 Which manager sold the inspirational Eric Cantona to Manchester United for £1m?

And some harder or two-part questions for 2 points

11 Name the 4 former Porto players who have played for Chelsea under the former Porto manager, Mourinho.

12 Which 3 Chelsea players scored 10 league goals or more in their title-winning season of 2004–05?

13 How many goals did Chelsea concede in the Premiership when they won the title in 2004–05? (1 pt for one either side)

14 Before Jose Mourinho arrived at Chelsea, who were the 2 other managers to lift the Premiership title apart from Messrs Ferguson and Wenger?

15 Who left Leicester City in 2000 after the most successful spell in their history? Who replaced him?

Questions 1-10, for 1 point each

1 Which 34-year-old Irishman was voted PFA Player of the Year in 1992–93 after his side finished 2nd in the Premiership?

2 Who spent 2005–06 on loan at Bolton, played in the WCFT in 2006 and promptly retired, aged only 30?

3 Where was Ruud Gullit's disastrous second foray into management in the Premiership?

4 Who played in the Premiership in 2000, aged 41, after being pressed into emergency service at injury-hit Bradford City?

5 Who played 171 league games for Fulham before moving on a free transfer to Tottenham in 2006?

6 To which Premiership side did West Ham suffer a humiliating 6-0 defeat on New Year's Day, 2007?

7 Which player has won most caps for his country whilst an Arsenal player?

8 Who moved from QPR to Newcastle for £6m in 1995?

9 In 2004–05, who became the first team to stay up despite being bottom of the Premiership at Christmas?

10 Who was manager of Newcastle United when they achieved their highest Premiership finish of second in 1996?

And some harder or two-part questions for 2 points

11 Name Craig Bellamy's 5 previous clubs (inc loan deals) prior to his joining Liverpool. (3 or 4 gets you 1 pt)

12 As of June 2007, Nicolas Anelka is the most expensive purchase for which 2 Premiership clubs?

13 Who were Chelsea's top 2 scorers in the League in their Premiership-winning season in 2004–05?

14 Which are the only 3 clubs to have been promoted together and survive the first season in the Premiership?

15 In summer 2001 Alex Ferguson made two expensive signings to the tune of nearly £50m. Who were the 2 players, destined for contrasting fortunes in England?

Questions 1-10, for 1 point each

1 Who sold Tim Flowers when he became Britain's most expensive goalkeeper after joining Blackburn in 1994?

2 With which Premiership club is Swedish international defender Olof Mellberg a crowd favourite?

3 Joe Cole, Jermaine Defoe and Rio Ferdinand all started out at which club?

4 Who came off the bench to score 4 goals for Manchester United against Nottingham Forest in a Premiership match?

5 As of the end of February 2007, Alberto Luque has scored how many league goals since his £9.5m move from Deportivo in 2005?

6 Who swapped Fulham for West Ham in January 2007 but was being jeered for lack of effort within a month?

7 Who was Portsmouth's top scorer in 2006-07?

8 Which manager took David Ginola and Benito Carbone to Villa Park, but got little from them in return?

9 Who scored a hat-trick in less than 5 minutes for Liverpool against Arsenal in 1994?

10 How many seasons have Wolverhampton Wanderers spent in the Premiership?

And some harder or two-part questions for 2 points

11 Who were the only 2 English players to play first-team football for Arsenal in 2006-07?

12 The 1997-98 season saw which 3 players from Blackburn Rovers, Coventry City and Liverpool finish joint top scorer?

13 Name the 3 people who managed Leeds in 2003.

14 Who scored in 7 consecutive Premiership games for Chelsea in 1993-94, and who broke the record in 2001-02?

15 Which 2 Arsenal stalwarts announced their retirement at the end of the 2001-02 double-winning season?

Questions 1-10, for 1 point each

1 Who replaced Terry Venables as Tottenham manager in 1993-94?

2 From which European giants did Chelsea buy Claude Makelele?

3 Who was the manager when Jurgen Klinsmann returned for a brief second spell at Spurs to help them stave off relegation in 1997-98?

4 Ian Taylor played in the Premiership for almost a decade with which club?

5 With which club did Nolberto Solano spend 2½ seasons in between his 2 spells at Newcastle?

6 Who was the always-positive Watford manager during 2006-07?

7 For whom did Arsenal pay Bordeaux £11m in 2000, one of Arsène Wenger's least successful purchases?

8 Who scored 5 times in Manchester United's record Premiership victory, 9-0 against Ipswich Town in 1995?

9 The SAS partnership was used to describe Shearer and Sheringham for England but the phrase was coined to describe Shearer's club partnership with which other forward?

10 Whose Premiership placings between 1995 and 2004 were: 11, 11, 6, 4, 3, 5, 6, 6, 4, 2?

And some harder or two-part questions for 2 points

11 Which 2 players left Arsenal for Villareal in summer 2006?

12 Which 3 sides were promoted in 1996-97 and relegated en masse the following season?

13 With which 4 clubs has Chris Sutton played top-flight football in England?

14 Name the 3 players to have scored 30 goals in a Premiership season since it was reduced to 20 teams in 1995-96?

15 Which 3 managers took charge of Sunderland in their relegation season of 2002-03?

Questions 1-10, for 1 point each

1 Who was the East Germany international who joined Manchester City in 1993-94 and became a bit of a cult hero?

2 Ignoring any clubs promoted in 2007, which 3 clubs have spent only a single season in the Premiership?

3 With which side did Henrik Larsson make a handful of appearances in the Premiership in 2006-07?

4 Which former player of his at Monaco recommended Arsène Wenger to the Arsenal board?

5 Who is the Austrian hard-man at the heart of the Middlesbrough defence?

6 Which Newcastle player was called to account for alleged racist remarks in 2 Premiership games in 2006-07?

7 What was Aston Villa's highest Premiership finish?

8 Rangers stalwart Barry Ferguson spent a year with which Premiership club?

9 Who might have regretted a summer 2005 £3m move from Wigan to West Brom as the season worked out very differently for the two sides?

10 Arsenal's worst-ever Premiership finish came in 1995; where did they finish? (1 pt for within 1 place)

And some harder or two-part questions for 2 points

11 Who made a surprise return to the Premiership when Reading signed him from Stoke in January 2007? With which club had he made his last Premiership appearance 3 years earlier?

12 Who scored the goal that preserved Everton's top-flight status on the last day of the 1993-94 season? Which side let slip a 2-goal lead against them on that last day?

13 Which 2 Premiership managers (2005-06) were at West Brom as players in 1981-82?

14 How much did Chelsea pay for Shaun Wright-Phillips, their reserve winger? (1 pt for £1m either way)

15 Which Premiership manager collapsed in 2003 and was treated for a brain tumour? Who took temporary charge of the club?

Questions 1-10, for 1 point each

1 In a scandal-laden season, which manager was sacked in February 1995 after bribery was proved?

2 Who became the first goalkeeper to score in the Premiership when he netted against Everton for Aston Villa in October 2001?

3 Who did Martin O'Neill replace as manager of Aston Villa?

4 Gabriel Agbonlahor emerged as a talented wide player at which club in the 2006-07 season?

5 How many Premiership goals had £8m striker Ashley Young scored for Watford before signing for Aston Villa in January 2007?

6 West Brom bought the energetic midfielder Jonathan Greening from which Premiership club in 2004?

7 Which Bulgarian international failed to illuminate the English game after a £1.5m move from Partizan Belgrade to Barnsley in 1997?

8 Who avoided falling out of the top flight on goal difference in 1997-98?

9 Which Fulham player (2006-07) has played over 80 matches for his country?

10 Which on-loan striker was Birmingham City's top scorer in 2003-04?

And some harder or two-part questions for 2 points

11 Who started the 2005-06 season as Portsmouth manager, and who took temporary charge before Harry Redknapp was brought in?

12 When Ronaldinho was named European Footballer of the Year in 2005, which 3 Premiership players were 2nd, 3rd and 4th?

13 Who became one of the earliest African big-name stars on the scene in 1995 when he signed for Leeds, and where did they sign him from?

14 Whose 2006-07 Premiership ground had the smallest capacity? What is the lowest capacity ground to have hosted Premiership football?

15 Who took over as Director of Football at Tottenham in 2004? Where did he move to fulfil the same role a year later?

Questions 1-10, for 1 point each

1 Who replaced Kenny Dalglish as day-to-day manager of Blackburn when Dalglish moved 'upstairs' after winning the 1995 premiership title?

2 Which Premiership ground has the largest capacity?

3 Who took over as manager of Middlesbrough when Steve McLaren left to take the England job?

4 Which centre-back moved to West Ham in the 2007 transfer window and promptly injured himself in his first match?

5 In the 2002–03 Premiership season, which Middlesbrough defender earned 3 red cards and a further 7 yellow cards in the league?

6 Diomansy Kamara took the Championship by storm in 2006–07. How many goals did he score in 26 Premiership appearances the previous season?

7 Who missed a game on New Year's Day, 2006, thus ending a run of 164 Premiership appearances, a record?

8 For which Premiership club did Scottish PFA Player of the Year (2005–06) Shaun Maloney sign in January 2007 after a contract dispute with Celtic could not be resolved?

9 Which colourful winger, who had good spells with Everton and Bradford City, was one of the first Premiership players to perform acrobatic goal celebrations?

10 Which club in 2005 became the first to be relegated from the Premiership on four occasions?

And some harder or two-part questions for 2 points

11 Which 3 players did Portsmouth buy from Tottenham in a job lot in the January 2006 transfer window?

12 In the first Premiership season, what position did title-holders Leeds finish? (1 pt for within one)

13 Who broke his leg 3 games into his Premiership career with Aston Villa in 2000 and never played again? And who was his strike partner in a prolific season at PSV in 1998–99?

14 Wimbledon equalled their highest ever league placing (6th) in 1993–94. Who was their manager and who finished as their top scorer?

15 Who surprisingly resigned as manager of Southampton in March 2004? Who started a short-lived tenure as his replacement?

Questions 1-10, for 1 point each

1 From which other North-West club did Manchester United buy Dennis Irwin?

2 Who moved to Aston Villa after an outstanding Euro 2004 with the Czech Republic?

3 Who scored twice for Everton against Wrexham on 1st October 2002, becoming their youngest-ever scorer?

4 Which former Liverpool player took over from Sam Allardyce at Bolton?

5 Which Welsh international did Fulham buy from Everton in the 2007 January transfer window?

6 Who was suspended by his own club after hospitalising a team-mate in training 2 weeks before the end of the 2006-07 season?

7 Who scored the Premiership's fastest goal, for Tottenham after 10 seconds of a 2000 match against Bradford City?

8 Which goalkeeper scored with a long clearance which bounced over Watford keeper Ben Foster's head in March 2007?

9 Which striker was signed by Arsenal not too long after being top scorer at the 1998 World Cup, but failed to make his mark in England?

10 Who scored the first Premiership hat-trick, for Leeds against Tottenham in August, 1992?

And some harder or two-part questions for 2 points

11 Which potent strike partnership started to gel for Middlesbrough in 2006 as they hauled themselves up the Premiership table?

12 Who took temporary charge of Fulham when Chris Coleman was sacked towards the end of the 2006-07 season? With which other role did he combine this job?

13 Name the 3 managers who looked after Tottenham in 2004.

14 Which club did Alan Ball leave for Southampton in 1994, and for which other club did he move on in summer 1995?

15 From which 2 European clubs did Chelsea and Liverpool recruit Jose Mourinho and Rafa Benitez in summer 2004?

Questions 1-10, for 1 point each

1 Who was the first player to play his 500th Premiership match, in 2006–07?

2 In Arsenal's unbeaten Premiership season (2003–04), how many of their 38 matches did they win?

3 With which other Premiership club did James Milner have a successful season on loan in 2005–06 before returning to Newcastle?

4 Which young player was at the centre of a disputed transfer involving Manchester United and Chelsea in 2006?

5 Who received maybe the most pointless red card of 2006–07, getting himself sent off in the last minute of Fulham's cup match against Tottenham, when his team were already 4-0 down?

6 In 1994–95, who finished 3rd in the top flight, the best-ever Premiership finish by a newly promoted side?

7 Who hold the record for both the biggest home win and the biggest away win in the Premiership?

8 Brian Kidd resigned as Alex Ferguson's No2 at Manchester United to become manager at which club?

9 Which much-maligned former Chelsea player has won 64 caps for Serbia (inc Yugoslavia)?

10 Which goalkeeper did Liverpool let go on a free transfer in 2000?

And some harder or two-part questions for 2 points

11 Which three of Aston Villa's 2006–07 squad have won a solitary England cap each?

12 In 1996–97 Middlesbrough were relegated after being deducted 3 points after failing to fulfil a fixture against which side? Who would have gone down if the penalty had not been imposed?

13 Name the 3 former Premiership clubs playing in the 3rd tier in 2006–07.

14 Which 2 experienced international players did Bruce Rioch sign from Italy in 1995?

15 Which of the Premiership's ever-present clubs has accumulated the fewest points?

Answers on page 198

Questions 1-10, for 1 point each

1. The loss of which proven goalscorer through injury severely hampered Watford in 2006-07?

2. In 2003-04, whose penalty miss sparked off a free-for-all towards the end of the Man United v Arsenal match in the Premiership?

3. Who was in goal for most of the season when Blackburn won the Premiership in 1995?

4. Who was the expensive Chilean winger who struggled in his first season at Liverpool after his transfer from Albacete in 2006?

5. From March 2006 until 31 December that year, Darius Vassell scored only 3 goals for Manchester City, all against which club?

6. Who was manager when Bradford City reached the Premiership in 1999?

7. Who received a red card before he had touched the ball playing for Sheffield United against Reading in January 2007?

8. Who scored the goal as Jose Mourinho's reign at Chelsea started with a significant 1-0 win over Manchester United in August 2004?

9. Which former England striker scored his 100th Premier League goal in 2002-03?

10. In August 1993, who scored a hat-trick as Coventry started the Premiership season with a shock 3-0 win over Arsenal?

And some harder or two-part questions for 2 points

11. Who joined Fulham in summer 2006 but broke his leg 4 games into the new season? From which club did he join?

12. Name the 4 former England internationals who managed in the Premiership in 2006-07.

13. Against which team did David Beckham score from the half-way line in 1996, and who was in goal?

14. In 1995, Newcastle paid £10m for two London-based players, a defender and a centre-forward. Who were they?

15. Which overseas coach had a rough year as Tottenham manager in 1997, and which chairman hired and fired him?

Answers on page 198

FA Cup

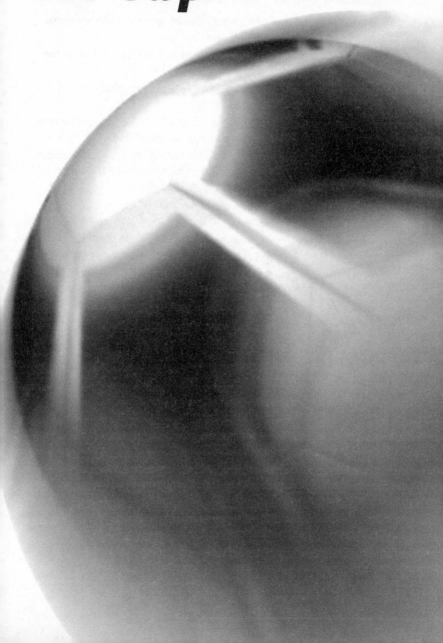

Questions 1–10, for 1 point each

1 Who is best remembered for lying prostrate on the Wembley turf after scoring for Arsenal in the 1971 FA Cup Final?

2 Which teenager kept goal for Leicester City when they lost the 1969 FA Cup Final?

3 Who knocked Liverpool out of the FA Cup in the 3rd round in 2004–05?

4 Who was the legendary figure who played in 9 FA Cup Finals in the Victorian era (winning 5) and became President of the FA from 1890 until his death in 1923?

5 In his playing days Ron Atkinson was a key player in which lower division side's impressive FA Cup run in 1963–64?

6 Who captained Manchester United in the 2007 FA Cup Final?

7 Who scored for Manchester United against Liverpool in the 1977 FA Cup Final, and then scored the winner against them in the SF two years later?

8 Who lost an FA Cup 1st round 2nd replay to Northern Premier League Chorley at Burnden Park in 1986–87?

9 Who scored the fastest goal in an FA Cup Final, for Chelsea against Middlesbrough in 1997?

10 Who missed the crucial penalty as Arsenal beat Manchester United in a shoot-out at the end of the 2005 FA Cup Final?

And some harder or two-part questions for 2 points

11 Which Division 1 side overturned a 3-goal deficit to beat Premiership Southampton in a 2001 FA Cup tie? Which veteran striker scored a hat-trick for the winners?

12 Which 2 teams contested the FA Cup Final with the now-legendary piece of commentary '... and Smith must score'? (he didn't)

13 In the 1982 FA Cup Final, who scored Tottenham's goals both in the original Final and the replay? And which future Spurs player scored the QPR goal which forced the replay?

14 Les Allen, son Clive and nephew Paul played in how many FA Cup Finals between them?

15 Who were the losing teams in the 2007 FA Cup SFs?

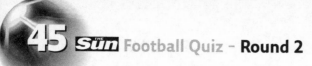

Questions 1–10, for 1 point each

1 How many FA Cup Winners medals did George Best win?

2 Goals by Ronnie Radford and Ricky George helped which lowly club overcome Newcastle in the FA Cup in 1972?

3 Who, in 1983, became (and remains) the youngest player to score in an FA Cup Final?

4 Which cheeky striker led his non-league side on a cup run and earned the nickname 'The Leatherhead Lip'?

5 Which of these sides has never won the FA Cup: Bradford City, Fulham, Sheffield United, Sheffield Wednesday?

6 Who, in 1969–70, was the last player to score in every round of the FA Cup?

7 Roger Osborne scored the only goal of the game in an FA Cup Final to give which side their only victory in the competition?

8 In 1986–87 Welsh valleys side Ton Pentre reached the first round proper for the only time. Who did fate pair them with in that tie, which they lost 4–1?

9 Who came on as a sub and scored a hat-trick as Tottenham overturned a 2–0 deficit to win 6–2 against Southampton in the 1994–95 FA Cup?

10 Which non-league side held Manchester United to a 0–0 draw at Old Trafford in a 3rd round FA Cup tie in 2004–05?

And some harder or two-part questions for 2 points

11 Who overturned a 3-goal half-time deficit with only 10 men against Tottenham in the FA Cup 4th round in 2004? Who had been sent off in the first half?

12 Who won Goal of the Season in 1996–97 for an extraordinary bicycle kick volley in an FA Cup match against Barnsley? For which team?

13 Who became the youngest player in an FA Cup Final when he played for Preston in 1963–64? And with which club did he win another loser's medal in 1968?

14 Who scored a controversial last-minute goal for Liverpool to take their 1984 FA Cup SF against Manchester United to a replay? Who scored United's winner in the replay?

15 Which of the 92 league clubs failed to take part in the 1999–2000 FA Cup? Why?

Answers on page 199

Questions 1-10, for 1 point each

1 Don Revie won an FA Cup winner's medal in 1956 as a clever inside-forward in which team?

2 Whose outstretched leg diverted a cross over Ray Clemence to hand the FA Cup to Coventry in 1987?

3 Who scored the winning goal when Wrexham stunned Arsenal with a 2-1 win in the 1992 FA Cup?

4 Which member of Chelsea's 1997 FA Cup Final winning team had scored against them in a previous Final?

5 Which of these sides has never reached an FA Cup Final: Nottingham Forest, Ipswich Town, Leyton Orient, Middlesbrough?

6 In the SF of the FA Cup in 1970, Leeds took 3 attempts to beat Manchester United. What was the aggregate score over the 3 matches?

7 Which non-league side were denied a unique place in the QF of the FA Cup in 1978 when Wrexham equalised from a corner which referee Alf Grey inexplicably ordered to be retaken twice?

8 Who scored twice as Liverpool won the first Merseyside derby FA Cup Final 3-1 in 1986?

9 Who nearly went out to Gretna in the first round of the FA Cup in 1993-94, but went on to beat three Premiership sides, including holders Arsenal, en route to the QF?

10 Who scored the opening headed goal in the 2004 FA Cup Final as Manchester United beat Millwall at a canter?

And some harder or two-part questions for 2 points

11 Which 2 teams contested the first FA Cup Final at Wembley, in 1923?

12 With which 3 clubs did Dennis Wise play in an FA Cup Final?

13 Which 2 West Midlands sides contested 3 FA Cup Finals in the 19th century?

14 Who, in 1977, became the first man to have lifted both the Scottish FA Cup and the FA Cup as captain? Which was the Scottish side?

15 When did sponsorship of the FA Cup begin: was it 1979, 1988 or 1995? Who were the first sponsors?

Answers on page 199

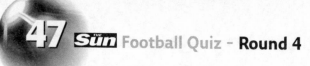

Questions 1-10, for 1 point each

1 Which side did Liverpool beat in the 1986 FA Cup Final to clinch the double?

2 An embarrassing FA Cup defeat by which lower-division side heralded the end of Graeme Souness' time as Liverpool manager?

3 Which side won 5 of the first 7 FA Cup Finals?

4 Which side played in 5 FA Cup Finals in 7 years between 1905 and 1911, but won only 1?

5 Who lost an FA Cup SF in 1965 and 1966, and the Final a year later?

6 Which junior commentator got his big break getting over-excited at the Newcastle-Hereford FA Cup tie in 1971-72?

7 Why was everyone so amused by Trevor Brooking's winning goal against Arsenal in the 1980 FA Cup Final?

8 Who played in his 6th FA Cup Final in 1987, 16 years after his first?

9 An injury to which player allowed Teddy Sheringham to come off the bench and score in Manchester United's 2-0 win in the 1999 FA Cup Final?

10 Who took over as sponsors of the FA Cup at the start of the 2006-07 season?

And some harder or two-part questions for 2 points

11 Who pulled off one of the great FA Cup shocks when they knocked out Leeds 3-2 in 1971? Which veteran striker scored 2 of the goals?

12 Who was the first goalkeeper to save a penalty in the FA Cup Final? Which Liverpool player had his shot saved?

13 Who scored the winner in the FA Cup Final replay in 1970 between Chelsea and Leeds? Where was the replay held?

14 Who fell to Liverpool in the 1992 FA Cup SF after 2 matches finished in stalemate? Who scored their goal in the original 1-1 draw?

15 Who were the last non-Premiership team left standing in the 2006-07 FA Cup? Who knocked them out?

Answers on page 199

Questions 1–10, for 1 point each

1 Who beat mighty Arsenal 2–0 in one of the FA Cup's greatest shocks back in 1933?

2 What was remarkable about Bert Trautmann's performance in goal during Manchester City's FA Cup Final win in 1956?

3 Who are the earliest FA Cup-winning side still playing?

4 What was unique (at the time) about 1 of Albert Shepherd's 2 goals in the FA Cup Final for Newcastle in 1910?

5 Ian Storey-Moore announced his potential when he scored a hat-trick for which club against holders Everton to knock them out of the 1966–67 FA Cup?

6 Who scored the deciding goal as Leeds finally won the FA Cup, beating holders Arsenal 1–0 in the Final in 1972?

7 Which Arsenal central defender ought to have received the first red card in an FA Cup Final when he cynically tripped West Ham's Paul Allen in the 1980 Final?

8 Who scored twice as a substitute for Everton against Liverpool in the 1989 FA Cup Final but still finished on the losing side?

9 Who scored a scintillating double as Liverpool beat Arsenal 2–1 in the 2001 FA Cup Final after being outplayed for much of the game?

10 Which 4th-tier side won 2–1 away at Premiership Fulham in the 2005–06 FA Cup?

And some harder or two-part questions for 2 points

11 'The Crazy Gang have beaten the Culture Club' was John Motson's take on which FA Cup Final?

12 Which 3rd-tier league side reached the FA Cup SF in 2001, and who was their manager?

13 Which 2 Northern sides knocked Arsenal out of the FA Cup in 2005–06 and 2006–07?

14 Which 2 sets of local rivals contested the 1993 FA Cup SF?

15 Prior to meeting in the Final in 2007, Manchester United and Chelsea had won the FA Cup 14 times between them. In what proportion?

Questions 1-10, for 1 point each

1 Who scored both Bolton's goals when they beat Manchester United in the 1958 FA Cup Final?

2 Which current manager scored the winning goal for Crystal Palace in a 4-3 thriller against Liverpool in a 1990 FA Cup SF?

3 How did the FA Cup leave England in 1926-27?

4 Who were the last West Midlands side to win the FA Cup?

5 Who scored 9 of West Brom's 16 goals as they won the FA Cup in 1967-68?

6 Goals by Vic Halom and Billy Hughes in a SF win over Arsenal ensured an FA Cup Final place for which team?

7 Who scored at both ends as the 1981 FA Cup Final between Tottenham and Manchester City ended 1-1?

8 Which defender lost 3 FA Cup Finals as an Everton player but finally won a winner's medal with Tottenham in 1991?

9 Who scored with an outrageous back-heeled flick from a corner in an FA Cup 3rd round replay against Norwich City in 2001-02?

10 How did Millwall's Curtis Weston outdo James Prinsep in 2004?

And some harder or two-part questions for 2 points

11 Who scored a classic winning goal for Manchester United in extra time of an FA Cup semi-final against Arsenal in 1999? Who saved an injury-time penalty to ensure the game went to extra time?

12 Who were thrown out of the 2006-07 FA Cup after fielding an ineligible player? Which side benefited as they were reinstated to the competition?

13 Which 3 sides have scored 3 times in an FA Cup Final and not won the trophy?

14 Which pair of notoriously truculent players scored the goals that earned Arsenal a 2-0 win in the 1998 FA Cup Final against Newcastle?

15 Who became the first overseas coach to win the FA Cup in 1997? And which other overseas coach matched him the following season?

50 The Sun Football Quiz - **Round 7**

Questions 1-10, for 1 point each

1 Which goalkeeper gave a flawless performance as Sunderland beat mighty Leeds 1-0 in the 1973 FA Cup Final?

2 Who were the opponents for Liverpool's ill-fated FA Cup semi-final at Hillsborough that ended in tragedy?

3 How many teams have won the FA Cup for 3 consecutive years since 1900?

4 Which non-league side took their 6th and most impressive League scalp in the FA Cup when they beat 1st-division Sunderland in 1948–49?

5 Who were the only side to win the FA Cup twice in the 1970s?

6 Whose towering performance for Sunderland in the 1973 FA Cup Final earned a move to Everton and a regular place at the heart of the England defence?

7 Who finished on the losing side in 2 FA Cup Finals against Manchester United in 1977 and 1983?

8 Whose 35-yard free-kick set Tottenham up for a 3-1 win over rivals Arsenal in the 1991 FA Cup SF?

9 Whose goal won the all-London FA Cup SF for Chelsea against Fulham in 2002?

10 Who scored Liverpool's opening goal in the 2006 FA Cup Final?

And some harder or two-part questions for 2 points

11 Which 2 Scottish strikers scored the goals that won Everton the FA Cup Final in 1984?

12 Who, in 2005, became only the second player to be sent off in an FA Cup Final? Who was the referee?

13 Who was the manager of Sunderland when they won the FA Cup as a 2nd-tier side in 1973? With which rival team had he won a winner's medal as a player in 1955?

14 Which 2 sides were involved when an FA Cup 5th-round tie was voluntarily replayed in 1998–99 because a goal had been scored when one side took advantage of possession conceded so an injured player could be treated?

15 Who scored a record 44 goals in the FA Cup? How many came in Finals?

Questions 1–10, for 1 point each

1 Who scored for Newcastle in the 1st minute of the 1955 FA Cup Final against Manchester City?

2 Against which non-league side did Ted Macdougall once score 9 times for Bournemouth in an 11–0 FA Cup thrashing?

3 Who scored twice from the penalty spot in the 1994 FA Cup Final against Chelsea?

4 With which club did Stan Seymour win FA Cup winner's medals as a player in 1924 and a manager in 1951?

5 How did Dennis Clarke make FA Cup Final history in the 91st minute in 1968 for West Brom?

6 In which year were FA Cup ties first played on a Sunday: was it 1974, 1981 or 1989?

7 When was the last time none of today's Big Four (Arsenal, Chelsea, Liverpool, Manchester United) or even Cup specialists Tottenham reached the last 16 of the FA Cup: was it 1929, 1953 or 1984?

8 Paul Gascoigne was stretchered off during the 1991 FA Cup Final after his own horrendous tackle on which Nottingham Forest player?

9 In the 2002 Final against Chelsea, which Arsenal player became the first man to score in successive FA Cup Finals for 40 years?

10 Whose extra-time SF goal took Chelsea into the 2007 FA Cup Final?

And some harder or two-part questions for 2 points

11 Who scored a hat-trick for Blackpool in the 1953 FA Cup Final against Bolton? What was the final score?

12 The last FA Cup Final before WWII and the first after the war were won 4–1. By which two sides?

13 Which shooting star scored both West Ham's goals in their 2–0 win in the 1975 FA Cup Final? Who were the opponents?

14 Who was sent off in the classic SF replay between Arsenal and Manchester United in 1999? Which Arsenal defender was dismissed in the first game?

15 Who did Arsenal beat in both domestic Cup Finals in 1993? Who scored for Arsenal in both the original FA Cup Final and the replay?

Questions 1–10, for 1 point each

1 Which non-league side knocked 1st-division Coventry out of the FA Cup in 1989, only 2 seasons after Coventry won the competition?

2 Who was manager of Wimbledon when they won the FA Cup in 1988?

3 Who scored the only goal of the 1996 FA Cup Final as Manchester United beat Liverpool 1–0?

4 When was the last time Wolves reached the FA Cup Final: was it 1933, 1955 or 1960?

5 Who are the only club to have played in 4 FA Cup Finals and lost the lot?

6 Whose volley for Fulham against Leicester in the FA Cup in 1973–74 was the Goal of the Season: Bobby Moore, Alan Mullery or Keith Weller?

7 Which unfancied side knocked mighty Liverpool out of the FA Cup in successive seasons in 1982–83 and 1983–84?

8 Who missed a penalty in the 1991 FA Cup Final?

9 Who did Arsenal beat for the 4th year in succession in the FA Cup in 2003–04?

10 Who are the only team to have beaten Tottenham in an FA Cup Final?

And some harder or two-part questions for 2 points

11 Who scored twice as Tottenham won a thrilling FA Cup Final replay 3–2 against Manchester City in 1981? Which latter-day TV reporter scored their other goal?

12 Which 3 sides have won the FA Cup in consecutive years since WWII?

13 Which 3rd-tier side won away at Leeds, Chelsea and Sunderland before falling to 2nd-tier Southampton in the SF in 1976? Who was their manager at the time?

14 In which year was the last FA Cup Final at the old Wembley Stadium? Who was the winning captain?

15 'The other semi-final is a bit of a joke.' Who said this before his side beat Derby 2–0 in 1976? And which 2nd-tier team had the last laugh when they beat the hot favourites in the Final?

Answers on page 200

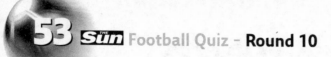

Questions 1–10, for 1 point each

1 Who was manager of Burton Albion when they took Manchester United to a replay in the FA Cup in 2005–06?

2 Who won their only 2 FA Cup Finals in the early part of the 20th century by the handsome margins of 4–0 and 6–0?

3 Dickie Guy kept a clean sheet at top-flight Burnley and Leeds in the 1974–75 FA Cup for which team?

4 Which of these sides has reached the FA Cup Final: Oldham Athletic, Oxford United, Norwich City, Barnsley?

5 Which 2nd-division side beat Liverpool in an FA Cup QF in 1970 with a Barry Endean header?

6 Who was sacked 6 weeks after his side won the FA Cup in 1977?

7 For which club did Scottish international striker Mo Johnston make an FA Cup Final appearance?

8 Whose headed goal settled the 1993 FA Cup SF between Arsenal and Tottenham?

9 Who did Arsenal destroy 5–1 in a 2003–04 FA Cup QF, a display so good that even the home support gave them an ovation?

10 In 2007, in a humdinger of a tie at White Hart Lane, whose late equaliser against Tottenham earned Chelsea a replay which they duly won?

And some harder or two-part questions for 2 points

11 Terry Venables won the FA Cup playing for which club? Which former club of his did they beat 2–1 in the Final?

12 Which 2 sides have lost consecutive FA Cup Finals since 1900?

13 Which 2 members of Southampton's FA Cup-winning side from 1976 had scored in previous Finals for Sheffield Wednesday and Chelsea?

14 Gary Neville was sent off in an FA Cup Manchester derby in 2003–04 for headbutting which City player? What was the result of the match?

15 Who enjoyed a brief moment in the sun with 2 goals for Everton in their 3–2 FA Cup Final victory in 1966? Who was the manager who boldly selected him ahead of fit-again first choice, Fred Pickering?

European
Championships

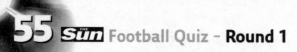

55 *Sun* Football Quiz - **Round 1**

Questions 1–10, for 1 point each

1 What *Sun* headline greeted England's defeat by Sweden at Euro 92?

2 Denmark won Euro 92 despite not qualifying; the disqualification of which war-torn country allowed them to sneak into the finals?

3 Who was the Portugal goalkeeper at Euro 2004, with a penchant for saving and scoring penalties?

4 Who put the ball in the net only to have the 'goal' ruled out during injury time in England's Euro 2004 match with Portugal?

5 Who were the last team to win the European Championships in their own country?

6 Who have won the European Championship on the only occasion they qualified for the Finals?

7 Who beat Scotland in a 2-leg play-off to qualify for Euro 2000?

8 Whose clinical finishing destroyed England in a group match against Holland in the 1988 Finals?

9 Who scored England's crucial equaliser in Poland to ensure qualification for the 1992 European Championship Finals?

10 Who was the attention-seeking referee who sent off two Dutch players and one Czech in a European Championship SF in 1976?

And some harder or two-part questions for 2 points

11 Name 2 of the 3 midfielders who played alongside Michel Platini in the France team that won the 1984 European Championship Final.

12 Which 2 countries will jointly host the 2012 European Championships?

13 Which country denied England a European Championship Finals appearance in France in 1984? Who was the England manager?

14 Who beat Ireland in a one-off play-off for the last place at Euro 96, and where was the game played?

15 Who did France beat 3–2 in a thrilling SF in the 1984 European Championships? Who scored the late winner?

Questions 1-10, for 1 point each

1 Who did West Germany beat 2-1 in the European Championship Final in 1980?

2 Before losing to Germany in a penalty shoot-out at Euro 96, England actually won a shoot-out in the QF - against which opponents?

3 Who missed a penalty for England against France in the Euro 2004 group match?

4 Who was England's referee at Euro 2004 (he was sent home early after a couple of inadequate displays)?

5 Who scored the only goal of the game when Scotland recorded a memorable 1-0 win over France in a Euro 2008 qualifier in October 2006?

6 Whose victory in the 1964 European Championships remains their only success in a major championship?

7 How many points did England get in their group in the European Championship Finals in 1988?

8 Which French player found consolation at Euro 2000 having missed the World Cup Final through an unjust suspension?

9 Who scored a hat-trick in a 3-1 win over Poland at Wembley in a 1999 European Championship qualifier?

10 Who was the manager of Scotland when they qualified for Euro 92?

And some harder or two-part questions for 2 points

11 At Euro 2000, which two sides came from behind to beat England and eliminate them in the group stages?

12 Who will be the joint hosts of the 2008 European Championships?

13 Which home nation reached the QF of the 1976 European Championship, and who beat them over two legs?

14 Who became the first team to hold both the European Championship and World Cup at the same time? Who have subsequently matched this feat?

15 Who beat England in a tetchy SF in the 1968 European Championships? Which England player was sent off in the last minute?

Questions 1-10, for 1 point each

1 Everyone remembers England's defeat by Germany on penalties at Euro 96. Who lost the other SF against the Czech Republic, also on penalties?

2 Who beat hot favourites West Germany in a penalty shoot-out in the final of the 1976 European Championships?

3 Who missed the rest of Euro 2004 after he was given a 3-match ban for spitting at Denmark's Christian Poulsen in Italy's opening game?

4 Who failed to impress as manager of France at Euro 2004 and was equally unimpressive in a brief stint at Tottenham the following season?

5 Who scored Scotland's only goal in their Euro 96 campaign?

6 Who were the only team England beat in the Euro 2000 Finals?

7 Apart from Germany, which other country has won the European Championships twice?

8 What nationality is Urs Meier, the referee who disallowed Sol Campbell's header in the QF of Euro 2004?

9 Who suffered a sad end to a great career when he was sent off for Romania against Italy in a Euro 2000 QF?

10 Which player, the only team member based overseas at the time, scored England's only goal in the Euro 92 Finals?

And some harder or two-part questions for 2 points

11 Who was the only member of Greece's winning side at Euro 2004 who was playing in the Premiership at the time? For which side?

12 Who scored England's goals in the QF defeat by Portugal at Euro 2004?

13 Since the expansion of the European Championships to a group-based Finals in 1980, only Germany (who else?) have qualified for all 7 tournaments. Which 4 sides have qualified 6 times?

14 Which 2 sides did England play for the first time during qualifying for Euro 2008?

15 Which England manager substituted Gary Lineker in England's disastrous match against Sweden in Euro 92; who came on?

Questions 1-10, for 1 point each

1 Which Tottenham reject scored the goal against England which took the Euro 2004 QF into extra time?

2 What fate was shared by Peter Beardsley, Chris Waddle and Ian Wright at the 1992 European Championships?

3 The Swedish President of UEFA, Lennart Johansson, was instrumental in persuading which retired striker to play for his country at Euro 2004?

4 Who was the German coach who masterminded Greece's victory at Euro 2004?

5 At the 1984 European Championship, who scored 9 goals in 5 games from midfield?

6 Who missed the crucial penalty in the SF shoot-out against Germany at Euro 96?

7 Which side missed 2 penalties in open play and 3 out of 4 in a shoot-out to lose their Euro 2000 SF against Italy?

8 How many times have the Republic of Ireland qualified for the Finals of the European Championship?

9 Who scored the Golden Goal in the Final against Italy to clinch Euro 2000 for France?

10 Who gave away the late penalty that saw his side eliminated from Euro 2000 by Romania?

And some harder or two-part questions for 2 points

11 Who scored 2 goals each as England destroyed Holland 4-1 at Euro 96?

12 Which unfancied side embarrassed Ireland with a 5-2 thrashing in a Euro 2008 qualifier in October 2006? Which Irish defender got a red card in that game?

13 Who were the tournament's first winners in 1960? And in which country were those first Finals played?

14 Who scored a brilliant solo goal for England when they beat Scotland 2-0 at Euro 96, and who missed a penalty for Scotland a minute before?

15 Who scored a last-minute penalty for Spain to decide a 4-3 classic with Yugoslavia at Euro 2000? And who took and missed a last-minute penalty in the QF against France, with Spain 2-1 down and the main penalty-taker off the field?

European Trophies

Questions 1-10, for 1 point each

1 In which year did the European Cup become the Champions League?

2 Who destroyed Johann Cruyff's Barcelona, winning 4-0 in the 1994 Champions League Final?

3 Which Italian side made sure West Ham's 2006-07 UEFA Cup adventure lasted only one round?

4 Who were the first team to win the European Cup in a penalty shoot-out?

5 Which Scottish side were one of the losing semi-finalists in the very first European Cup in 1956?

6 What nationality was Owe Kindvall, scorer of Feyenoord's winning goal in the 1970 European Cup Final?

7 Which Brazilian playmaker scored twice as Milan lost 2-3 to Manchester United in a 2007 Champions League SF?

8 Which Blackburn player was sent off in their Champions League tie with Spartak Moscow in 1995-96?

9 Who won a European Cup winner's medal in 1963, 40 years before his son won his fourth?

10 Who refereed Manchester United's Champions League Final against Bayern Munich in 1999?

And some harder or two-part questions for 2 points

11 Who were the Dutch trio at the heart of AC Milan's success in the late 1980s and early 90s?

12 Whose last-minute goal for Porto eliminated Manchester United from the 2004 Champions League? Who had a 'goal' wrongly disallowed for offside minutes earlier?

13 In 1978-79 the 2 pre-tournament favourites, Liverpool and Juventus, were eliminated in the First Round of the European Cup. Which 2 British clubs knocked them out?

14 Dejan Savicevic and Marcel Desailly were both second-time winners of the European Cup when they played for Milan in 1994. With which 2 sides had they won the trophy before?

15 In 2003, Clarence Seedorf became the first player to win the Champions League with 3 different clubs; which 3 clubs? (They are all from different countries)

Questions 1-10, for 1 point each

1 Who scored both Ajax goals in their 2-0 European Cup win over Inter Milan in 1972?

2 Along with Roy Keane, which key Manchester United player missed the 1999 Champions League Final?

3 Who scored 5 times for Aston Villa in a two-legged tie against Dinamo Bucharest in the 1982-83 European Cup?

4 Which German international scored twice for Borussia Dortmund when they won the Champions League Final in 1997?

5 Which famous English referee took charge of the first European Cup Final in 1956: was it Jack Taylor, Stanley Rous or Arthur Ellis?

6 Who scored for Celtic in both their European Cup Final appearances?

7 Which English side lost 4-2 to Anderlecht in the 1976 European Cup Winners Cup (ECWC) Final?

8 Who scored a hat-trick for Manchester United in a 1997-98 Champions League match with Feyenoord?

9 Who turned around a 4-1 deficit from the first leg in Milan in a Champions League QF?

10 In which city was the Heysel Stadium, scene of the terrible disaster at the 1985 European Cup Final between Juventus and Liverpool?

And some harder or two-part questions for 2 points

11 Who was manager of Aberdeen when they won the ECWC in 1983? Who did they beat in the Final?

12 Who was the only member of the 2006-07 Everton squad to have played in a Champions League Final, and for which club?

13 In the 1980-81 European Cup, the English champions beat the Scottish champions 5-0 on aggregate. Which two teams were involved?

14 In 1995, which side appeared in their 5th European Cup Final in 7 years? Who was the only player to appear in all 5?

15 What was the score in the group matches between Manchester United and Rangers in the 2003-04 Champions League?

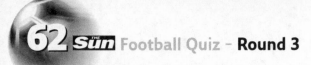
Questions 1-10, for 1 point each

1 Who is the all-time top scorer in the Champions League, as of May 2007?

2 Which side were ejected from the 2006-07 UEFA Cup after crowd trouble, giving Tottenham a bye into the last 16?

3 Who qualified for the Champions League in 2005 for the first time since 1970?

4 Who contested 3 consecutive Champions League Finals in 1993, 94 and 95, winning only the middle one?

5 Who was the great Uruguayan playmaker of the 1950s who appeared for AC Milan in the 1958 European Cup Final?

6 Who, in 1971, became the first (and last) Greek side to reach the European Cup Final, losing to Ajax?

7 Whose penalty settled the meaningless European Cup Final played out after the Heysel tragedy?

8 Which German goalkeeper won a Champions League winner's medal with Real Madrid in 1998?

9 Who scored all 4 goals for Manchester United in a 4-1 Champions League win in 2004-05?

10 Who scored in injury time against Rotor Volgograd in the 1995 UEFA Cup to save what was then an unbeaten home record in European competition for Manchester United?

And some harder or two-part questions for 2 points

11 In the 1999 Champions League Final, both Manchester United scorers were substitutes; who started the game as the twin strikers?

12 Which two Chelsea players were dismissed in the spicy Champions League ties against Barcelona in 2004-05 and 2005-06?

13 Which two England internationals have played for Real Madrid in a European Cup Final?

14 Which future Premiership star captained the Juventus side that won the 1996 Champions League? Which other future Premiership player scored Juve's first goal?

15 Which two English sides beat Internazionale and Lazio 5-1 and 4-0 respectively, both away from home, in the 2003-04 Champions League?

Questions 1-10, for 1 point each

1 Which side won the first 5 European Cup Finals?

2 Which Brazilian kept goal for Milan in the 2007 Champions League Final?

3 When Ruud Van Nistelrooy took his goal tally for Manchester United in European competition to 35 in 2004-05, whose club record did he break?

4 Which British club side featured in the very first ECWC Final in 1961?

5 Which French side lost the 1956 and 1959 European Cup Finals to the mighty Real Madrid?

6 In 1971-72, who lost a European Cup tie 7-1 and yet won the tie?

7 After the ban imposed on English clubs following the Heysel tragedy, when did Liverpool next play in the European Cup?

8 Who celebrated Manchester United's winning goal in the 1999 Champions League Final with a somersault?

9 Whose headed goal saw Chelsea past Barcelona 5-4 on aggregate in a 2004-05 Champions League last-16 tie?

10 Who won their only European trophy when they lifted the 1972 ECWC, beating Moscow Dynamo in the Final?

And some harder or two-part questions for 2 points

11 Which 2 players shared all 7 goals as Real Madrid beat Eintracht Frankfurt 7-3 in the 1960 European Cup Final?

12 Who beat Middlesbrough in the 2006 UEFA Cup Final and what was the score?

13 Who are the only Turkish side to win a major European trophy, and who did they beat on penalties in the 2000 UEFA Cup Final?

14 In their successful 1998-99 Champions League campaign, which 2 other European giants were drawn in Manchester United's difficult 1st-phase group?

15 Who beat Chelsea in the 2003-04 and 2004-05 Champions League?

Questions 1–10, for 1 point each

1 Which British ground was the setting for Real Madrid's 7–3 demolition of Eintracht Frankfurt in the European Cup Final of 1960?

2 Which English side hold the record for an aggregate victory in a two-legged tie after thrashing Jeunesse Hautcharage of Luxembourg 21–0 in the 1970s?

3 Who eliminated Arsenal from the Champions League in 2006–07, ending the club's chances of a trophy in March?

4 Which Dutch striker scored twice in each game as Anderlecht won the ECWC in 1976 and again in 1978?

5 Which British club lost the Fairs Cup (UEFA Cup) Finals in 1960 and 1961?

6 Accusations of bribery marred which Italian club's win over Derby County in the 1973 European Cup SF?

7 Why did AC Milan supporters sing 'You'll Never Walk Alone' before their 1989 European Cup SF against Real Madrid?

8 Whose goals put out holders Real Madrid on a very cold night in Kiev in a 1998–99 Champions League QF?

9 Who beat Celtic in the 2006–07 Champions League after they reached the knockout phase for the first time since the new format was introduced?

10 Two goals from which striker won the 1991 ECWC for Manchester United against Barcelona?

And some harder or two-part questions for 2 points

11 Who beat Celtic 3–2 in the 2003 UEFA Cup Final? Who scored both Celtic goals?

12 Who became the first Russian club to lift a European club trophy when they won the UEFA Cup in 2005? And who lost the final in their home city in Portugal?

13 Who scored a memorable hat-trick for Newcastle against Barcelona in a Champions League match? For which country was he an international?

14 Who were the opponents when Manchester United came from behind to win 3–2 in the SF of the 1999 Champions League after a 1–1 draw at Old Trafford? Whose goals had given United a seemingly impossible task?

15 Which much-maligned Liverpool defender made a vital goal-line clearance in the closing stages of the 2005 Champions League Final? And who made the vital saves in the penalty shoot-out?

Questions 1–10, for 1 point each

1 With which club did Aston Villa manager, Martin O'Neill, win the European Cup as a player?

2 Who did Everton beat in the Final of the ECWC in 1985?

3 In the QF of the 2005–06 UEFA Cup, who were 3–0 up on aggregate with an hour to play against Middlesbrough and still lost the tie?

4 Who scored the winning goal for Arsenal when they beat Parma 1–0 in the 1994 ECWC Final?

5 Which of the following sides has never played in the European Cup or Champions League: Burnley, Ipswich Town, Norwich City, Wolverhampton Wanderers?

6 A 30-yarder from Georg Schwarzenbeck took which side to a European Cup Final replay (which they won) with Atletico Madrid in 1973–74?

7 Who was manager of Benfica when they reached the 1990 European Cup Final?

8 Who scored 3 times for Chelsea in the 1999–2000 QF tie against Barcelona, only to see his side lose 6–4 on aggregate?

9 Who scored Chelsea's late winner as they came from 1–0 down to win 2–1 in Valencia in a 2006–07 Champions League QF?

10 Bruno N'Gotty's goal meant which team became the first French side to win the ECWC in 1996?

And some harder or two-part questions for 2 points

11 Who lifted the Champions League Trophy at Old Trafford as captain of Milan in 2003? What was the connection with the 1963 Final of the competition at Wembley?

12 Which member of the 2006–07 Rangers squad played in the 2004 Champions League Final for AS Monaco? For which country does he have over 30 caps?

13 Which 2 English clubs did Celtic overcome on their way to the 2003 UEFA Cup Final?

14 Which 2 sides contested the first Champions League Final between two teams from the same country, in 2000?

15 Which 2 sides contested the 1972 UEFA Cup Final, the only one between 2 English clubs?

Answers on page 202

Questions 1-10, for 1 point each

1 With which club did French World Cup winner Bixente Lizarazu win the Champions League?

2 Which Scottish international defender scored only 3 goals in nearly 300 league games for Newcastle, but managed another 3 in the 6-2 aggregate win over Ujpest Dozsa in the 1969 Fairs Cup Final?

3 Who lost 8-0 to FC Cologne in the 1995 Intertoto Cup, the club record defeat?

4 Everyone remembers Nayim beating David Seaman from the half-way line in the 1995 ECWC Final; but for which club was Nayim playing?

5 Which new sensation scored twice as Benfica won the 1962 European Cup Final 5-3 against Real Madrid?

6 Who was manager of Leeds United when they reached the 1975 European Cup Final?

7 Which young goalkeeper was in goal for Olympique Marseille in the 1993 Champions League Final?

8 Who scored a crucial goal in each leg as Real Madrid squeezed past Bayern Munich in the 2000 Champions League SF?

9 Who did Ipswich Town beat in the 1981 UEFA Cup Final to clinch their only European trophy?

10 Which English ground hosted the last ever ECWC in 1999?

And some harder or two-part questions for 2 points

11 Who did Liverpool beat to win the 2001 UEFA Cup, and what was the score?

12 Name the 2 non-English players in the team that won Liverpool the European Cup for the first time in 1977.

13 Which Scottish side fell at the SF stage, thus preventing an all-British European Cup Final against Liverpool in 1984? Who did Liverpool beat in the Final?

14 Who beat eventual Champions League winners Real Madrid 4-2, 4-1 and 2-1 during the course of the competition, but were still eliminated by the Spaniards? Explain

15 Where was the 2002 UEFA Cup Final held, and which side beat Borussia Dortmund on their own ground?

Questions 1-10, for 1 point each

1 Who beat Leeds in the 1975 European Cup Final?

2 Which future Premiership player scored both of Sampdoria's goals in their 1990 ECWC triumph?

3 Who scored the only goal of Liverpool's two-legged Champions League win over Chelsea in 2004-05?

4 Eintracht Frankfurt lost a memorable European Cup Final 7-3 to Real Madrid. Which side did they beat 12-4 on aggregate in the SF, thus preventing that team playing in the Final in their home city?

5 Defeat by which Italian side in the 1964-65 European Cup SF left Liverpool manager Bill Shankly fuming about a highly debatable refereeing display?

6 Which French side did Bayern Munich beat in the European Cup SF in 1975 and the Final in 1976?

7 In the 1990-91 European Cup, why were Olympique Marseille awarded the second leg of their tie against Milan 3-0?

8 Who lost successive Champions League Finals in 2000 and 2001?

9 By what name is the pre-qualifying competition for the UEFA Cup known?

10 How many European Cup Finals were held at the old Wembley: was it 2, 5 or 11?

And some harder or two-part questions for 2 points

11 Who scored Nottingham Forest's winning goals in the 1979 and 1980 European Cup Finals?

12 Who are the 2 East European sides to have won the European Cup?

13 Which side won the 1991 ECWC, the first year after the Heysel ban was lifted? Who were England's representatives in the European Cup that year?

14 Which three English sides reached the QF of the 2000-01 Champions League?

15 Who ended Everton's first venture into the Champions League, and which former Premiership striker scored against the Merseysiders?

Answers on page 202

Questions 1-10, for 1 point each

1 After completing a hat-trick of European Cup wins in 1976, how long did Bayern Munich have to wait before lifting the trophy again?

2 Who played only his 2nd game for Aston Villa in the 1982 European Cup Final after Jimmy Rimmer injured himself in the warm-up?

3 Who scored twice for AC Milan in the 2005 Champions League Final but finished on the losing side?

4 Who became the first British side to win the Fairs Cup (later UEFA Cup) in 1967?

5 Who did Manchester United beat 5-1 away from home after a brilliant display in the QF of the 1965-66 European Cup?

6 Which side were the losers when Liverpool won their first European Cup, and again in the following season's SF?

7 Who, in 1991, became the first English player to appear in a European Cup Final since the Heysel ban when he played for Marseille against Red Star Belgrade?

8 Whose path to their only Champions League Final included goals from Bernd Schneider, Dimitar Berbatov and Brazilian centre half, Lucio?

9 Who scored the solitary goal in the 2006 Champions League SF tie that saw Arsenal reach the Final at the expense of Villareal?

10 Who scored the game's only goal as Chelsea beat VFB Stuttgart to win the 1998 ECWC?

And some harder or two-part questions for 2 points

11 Who scored a hat-trick for Real Madrid, aged 35, in the 1962 European Cup Final against Benfica? What was the final score?

12 Name the 2 Nigerians who appeared in Ajax's Champions League Final win in 1995.

13 Which 2 sides played out the first goal-less draw in a European Cup Final in 1985-86?

14 Who, in 2001-02, became the first Welsh club to win a European Cup tie when they beat Shamkir from Azerbaijan? Which former winners of the competition beat them 8-0 on aggregate in the next round?

15 Which English side progressed the furthest in the 2006-07 UEFA Cup? Who eliminated them?

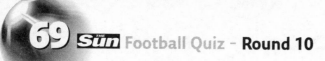

Questions 1-10, for 1 point each

1 Who was the only member of the Alaves team that played in the 2001 UEFA Cup Final with previous Premiership experience, having had an unsuccessful spell with Manchester United?

2 Whose goal from a quickly taken free-kick sparked off controversy in Manchester United's Champions League match against Lille in 2007?

3 Whose penalty miss in the shoot-out at the end of the 2005 Champions League Final was the cue for Liverpool's victory celebrations?

4 Between 1967 and 1973, only British clubs won the Fairs Cup/UEFA Cup. Which side won twice in that period?

5 Who announced themselves as a force in Europe when they beat Bill Shankly's Liverpool 5-1 in a European Cup QF in 1966-67?

6 In the 1975-76 European Cup, who were beaten 4-1 by Derby County only to win the second leg 5-1 and go through?

7 Which Marseille striker's 7 goals in 2 ties made him the leading scorer in the 1991-92 European Cup, despite his side not even reaching the group stage?

8 Craig Bellamy's injury-time winner at Feyenoord saw which side squeeze into the second phase of the 2002-03 Champions League?

9 Whose dismissal in the 2006 Champions League Final left Arsenal playing most of the match with 10 men?

10 Which Italian side won their only European trophy when they lifted the final ECWC in 1999, a year after losing the UEFA Cup Final to Inter?

And some harder or two-part questions for 2 points

11 Didier Drogba played in the 2004 UEFA Cup Final for which team? Who managed the victors, Valencia, that day?

12 Name 3 of the 5 British players who played for Chelsea in the 1998 ECWC Final victory over Stuttgart.

13 Which 2 Steaua Bucharest players scored 13 goals between them in the 1989 European Cup?

14 Which 20-year-old Real Madrid goalkeeper came on as a substitute and lit up the 2002 Champions League Final with a series of stunning saves? Whose acrobatic volley clinched the match for Real?

15 Who did Chelsea beat in the Final of the 1971 ECWC after a replay? Who scored for Chelsea in both matches?

Questions 1-10, for 1 point each

1 Which former Dutch international was manager of the Barcelona side that won the 2006 Champions League?

2 For which club did Michael Ballack play in a Champions League Final prior to joining Chelsea?

3 Which side beat Leeds in the 1973 ECWC, largely due to a scandalous and highly suspicious refereeing performance?

4 Which of these clubs has never played in European club competition: Burnley, Blackburn Rovers, Stoke City, Sheffield United

5 Who did Manchester United beat in the SF when they won the European Cup in 1968?

6 Which midfield player scored 2 hat-tricks for Liverpool in the 1980-81 European Cup?

7 Who was Milan's £13m 'wonderkid' who played (and flopped) in the 1993 Champions League Final?

8 Who won a Champions League SF by scoring an away goal in their own stadium?

9 Fernando Morientes reached the Champions League Final whilst on loan at which club in 2004?

10 Apart from Dynamo Kiev, which other team from outside Russia won a European trophy (ECWC, 1981) whilst part of the Soviet Union?

And some harder or two-part questions for 2 points

11 Which 2 players scored Liverpool's goals in the Champions League win in Barcelona in February 2007?

12 Which Scottish side reached their only European Final (UEFA Cup) in 1987? Which Swedish side beat them to become the first Swedish winners of a European club trophy?

13 Who won the 1993 Champions League but were unable to defend their trophy after being found guilty of match-fixing? Who was the outspoken club President at the heart of the scandal?

14 In the 2002-03 Champions League Liverpool were eliminated in the preliminary groups after losing twice to which Spanish side and failing to beat which unfancied Swiss team?

15 Which English side won the 1971 ECWC? Who beat them the following season in the SF?

Questions 1–10, for 1 point each

1 Wayne Rooney scored a hat-trick on his Manchester United debut; who were the opponents?

2 In the 2004 Champions League, which Spanish team lost 4-1 in Milan, but came back to win the 2nd leg 4-0 and go through?

3 Which European side have played in 7 European Cup Finals, but lost all except the first 2?

4 Which is the only one of these clubs to have played in European competition: Bristol City, Portsmouth, Swansea City, Tranmere Rovers

5 Who beat the holders, Manchester United, in the 1968-69 European Cup SF?

6 Who was manager of Aston Villa when they won the European Cup in 1982?

7 Whose 2 goals against Liverpool in the final saw Milan clinch the 2007 Champions League?

8 Which goalkeeper saved 3 penalties in the shoot-out as Milan beat their compatriots, Juventus, in the 2003 Champions League Final?

9 Which former World Cup winner managed Monaco when they reached the Champions League Final in 2004?

10 Which Italian side surprisingly beat Juventus over 2 legs in the Final of the 1995 UEFA Cup and then won the trophy again in 1999, beating Marseille 3-0?

And some harder or two-part questions for 2 points

11 Name the 3 members of the Real Madrid side that won the Champions League Final in 2000 who have subsequently played for Bolton Wanderers.

12 Which 2 namesakes scored 5 of the 6 Juventus goals when they hammered Dortmund 6-1 on aggregate in the 1993 UEFA Cup Final?

13 Who eliminated Manchester United on away goals on United's return to the Champions League in 1993-94? Who was given a red card after the final whistle for a gesture made to the Swiss referee?

14 Who was applauded from the field by the home fans after scoring a superb hat-trick for Real Madrid at Old Trafford in the 2002-03 Champions League QF? Who scored twice for United after coming off the bench?

15 Which 2 sides lost UEFA Cup Finals to Liverpool and later lost European Cup Finals to them?

Answers on page 203

Overseas

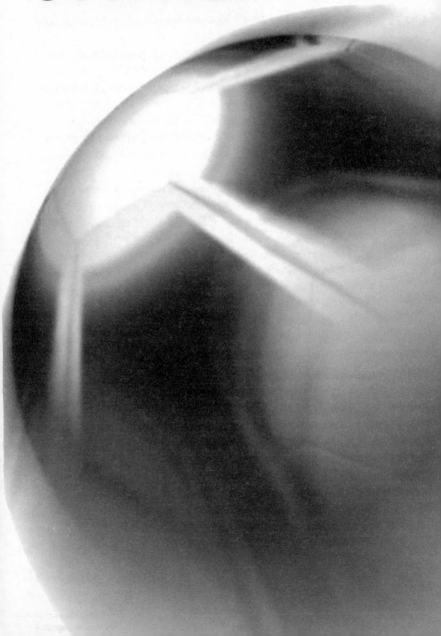

73 ☀ The Sun Football Quiz - **Round 1**

Questions 1-10, for 1 point each

1 In which city could you watch a game in the Nepstadion?

2 Ubaldo Fillol is rated as probably the best South American goalkeeper ever; for which country did he play?

3 Bayern Munich provided the backbone of the great West Germany side of the early 1970s, but for which rival side did Berti Vogts and Rainer Bonhof play?

4 Which was Lothar Matthaus' only European club outside Germany?

5 Luis Nazario de Lima is known simply by his first name, which is what?

6 Which Italian goalkeeper was unbeaten in internationals for 1,143 minutes, until conceding against Haiti in 1974?

7 Who was the Bulgarian international signed by Martin O'Neill from his former employers, Celtic, in 2006?

8 Whose goal-scoring for Auxerre in France earned him a (reported) £14m move to Liverpool in 2004?

9 Which side have won the French league most often, having dominated in the 1960s and 70s?

10 Honved were a legendary club side in which country in the 1950s and 60s?

And some harder or two-part questions for 2 points

11 Which 2 famous German internationals were known as Der Kaiser und Der Bomber?

12 Which Sardinian side won their only league title in 1970, and who was the flying winger, a star of the 1970 WCFT, whose goals were vital to their success?

13 Which Danish striker won the European Footballer of the Year award in 1977, and for which German club was he playing that season?

14 Which coach won the European Cup with Feyenoord in 1970 and Hamburg in 1983, as well as reaching the World Cup Final with Holland in 1978? For which country was he a seriously good player in the years after the war?

15 Which French-born player was top scorer for title-chasing Sevilla in 2006-07? For which country did he opt to play international football?

Answers on page 203

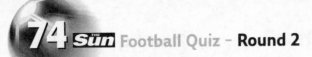

Questions 1-10, for 1 point each

1. The art of the deep-lying 'playmaker' centre-forward was pioneered by Nandor Hidegkuti for which country's national team?

2. Which of these sides does NOT play in UEFA competition as the result of the break-up of Communist Yugoslavia: Montenegro, Slovenia, Estonia, Croatia?

3. Inter Milan, AS Monaco, Tottenham, Bayern Munich: whose impressively cosmopolitan sequence of clubs was this in the 1990s?

4. Which resilient Cameroon international was African Player of the Year in 1976 and then again 14 years later, in 1990, aged 38?

5. Which German striker was European Player of the Year in 1980 and again in 1981?

6. How many caps did Gianfranco Zola win in his career: was it 12, 35 or 66?

7. Fulham's full-back Carlos Bocanegra has over 40 caps for which national team?

8. From which Spanish side did Newcastle buy Patrick Kluivert in 2005?

9. Who were awarded the Italian Serie A title after it was stripped from Juventus following the bribery scandal in 2005-06?

10. Who was Manager of the Year in the Japanese League in 1995?

And some harder or two-part questions for 2 points

11. Which 2 Australian internationals have won the European Cup with Liverpool?

12. Which were Marco Van Basten's only 2 clubs before his premature retirement through injury?

13. Which 3 Brazilian players have been named European Footballer of the Year in the last 10 years?

14. Before his move to Arsenal, at which club had Thierry Henry previously played under Arsène Wenger? Which other current Arsenal star was bought from the same club in January 2006?

15. Where was Portuguese international Deco born? From which club did Barcelona buy him in 2004?

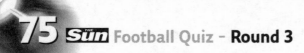

Questions 1-10, for 1 point each

1 Where was Portugal legend Eusebio born?

2 Italian legend Franco Baresi was revered at which club, the only one he played for?

3 Which Frenchman, a star of the 1958 World Cup, and later a star with Real Madrid, was voted European Footballer of the Year in 1958?

4 How many goals did Gerd Muller score in his 62 matches for West Germany: was it 37, 55 or 68?

5 Marian Pahars of Southampton played international football for which country?

6 Andoni Zubizaretta won 126 caps playing in goal for which country?

7 From which Dutch club did Manchester City sign the experienced Tunisian international Hatem Trabelsi in 2006?

8 For which country did Shaun Goater play international football?

9 In which Italian city do Juventus play?

10 Perennial Norwegian champions Rosenborg are based in which city?

And some harder or two-part questions for 2 points

11 In which 2 European countries did Mark Viduka play club football before joining Leeds?

12 From which club did Manchester United buy Ruud Van Nistelrooy? And which other player did they buy from the same club in 2005?

13 Who are the two Portuguese players to have been named as European Footballer of the Year?

14 Who captained Nigeria to Olympic glory in 1996, aged only 20? Which 18-year-old future Premiership player scored the opening goal in the Final?

15 Which PSV star won his 100th cap for Holland against Argentina in the 2006 WCFT? For which European giants did he make over 200 league appearances?

Questions 1-10, for 1 point each

1   To which Italian club did Hernan Crespo return after his patchy spell at Chelsea?

2   Which Argentinian legend earned the devotion of Fiorentina supporters when he stayed with the club after their relegation in the early 1990s and led them back into Serie A?

3   For which Premiership club did Brian Laudrup have a brief but impressive spell?

4   With which Italian side did Pavel Nedved win a league and cup double before leaving for Juventus?

5   Enzo Scifo won 84 caps for which adopted country?

6   Patrice Evra was born in Senegal but plays international football for which country?

7   Who swapped industrial Donetz (with Shakhtor) in Kiev for industrial Wigan in January 2007?

8   West Ham paid Fiorentina £5m in 2001 for which defender?

9   In which Italian city do Fiorentina play their home games?

10   Newcastle's Nolberto Solano was the only representative of which country active in the Premiership in 2006-07?

And some harder or two-part questions for 2 points

11   Which Russian club sold Nemanja Vidic to Manchester United; and for which country does he play international football?

12   Which goalkeeper won 78 caps for the Soviet Union in the 1960s? What was characteristic of his attire?

13   Which side have won the French league for the last 6 seasons? Who was their manager in 2006-07?

14   Who holds the record for most caps for Italy? Who became the third Italian player to reach 100 caps during the 2006 WCFT?

15   Who left Manchester United for Lazio in 2001, and for which club in his homeland was he playing in 2006-07?

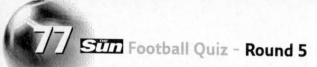

Questions 1-10, for 1 point each

1 Which French club took Djibril Cissé on loan from Liverpool after an unsuccessful spell in the Premiership?

2 Which world star of the 1990s was nicknamed 'Batigol' and had as many websites run by adoring female fans as male ones?

3 Which Italian club signed Denis Law from Manchester City in 1960?

4 The great Italian defender Guiseppe Bergomi played over 750 matches for which club, his only one?

5 Which Serbian international spent just one season at Chelsea after a £5m move from PSV Eindhoven in 2004?

6 Michael Essien was bought from Lyon in 2005; which Chelsea player went the other way as part of the deal?

7 Which quick international winger joined Charlton from PSV in 2004?

8 Who won the 2004 Olympic soccer tournament?

9 Of which league have Linfield been the most frequent winners?

10 Middlesbrough's Fabio Rochemback has been capped by which country?

And some harder or two-part questions for 2 points

11 Which 2 countries played each other for the first time at Hamburg's Volkspark Stadium in 1974, but are unlikely to play each other again?

12 Apart from England, in which 2 countries did Gary Lineker play professional football?

13 Which side won their first and only Spanish league title in 2000? Which Dutch striker was their top scorer that season?

14 Who was the great Mexican player with a trademark somersault celebration? With which club was he a cult hero for much of the 1980s?

15 In which country was England star Owen Hargreaves born? For which side has he played all his club football up to 2007?

Answers on page 204

Questions 1-10, for 1 point each

1 Which top club side formed the basis of the USSR's team for the 1986 WCFT?

2 Who was coach of the Italian national side from 1975 to 1986, winning the World Cup in 1982?

3 With which Premiership club did Jari Litmanen spend 2 years, most of it, mystifyingly, on the bench?

4 Which club boasted Pele on its books for most of his career?

5 Uwe Seeler was a 1960s legend with which country?

6 What nationality is Chelsea's Khalid Boulahrouz?

7 How many international goals has Jimmy Floyd Hasselbaink scored in his 23 matches for Holland: is it 2, 9 or 16?

8 Which occasionally eccentric goalkeeper played over 100 matches for Sweden and kept goal for them at the 1990 and 1994 WCFT?

9 Which side have won the Norwegian league every year since 1991, barring 2005 when Valerenga pipped them?

10 Which Argentinian defender has played over 400 matches for Internazionale, as well as having over 100 caps for the national team?

And some harder or two-part questions for 2 points

11 Which Czech player was European Footballer of the Year in 2003 and with which club was he playing?

12 Who is the only New Zealand international regularly getting a game in the Premiership, and for which club?

13 A game between Servette and the Grasshopper Club would be between teams representing which Swiss cities?

14 Tottenham's Steed Malbranque has won how many caps for France? (1 pt if within 2)

15 Who was sacked by Chelsea after drug-taking revelations in 2004? For which Serie A side was he scoring regularly in 2006-07?

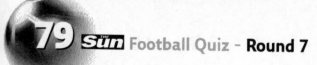

Questions 1-10, for 1 point each

1 With which French club did Eric Cantona win the French League title?

2 Which Italian side are known as the Bianconeri (black & whites)?

3 What connects Serie A clubs Milan, Lazio, Fiorentina and Reggina in the 2006–07 season?

4 Which club once featured Franz Beckenbauer and Pele in the same team?

5 Who was the Ukrainian striker with whom Andriy Shevchenko formed a deadly partnership at Dynamo Kiev?

6 From which Spanish club did Rafa Benitez buy Xavi Alonso?

7 Who was the only Belorussian international playing in the Premiership in 2006–07?

8 Brehme, Klinsmann and Matthaus, all key members of West Germany's 1990 WCFT squad, were all playing for which Italian club at the time?

9 Portuguese club Benfica play in which city?

10 Who made a comeback after a lengthy injury lay-off for Real Madrid in 2005–06, but scored an own-goal and got sent off in his first game back?

And some harder or two-part questions for 2 points

11 The retirement of which pair of brothers after the 1998 World Cup heralded a decline in Denmark's fortunes as a footballing power?

12 Which 2 players were the subject of a surprise move to West Ham at the start of the 2006–07 season?

13 Which former France manager had a disappointing spell as manager of Tottenham in 2004–05? Which club did he lead to a first French league title in 2002?

14 With which Italian side did Graeme Souness have a brief spell as a player? And which club did he manage after his acrimonious departure from the Liverpool job?

15 Which Portuguese international joined West Ham in January 2007? Where did he start his career in England?

Questions 1-10, for 1 point each

1 Whose nickname in Italy translates as 'The Golden Ponytail'?

2 How many times did Paolo Di Canio play for Italy: was it 0, 10 or 31?

3 For which country does Inter Milan's Zlatan Ibrahimovic play his international football?

4 With which Italian side did Michel Platini enjoy a triumphant spell in the 1980s?

5 Who was the prima-donna of the 1990s Bulgarian side who won 4 consecutive league titles and a European Cup with Barcelona?

6 Who was the powerful African midfielder that Rafa Benitez brought from his old club, Valencia, in 2005?

7 Which other La Liga club would Barcelona play in a local derby?

8 Dutch star Ronald Koeman was a favourite at which Spanish club?

9 Kaizer Chiefs and Orlando Pirates are teams in which country's football league?

10 A Rome derby would feature Roma and which other side?

And some harder or two-part questions for 2 points

11 Gunnar Gren, Nils Liedholm and Gunnar Nordahl were all part of which strong postwar national team? Which Italian club did the trio lead to a first Serie A title for 44 years in 1951?

12 Which talented Arsenal winger spent 2006-07 on loan at Birmingham City? For which national side did he make his debut that season?

13 Which former favourite overseas star returned to Juventus as manager in 2006-07? Who did he replace?

14 Who is this? He scored only 6 times in his 81 matches in midfield for Italy, but saved one for the 1982 World Cup Final (2 pts if you already have the answer); he won 5 Serie A titles with Juventus, his only club; he is one of the few players to have won all 3 major European club trophies.

15 Which Polish superstar was the first from his country to win a European Cup winner's medal? For which club?

Questions 1–10, for 1 point each

1 Who was the charismatic Paraguayan goalkeeper of the 1990s who doubled as their set-piece specialist?

2 Who was the Finnish international at the heart of the resurgence of Ajax in the early 1990s?

3 Which former Liverpool player scored 33 goals in 63 games for Real Sociedad between 1989 and 1991?

4 Who won his 100th cap for Spain in a friendly against Iceland in August 2006?

5 With which club has Francesco Totti spent his entire career?

6 Where was Tomasz Rosicky playing before his 2006 move to Arsenal?

7 In 2006–07, which Spanish top-division side didn't play home matches on the mainland?

8 Who was the USA international forward who played top-flight English football with Chelsea and Coventry City in the early 1990s?

9 Which side won the league title in the old Soviet Union most often?

10 What connects Steaua, Rapid and Dynamo?

And some harder or two-part questions for 2 points

11 Which English footballer was voted European Footballer of the Year whilst with a foreign club? Which was the club?

12 Which English manager was in charge of Switzerland when they qualified for the 1994 WCFT and Euro 96? Which national team did he take over as coach in 2006?

13 Which Belgian international succeeded Sepp Maier as Bayern Munich's goalkeeper? Who has held the position for the last decade and more?

14 Hermann Hreidarsson is which club's record transfer outlay AND record transfer receipt? Which club was he with in 2006–07?

15 Which 2 Romanian stars were signed by Tottenham after shining at the 1994 World Cup?

Questions 1-10, for 1 point each

1 Who was the manager of West Germany between 1966 and 1978?

2 With which club was Sven-Goran Eriksson manager immediately before taking the England job?

3 In which city is the Maracana stadium?

4 In which particular area of Italy was Gianfranco Zola born?

5 Which manager won 6 Serie A titles with Juventus between 1977 and 1986, and another with Inter Milan in 1989?

6 A fringe player in the Premiership he may be, but Portsmouth's Svetoslav Todorov is a regular in which international side?

7 Argentinian-born Roberto Colautti is the new Golden Boy of which soccer nation?

8 In which league might you find a side called Kashima Antlers?

9 Who are the bitter local Istanbul rivals of Galatasaray?

10 Which Ghana international was a rock in defence for a decade at Bayern Munich before moving to AS Roma in 2005?

And some harder or two-part questions for 2 points

11 Former Dutch coach Rinus Michels exerted his homeland's influence at Barcelona by importing which two Dutch stars?

12 Who were the 2 Egyptian internationals on Tottenham's books in 2006-07?

13 Oleg Blokhin won 101 caps for the USSR. Which country would he represent now? For which club did he play?

14 Which Premiership player made his debut for France in May 2006 against Denmark? Which club was he playing for at the time?

15 Who was appointed manager of Bayern Munich in 1998? From which other German club did he join?

Questions 1-10, for 1 point each

1 Rinus Michels was responsible for the transformation of which Dutch club into a European super-power in the 1970s?

2 Luis Figo enraged the supporters of which club when he left to join Real Madrid?

3 Which team did Diego Maradiona lead to their first-ever Serie A title?

4 Which European side did Rivaldo sign for in 2004, a year after being released by Milan?

5 In which country was Patrick Vieira born?

6 Which Tottenham player has over 30 caps for Finland?

7 Eddie Lewis of Leeds, and before that Preston, has over 70 caps for which country?

8 Which Chelsea player was the only English-based member of Italy's 1998 WCFT squad?

9 Penarol and Nacional are the two dominant sides in which South American league?

10 Which side play in the Santiago Bernabeu stadium?

And some harder or two-part questions for 2 points

11 Which Fiorentina player became the first striker to score over 30 goals in Serie A for over 50 years? What was the icing on his cake for the season?

12 Who were the 2 Israeli internationals on Bolton's books in 2006-07?

13 Since ending his disappointing stint at Manchester United, Diego Forlan has been a great success at which Spanish club? For which country does Forlan play?

14 Who were the two South African internationals playing with Blackburn Rovers in 2006-07?

15 Who was 2nd choice to the erratic Fabien Barthez at the 2006 WCFT, and for which club does he play?

Questions 1-10, for 1 point each

1 With which club did Kanu win a Champions League winner's medal before he was 21?

2 The World Club match between Racing Club and Celtic in 1968 turned into a fist-fight; in which city did the match take place?

3 Which club first brought a young Diego Maradona to Europe?

4 Who was Real Madrid's left-back for almost a decade after joining from Milan in 1996?

5 Which Italian-based player won his 100th cap for France in a friendly against Greece in November 2006?

6 Who did Newcastle buy from Internazionale in summer 2005 as cover for the injured Michael Owen?

7 What do German sides Hansa Rostock, Energie Cottbus and Carl Zeiss Jena have in common?

8 Twente Enschede against AZ Alkmaar would be a league match in which country?

9 Who was the legendary manager of the 1960s Inter side: was it Maldini, Ancelotti or Herrera?

10 Which veteran striker was Juve's top scorer in 2006–07 as they fought their way back out of Serie B?

And some harder or two-part questions for 2 points

11 Which 2 players did Barcelona pick up from Juventus in 2006 after the Italian side were relegated from Serie A for corruption?

12 Which disastrous signing from Lyon cost Fulham £11.5m in 2001, and which manager was responsible?

13 Who is this? He was an intimidating man-marker with Juventus and Italy in the 1970s and 80s, (2 pts if you already have the answer) winning 71 caps, a World Cup and 7 Serie A titles.

14 Name 3 of Barcelona's 4 Dutch coaches in the last 30 years.

15 Who were the 'Holy Trinity' of Dutch football in the 1980s?

Questions 1-10, for 1 point each

1 1960s star Florian Albert was a natural successor to the great forwards of the 1950s in which national team?

2 Which Italian side bought Paul Gascoigne from Tottenham?

3 Who was the 'Butcher of Bilbao' who almost ended Maradona's career with a savage tackle in 1983?

4 Who was manager of PSV Eindhoven when they won the Dutch league in 1991 and 1992?

5 For which striker did Inter pay Lazio £32m (then a world record) in 1999?

6 Apart from Mark Viduka, who was Middlesbrough's other Australian international in 2006-07?

7 Goalkeeper Mart Poom plays international football for which country?

8 Which team have been winners of the top division in Belgium most often?

9 In 1971-72 Celtic knocked Sliema Wanderers out of the European Cup; which country were Sliema representing?

10 Widzew Lodz and Gornik Zabrze are famous sides from which European country?

And some harder or two-part questions for 2 points

11 From which Spanish club did Arsenal buy Jose Antonio Reyes, and with which other Spanish club did he spend 2006-07 on loan?

12 Which 2 members of the Sweden WCFT squad in 1990 went on to play for Arsenal?

13 Who is this? His magical left foot earned him the nickname 'Maradona of the Carpathians'; (2 pts if you already have the answer); his skills lit up the Bernabeu and the Nou Camp and he is revered at Galatasaray as well as in his homeland; he scored 35 goals in 125 matches for his country – both records.

14 The Bundesliga in 2006-07 ended in a 3-way struggle between which sides?

15 Which US club signed David Beckham for the 2007 season, and which former US international is chairman of the club?

England

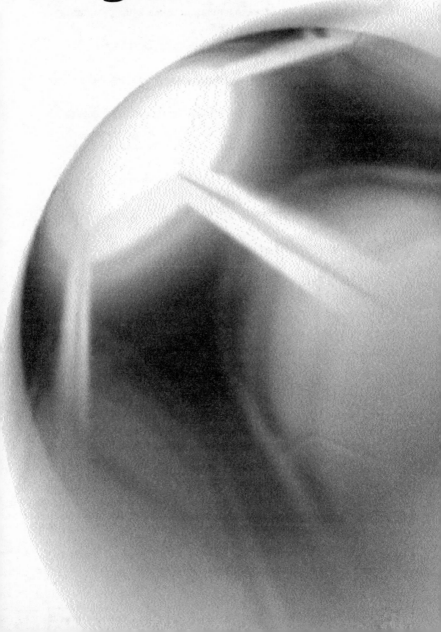

Questions 1-10, for 1 point each

1 Which club has provided the most England internationals over the years?

2 Which 2006-07 Premiership side has never provided an England international?

3 Willie Hall scored 5 times for England against Northern Ireland in 1938, including a hat-trick in 4 minutes. For which club side was Hall playing?

4 Which Liverpool player scored twice as England beat reigning World Champions Argentina 3-1 in a 1980 friendly?

5 Ignoring caretakers, who was England's least successful manager, with a win percentage of only 38.88?

6 How many of Tony Adams' 66 England caps were as captain of the side?

7 In which year did Bobby Moore make his England debut, was it 1959, 1962 or 1965?

8 Which former England international was killed in a car crash in Spain in 1989, aged only 33?

9 Who scored on his England debut against Scotland in 1958?

10 Who is the only player since 1970 to have made his England debut while playing for Fulham?

And some harder or two-part questions for 2 points

11 In which city did the first official England international take place? And was it in 1844, 1872 or 1898?

12 Name two of the three players who have played for England whilst on the books at Sampdoria in Serie A.

13 In which year was the last Home International played? (1 pt for 2 years either way)

14 Name the 4 post-war players to have won 20 caps whilst at Derby County.

15 Defeat at home to which country sealed the fate of Kevin Keegan as England manager in October 2000? Whose tame shot crept past David Seaman as England lost the game 1-0?

Questions 1-10, for 1 point each

1 Which England international of the 1970s earned the nickname 'Nijinsky' due to his prodigious stamina?

2 'The ..... are from another planet!' was a newspaper opinion on which side's remarkable 7-1 victory over England?

3 Who won most caps for England: David Batty, Mick Channon, Francis Lee or David James?

4 Who was capped by England whilst playing for 3 different Italian clubs?

5 Which recent England international sports Ivanhoe as one of his middle names?

6 Who was the first black player to win a full England cap?

7 Who scored 197 goals in 316 games for Blackpool in the 1940s and 50s, and an impressive 23 in 25 England appearances, including 4 on his debut?

8 Which England international was given the name 'Supermac' when he emerged as a top-class striker at Newcastle?

9 Which prolific striker of the late 1980s/90s won 13 caps for England without ever playing in the top flight?

10 Who is the only player since 1970 to have made his England debut while playing for Birmingham City?

And some harder or two-part questions for 2 points

11 Name 3 of the 4 members of Luton's League Cup-winning team of 1988 who played for England at some point in their career.

12 Which current but injury-prone striker scored on his only England appearance against Australia in 2003? What was the result of the match?

13 Who was the popular choice for England manager in the newspapers prior to Ron Greenwood's appointment in 1977? Whose tenure had just ended?

14 Name the three goalkeepers to have won solitary caps for England since WWII. (Discount Robert Green, as he is still playing.)

15 Who scored in his first competitive match as England captain in a 2001 World Cup qualifier against Finland? Which cult character scored for Finland?

Questions 1-10, for 1 point each

1 Which World Cup winner was known as 'The Ghost' due to his ability to steal in at the back post and score?

2 When Wayne Rooney became England's youngest-ever goalscorer in September 2003, whose record did he break?

3 Who achieved the unusual 'feat' of winning his first 4 England caps (beginning in 1995) under 4 different managers?

4 Who holds the record for the most England goals in one calendar year?

5 To the end of 2006, the Neville brothers have won 138 caps for England; how many goals have they scored between them?

6 How many games did England lose when Gordon Banks made his 73 appearances? Was it 9, 15 or 22?

7 Who played for England on his home ground against Germany in the 5-1 rout of 2001?

8 Who were the Wembley Wizards, who inflicted England's first defeat at Wembley – a 5-1 thrashing – in 1928?

9 How many goals did Peter Beardsley score in 59 games for England, was it 9, 13 or 19?

10 Who is the only player since 1970 to have made his England debut while playing for Oldham Athletic?

And some harder or two-part questions for 2 points

11 Who scored the fastest-ever goal in a World Cup match when they scored against England after 9 seconds of a qualifier in 1993? Who scored a hat-trick in the same match?

12 Which team did England beat 6-1 in a friendly in 2004? Which England-based striker scored the opponents' goal?

13 Which young goalkeeper made his England debut in a friendly against Spain in February 2007? Which club holds his registration?

14 Name the 4 England players capped whilst playing for Real Madrid.

15 In 1991, England played a friendly, their only one to date, against which Asian country on their way back from a tour of New Zealand and Australia? Who scored all 4 goals for England in their 4-2 win?

Questions 1-10, for 1 point each

1 Which legendary sportsman, capped for England in 1901, won 26 caps at cricket as well as representing Oxford at rugby union and holding the world long-jump record?

2 Who, in 1975, was the fourth and most recent England player to score 5 goals in a match (against Cyprus)?

3 In what role did Jimmy Mullen become the first player to play for England in a friendly against Belgium in 1950?

4 Which 18-year-old made his England debut in 2006?

5 Whose solitary England cap came whilst he was playing for Celtic in 2004?

6 How many England caps did Chelsea, Stoke and Arsenal maverick, Alan Hudson, win for England? Was it 2, 8 or 19?

7 Who beat England for the first and only time in 1981 in a World Cup qualifying match?

8 Who scored the winning goal for Northern Ireland when they beat England in a World Cup qualifier in 2005?

9 Which of these strikers has the best goals-per-game ratio for England: Michael Owen, Kevin Keegan, Gary Lineker, Alan Shearer?

10 'Only one team can win this game ... and that's England,' said Kevin Keegan. What happened next?

And some harder or two-part questions for 2 points

11 Which left-winger won his solitary England cap in 1999 whilst playing for Leicester City? And from which club had Leicester signed him?

12 Derek Statham won few caps for England as he spent most of the time understudying which long-serving and consistent left-back? Which was Statham's club?

13 With which club did Roy McFarland and Colin Todd form an outstanding defensive pairing, and which club did they jointly manage for a brief period?

14 Which goalkeeper made his only England appearance so far (May 07) against Greece in a friendly in August 2006? Which club did he join shortly afterwards?

15 In the 1980s England twice beat Turkey 8-0. Who scored a hat-trick from midfield in the first match, and which winger scored twice in each game?

Answers on page 206

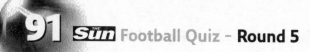

Questions 1-10, for 1 point each

1 Which TV personality scored 44 goals in 57 games for England between 1959 and 1967?

2 Which England manager won most caps as a player?

3 'The Battle of Highbury', a notoriously dirty 1934 international, was played between England and which other nation?

4 Who, in 2004, was the most recent former England international to receive a knighthood?

5 Which Newcastle centre-half won 4 caps in the mid-90s?

6 With which club was Steve Foster, the headband-wearing centre half, playing when he won his 3 England caps?

7 Don Revie left the England job to take a lucrative contract managing which other national side?

8 Which striker from the turn of the last century, the first great English goalscorer, remains Derby's all-time top league scorer?

9 Who got the most caps for England; Martin Chivers, Paul Mariner or Malcolm Macdonald?

10 Who scored 4 times on his England debut (against Portugal) in 1947?

And some harder or two-part questions for 2 points

11 What connects Jimmy Armfield, Peter Bonetti, Gerry Byrne, George Eastham, Ron Flowers, Norman Hunter and Ron Springett?

12 Which pair formed a central defensive partnership for Ipswich and, occasionally, England in the 1980s?

13 Name the 4 Leeds United players in England's 2002 World Cup Finals squad. They have all since crossed the Pennines.

14 Who were the opposition when an England 'friendly' in February, 1995 was abandoned after crowd trouble? What was the venue for the match?

15 Who scored a stunning solo goal as England pulled off a 2–0 win against Brazil in the Maracana Stadium in 1984? Which Italian-based player sealed the win with the second?

Answers on page 206

Questions 1-10, for 1 point each

1 Nat Lofthouse and Alan Shearer both scored 30 times for England. Who played the fewer games?

2 Who scored both England's fastest competitive goal and their fastest goal at Wembley stadium?

3 Who was the Inter Milan player in Glenn Hoddle's first England XI as manager?

4 Who appeared for England whilst playing club football in the league's third tier in 1948, after a strange transfer to Notts County from Everton?

5 Which Liverpool star waited 11 years between his first 2 England caps in 1966 and his last 2 in 1977?

6 Who was the last Bolton player to play for England?

7 Which future England manager scored twice on his debut as a player in a 4-0 win over France in 1957?

8 How many caps did Gareth Southgate win for England: was it 29, 40 or 57?

9 Which of these players has never captained England: Peter Beardsley, Terry Butcher, David Platt, Gareth Southgate?

10 Which of these famous Arsenal players has the most caps: Kenny Sansom, Tony Adams, David Seaman?

And some harder or two-part questions for 2 points

11 Against which side did England's Stan Mortensen make his first international appearance, in an unofficial wartime game?

12 Who scored England's equaliser with a stunning free kick against Greece in a crucial World Cup qualifier in 2001? And who had scored England's first goal with his first touch after coming on as a substitute?

13 Which two AC Milan players played together 15 times for England whilst at the Italian club in the 1980s?

14 Which powerful midfielder scored twice as England beat Scotland 5-1 in a 1975 Home International? Who had a disastrous game in goal for Scotland?

15 When England beat Northern Ireland 5-1 in October 1979, which 2 Nottingham Forest players scored twice each?

Questions 1-10, for 1 point each

1 How many caps did David Platt win for England: was it 42, 62 or 82?

2 Which of the following grounds has never hosted an England international: Craven Cottage, Upton Park, Selhurst Park, Burnden Park?

3 Who are England's official kit manufacturers?

4 'In The Name of Allah, Go!' was *The Sun*'s rather unkind exhortation to England manager Bobby Robson after a 1-1 draw against which country in 1988?

5 How many times did Bobby Charlton captain England during his 106 caps?

6 Which England manager was the first one to talk about the 'Christmas Tree' formation?

7 After Bobby Moore and Billy Wright, who has captained England in most international matches?

8 Which of these sides is the only one to have beaten England in a full international: Bulgaria, Finland, Switzerland, Turkey?

9 With which club side did England half-back Ron Flowers win 3 League titles in the 1950s?

10 Who scored both of England's goals in a 2-2 draw with Yugoslavia on his debut in 1950, but had to wait almost a year for his second cap?

And some harder or two-part questions for 2 points

11 Who scored a hat-trick as England destroyed Scotland 9-3 at Wembley in April, 1961? And who was the unfortunate Scottish goalkeeper who would never get picked again?

12 Which 2 Charlton Athletic full-backs made their England debuts under Sven-Goran Eriksson?

13 Name the 5 clubs with which Peter Shilton won his 125 caps.

14 Who scored both England goals as England won 2-0 in Glasgow in a Euro 2000 qualification play-off? Who scored Scotland's goal in their consolatory 1-0 win at Wembley in the return?

15 Who made his England debut against reigning World Champions West Germany in a 1975 friendly, and ran the game from midfield? How many more times did Don Revie pick him?

Answers on page 206

Questions 1-10, for 1 point each

1 Who recently became the tallest player ever to represent England?

2 In 2001 7 Manchester United players appeared in the same England match; who also supplied 7 players for a match in 1934?

3 'No better player ever wore the white shirt. I was proud to have him as a colleague and a friend.' Billy Wright pays tribute to which contemporary?

4 Who won 18 caps for England whilst playing for Olympique Marseille?

5 How many caps did Liverpool hard-man Tommy Smith win for England: was it 1, 8 or 22?

6 England cricketing great Denis Compton also played football for England and which London club?

7 Who were the first side to beat England after the 1966 World Cup win?

8 Who did England play in an unofficial international in 1996?

9 Which consistent full-back remains Blackpool's most-capped player, with 43 for England?

10 Who scored twice on his first start (second game) for England in a fine 3-0 win over West Germany in a tournament in the USA in 1985?

And some harder or two-part questions for 2 points

11 By the end of 2006, England had played 110 games against Scotland; how many had they won? (1pt for within 3)

12 Who are the most recent pair of brothers to have appeared in the same England team?

13 For which club was Teddy Sheringham playing when he made his England debut? And when he won his last cap?

14 As of 1 May, 2007, in how many of his 30 England games has Kieron Dyer played a full 90 minutes? How many goals has he scored?

15 How many caps did the following players win for England between them: Terry Phelan, Mark Stein, Kevin Ratcliffe, Robbie Earle? (1 pt for within 3 either way)

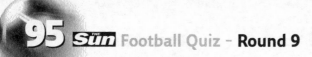

Questions 1-10, for 1 point each

1 Which future England manager made 3 appearances for them at the 1958 World Cup?

2 Which of these players won the most caps for England: Martin Keown, Terry Fenwick, Carlton Palmer or Steve McManaman?

3 Which band played on England's Euro 96 anthem 'Three Lions', along-side the songs' lyricists and promoters, comedians Baddiel and Skinner?

4 Which of these players has captained England the most times: Tony Adams, Kevin Keegan, Alan Shearer, David Beckham?

5 Two England strikers of the last 20 years have shared what name?

6 Which England striker became known as 'The Lion of Vienna' after scoring a memorable goal in a friendly against Austria in the 1950s?

7 Which player did Alf Ramsey refuse to drop after the first group match of the 1966 WCFT, despite an FA instruction to do so following a bad tackle in that first game against France?

8 With which club was Keith Curle when he won his 3 England caps?

9 Who scored on his England debut in 1934, a 4-0 win against Wales?

10 Who was the first player to reach 50 caps for England, in 1954?

And some harder or two-part questions for 2 points

11 Who was the last player from the league's third tier to play for England?

12 In which position did Alf Ramsey win 32 caps for England? With which club was he playing for all but the first of those 32?

13 How many caps for England did this flamboyant bunch win altogether: Frank Worthington, Stan Bowles; Duncan McKenzie; Peter Osgood? (1 pt for within 2)

14 Who scored 2 late goals to give England a 3-2 friendly win over Argentina in November 2005? Where was the game played?

15 When England played Brazil in May 1992, what were the international rankings of the 2 countries?

Answers on page 206

Questions 1-10, for 1 point each

1 Who was the first England player to reach the 100-cap landmark?

2 How many caps did Matthew Le Tissier win for England: was it 8, 18 or 24?

3 Who missed the crucial penalty with a particularly feeble effort against Portugal in the shoot-out during Euro 2004?

4 Which player scored 6 hat-tricks for England, more than any other?

5 Which goalkeeper made his England debut in a friendly against Spain in February, 2007?

6 Who was made caretaker manager of England when Sir Alf Ramsey was sacked in 1974?

7 Which club did Graham Taylor leave to become England manager?

8 *Addicted* was the characteristically honest autobiography of which former England captain?

9 How many goals did Michael Owen have for England before he scored his wonder goal against Argentina in the 1998 World Cup?

10 Who was the most recent Coventry City player to turn out for England?

And some harder or two-part questions for 2 points

11 Which 2 Channel Islanders made their England debuts in the same match in 1994, Terry Venables' first in charge?

12 Which 2 Nottingham Forest players were in Graham Taylor's first England team in 1990?

13 Name the 2 players capped for England whilst playing for Wimbledon.

14 Who took charge of England for 1 game each between Kevin Keegan's resignation and Sven-Goran Eriksson's start?

15 Who was appointed the first manager of England immediately after WWII? How long was he in charge?

Scotland

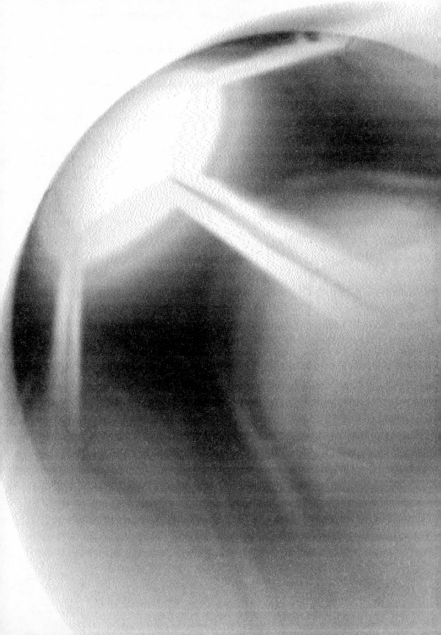

Questions 1-10, for 1 point each

1 What is the current capacity of Hampden Park in thousands: is it 52, 65 or 80?

2 At which ground were 66 people killed during a crush to celebrate a last-minute equaliser?

3 Goals by Gemmell and Chalmers sealed which famous victory?

4 Which Scottish goalkeeper has played the most times for his country?

5 Which SPL side play at Pittodrie?

6 Which side play at the Firhill Stadium in Glasgow?

7 Who won their first senior trophy when they beat Hibernian in the Scottish League Cup Final in 2004?

8 Which striker has maintained a hot scoring record for Rangers since his move from Kilmarnock in 2006?

9 Apart from Celtic and Rangers, which other side have never dropped out of the Scottish Premier League since it started in 1975-76?

10 How many players from Rangers and Celtic were in Scotland's 1986 World Cup squad: was it 3, 8 or 12?

And some harder or two-part questions for 2 points

11 Which two players followed Alex Ferguson from Aberdeen to Manchester United?

12 Which Scottish international played 330 league games for Chelsea between 1987 and 1998? What position did he hold in 2006-07?

13 Which English-based, 2nd-tier striker scored on his Scotland debut against Austria in April 1994? Which Aberdeen striker with a famous English namesake came on for him late in the game?

14 By what name is Javier Ignacio known in Scottish football? For which club did he make his debut in Scotland?

15 How many Scottish League titles did Graeme Souness win in 5 years as Rangers' manager? Who did he replace as manager?

Questions 1–10, for 1 point each

1   Which club side provided the entire Scotland team for the first-ever international between their country and England?

2   Which Celtic and Scotland winger was known as 'The Flea'?

3   Who was the Scottish forward whose 500-plus appearances in the postwar years saw him become a Liverpool icon long before the glory years?

4   Which former Celtic player became Rangers' first Catholic signing, under Graeme Souness' management?

5   Who scored 50 goals in 1935–36 for Celtic, still a club record?

6   Who were the most northerly SPL club in 2006–07?

7   Scottish league side Livingstone were born out of the ashes of which now-defunct Edinburgh club?

8   Which Scottish international was Newcastle United's top scorer with 36 goals when they won the league in 1926–27?

9   Who were relegated from the SPL with a record low of 18 points in 2005–06?

10   Which Dutch striker's goal clinched the Scottish FA Cup Final for Celtic against Airdrieonians in 1995?

And some harder or two-part questions for 2 points

11   Who was the Scottish winger with a thunderous shot who played on the right side of Don Revie's formidable Leeds midfield in the 1970s? And who was the other Scot on the left?

12   From which Scottish clubs did Everton buy Gary Naysmith and James McFadden?

13   Who started the 2006–07 season as Rangers manager? With which club had he made his reputation?

14   Who were the centre-back pairing at the heart of the great Aberdeen side of the 1980s?

15   Who was the first overseas coach of Rangers, appointed in 1998? To which post did he return when he left Rangers?

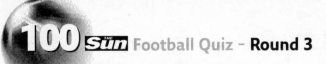

Questions 1-10, for 1 point each

1 For which Scottish side did George Best make 22 league appearances?

2 Which Danish striker was a revelation in the SPL when brought to Rangers by Graeme Souness?

3 What nickname was given to the victorious Celtic team who won the 1967 European Cup?

4 Who was the last player to win both the league and cup in both England and Scotland as a player?

5 Which player has won the most caps whilst a Celtic player? (Careful!)

6 Who were the most southerly Scottish league club in 2006-07?

7 Which English player's goal won the 2005 Scottish Cup Final for Celtic against Dundee?

8 Which Scottish maestro of the 1960s was known as the 'Wee Barra'?

9 Who was the second player (after Henrik Larsson) to score 100 SPL goals?

10 Who was the Celtic manager when they won all 4 major competitions they entered in 1966-67?

And some harder or two-part questions for 2 points

11 Who was appointed as Rangers manager after the departure of Paul le Guen in 2006-07? Who did he appoint as his assistant in January 2007?

12 What was the consequence of Scott McDonald's 2 late goals for Motherwell on the last day of the 2004-05 SPL season?

13 Who was Rangers' defensive stalwart and captain for much of their spell of dominance in the 1990s? From which Premiership club did he join?

14 Who were Celtic's 1996-97 Italian/Portuguese strike partnership?

15 Name the 3 Scottish managers in charge of 2nd-tier clubs at the end of the 2006-07 season.

Questions 1–10, for 1 point each

1 Who was embarrassingly sent off on his Rangers debut as player-manager?

2 With which Scottish club did Andy Gray start his career?

3 Before becoming a linchpin of Spurs' great side, Dave Mackay won a Scottish title in 1958 with which club?

4 Rudi Skacel signed for Southampton after a successful season in Scotland scoring goals for which club?

5 Which Scottish international won a Premiership title in 2006–07?

6 Which Scottish league side play their home games in the city of Perth?

7 Steven Pressley left which club for Celtic in 2006–07 after a dispute with that club's management?

8 Who were joint champions with Rangers in the first season of the Scottish League in 1891, and won the title outright the following year?

9 When Henrik Larsson missed the 1999–2000 season with a broken leg, who stepped in as SPL and Celtic top scorer?

10 Which SPL side (2006–07) are based in the town of Paisley?

And some harder or two-part questions for 2 points

11 Which out-of-favour Premiership striker did Martin O'Neill take to Celtic as a foil for Henrik Larsson? And where was he out of favour?

12 Which 2 sides contested the Scottish League Cup Final in 2006–07?

13 Who is this? He won the Scottish league both as player and manager with Rangers; he won 44 caps at half-back and centre-half for Scotland (2 pts if you've already got it); he lifted the ECWC in 1972.

14 How many caps did Alan Hansen win for Scotland? (1 pt if within 3)

15 Who was the only overseas manager of the Scotland team? Of which national side was he manager before being appointed to the Scottish post?

Questions 1–10, for 1 point each

1 From which Scottish league side did Liverpool sign Alan Hansen?

2 How many caps did Andy Gray win for Scotland: was it 12, 20 or 33?

3 Who was appointed manager of Scotland in January 2007 after the departure of Walter Smith?

4 Which former Scottish international goalkeeper went on loan from Leeds to Doncaster Rovers in January 2007?

5 Which striker who retired in 1998 after 15 years with the club, is Hearts' all-time top scorer?

6 Who ended Rangers' interest in the 2006–07 Scottish Cup, beating them 3–2 in the 3rd round?

7 Which hard-working player followed manager Gordon Strachan from Coventry to Southampton and on to Celtic?

8 Who were runners-up in the Scottish top division from 1922–23 to 1925–26, but never won the title?

9 Which club did Scotland goalkeeper Alan Rough play for when he was first selected for his country?

10 Who clinched a place in the 2007 Scottish Cup Final with a late penalty in a replay against Hibernian?

And some harder or two-part questions for 2 points

11 Which 2 members of the Bolton side of the mid-1990s carved out successful careers at Celtic?

12 Who joined Celtic from Real Madrid in 2006, after a couple of years on the fringe at the Spanish side? With which Premiership club did he establish a formidable reputation?

13 Which club did Rangers pay £4m for Duncan Ferguson in 1993? And which top-flight English club lured him south in 1994?

14 Which coach brought the SPL title back to Celtic after a gap of 10 years in 1997–98? Who was regarded as the crucial signing made by that coach?

15 Other than Alex Ferguson, who were the last 2 Scottish managers to win the FA Cup?

 **Sun** Football Quiz – **Round 6**

Questions 1-10, for 1 point each

1 Who earned a 3-month prison sentence after an on-field assault on Raith's John McStay?

2 In 1929, Arsenal paid Preston the astronomical sum of £8,750 for which brilliant Scottish inside forward?

3 Who was the talented former Rangers winger who tragically died aged only 39 whilst still playing lower-league football for Clydebank?

4 Who moved to Rangers from Chelsea for £12m in November 2000?

5 Which side gained a 4th successive promotion in 2006-07 to seal a spectacular rise to the SPL?

6 Who beat Celtic in a penalty shoot-out to win the 1995 Scottish League Cup?

7 Which former England international scored the winning goal in Rangers' 1-0 win over Celtic in March 2007?

8 Prior to Hearts in 2005-06, who were the last side outside Celtic and Rangers to finish in the top 2 of the Scottish league?

9 Who was Scotland manager at the 1982 WCFT?

10 Who was manager of Celtic for 43 years starting in 1897?

And some harder or two-part questions for 2 points

11 Which 2 sides would contest the Edinburgh derby in the SPL?

12 In 1982-83, who were the top 2 in the Scottish top division?

13 Who did Celtic beat 2-1 in a hard-fought Scottish Cup SF in 2007? Who scored both their goals?

14 Which former player took over from Jock Stein as Celtic manager in 1978? He returned in 1987 after a 3-year spell with which other former player in charge?

15 Who were the last 2 Scottish players to appear in an FA Cup Final?

World Cup

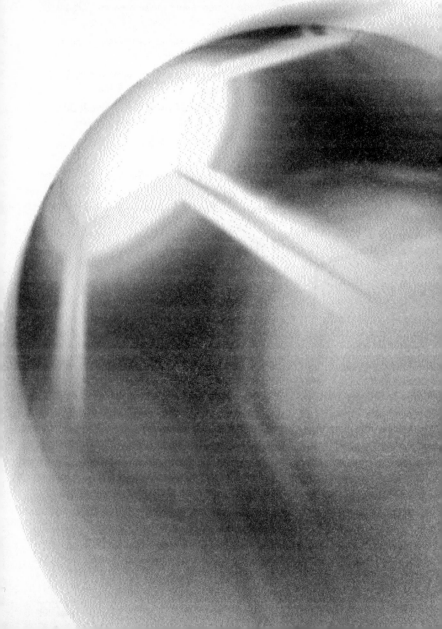

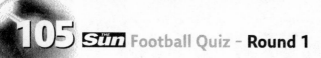
Questions 1–10, for 1 point each

1 Who is the only player to have scored in every match his country played in a particular World Cup Finals Tournament, including the Final?

2 Who played the long through-ball from which Geoff Hurst scored the final clinching goal in the 1966 World Cup Final?

3 What was unusual about Ernst Willimowski's 4 goals in 1 match for Poland against Brazil in the 1938 World Cup?

4 Cesar Luis Menotti managed which side to their first World Cup victory?

5 Who should have left the 2006 World Cup in disgrace, but was voted Player of the Tournament instead?

6 Which full-back was one of 2 Manchester City players (the other was Denis Law) in Scotland's 1974 World Cup squad?

7 Whose goal settled a dull SF between Brazil and Sweden at the 1994 World Cup?

8 England condemned Germany to a play-off by winning their qualifying group for the 2002 World Cup. Who did Germany beat in that play-off?

9 Who captained a side coached by his father at the 1998 WCFT?

10 Which WCFT had the highest average attendance?

And some harder or two-part questions for 2 points

11 Which future Liverpool player was sent off playing for Cameroon against Brazil in a World Cup match, aged only 17, in 1994? And what fate did he suffer at the World Cup Finals Tournament four years later?

12 Who was the leading scorer at the 1998 World Cup, and for which country was he playing?

13 The 1950 WCFT was decided by a Final Pool, or mini-league. Happily the last game was decisive; which Uruguayan legend scored a crucial equaliser to set up his side's victory, and who were the opposition?

14 Which 2 Belgian players appeared in the WCFT in 1986, 90, 94 and 98?

15 Who was the captain of the hardworking but ordinary German side that won the 1990 World Cup? Who scored the goal that settled a boring Final against Argentina?

Questions 1–10, for 1 point each

1 Which Wolves legend was England's captain at the 1954 World Cup?

2 Which Polish winger was the top-scorer at the 1974 World Cup?

3 Which future German manager came off the bench to equalise in the 1986 World Cup Final, only to see Argentina triumph with a late winner?

4 Who were the first African side to win a match in a WCFT when they beat Mexico 3–1 in 1978?

5 Who played at right-back for England in the 2002 World Cup in the absence of the injured Gary Neville?

6 An injury to which player gave Trevor Sinclair a chance to impress at the 2002 World Cup?

7 Who knocked Brazil out of the 1986 World Cup on penalties after a fabulous game ended 1–1?

8 A 0–0 draw away to which country sealed England's qualification for the 1998 World Cup?

9 Who won their first competitive international match when they beat Austria 1–0 in a World Cup Qualifier in 1990?

10 Chile qualified for the 1974 WCFT after which European side declined to play a match in a Santiago stadium recently used as a concentration camp under Pinochet's CIA-backed right-wing military dictatorship?

And some harder or two-part questions for 2 points

11 Injuries to which 2 key players hampered England's 1982 World Cup campaign? (They made 1 substitute appearance each)

12 Who caused a shock by eliminating Germany in the QF of the 1994 World Cup? And which country did they eliminate with a last-minute goal in the final game of their pre-tournament qualifying group?

13 Which side's squad in the 1998 World Cup featured players from clubs called Constant Spring, Harbour View and Violet Kickers? Which player left Harbour View for Bolton after the tournament?

14 Which other 2 home nations were in England's qualifying group for the 2006 World Cup?

15 Ulises De la Cruz played for which country in the 2006 World Cup? He moved from Aston Villa to which other premiership club soon after the tournament?

Questions 1-10, for 1 point each

1 Which side finished 3rd in the World Cups of 1974 and 1982?

2 Which dogged German full-back marked the great Johann Cruyff out of the 1974 World Cup Final?

3 Who scored the World Cup's first Golden Goal when his goal for France eliminated Paraguay in 1998?

4 Which young midfielder was assigned to man-mark Bobby Charlton in the 1966 World Cup Final? (He later admitted he was not ready but his day would come!)

5 Who was the Italian defender head-butted by Zinedine Zidane in the 2006 World Cup Final?

6 How many of Northern Ireland's heroic 1982 World Cup squad had played top-flight football in England the previous season: was it 2, 6 or 10?

7 In a table of World Cup performances, based on 3 points for a win and 1 for a draw (inc matches resolved by penalty shoot-outs), where do England lie?

8 Which winger scored in and won the UEFA Cup Final (with Real Madrid) and the World Cup Final (with Argentina) in 1986?

9 Who was manager of England when they failed to qualify for the WCFT in 1994?

10 Which US TV megastar tripped and fell flat on her face at the 1994 World Cup opening ceremony?

And some harder or two-part questions for 2 points

11 Bora Miljutinovic has coached 5 different sides in World Cups; which ones are missing from this sequence: 1986 Mexico, 1990 Costa Rica, 1994 ?, 1998 Nigeria, 2002 ?

12 Who beat a poor German side in the QF of the 1998 World Cup, and by what score?

13 Who were the scorers on the heavenly night for England fans when they beat Germany 5-1 away in a WCQ in 2001?

14 Which 2 British clubs had 2 players each in the Poland squad at the 2006 World Cup?

15 In the infamous penalty shoot-out against West Germany in 1990, who blazed England's last penalty high and wide to send them out? Who had scored a late equaliser to take the game into extra time?

Answers on page 208

Questions 1-10, for 1 point each

1 Who scored twice from the spot to see England past Cameroon in the QF of the 1990 World Cup?

2 Antonio Carbajal appeared in goal in 5 separate World Cups for which country?

3 Which Brazilian was sent off against England in the 2002 World Cup?

4 What is the prize awarded to the top scorer in each WCFT?

5 Which Argentine striker played in three World Cups, failing to score in 1974 and 1982, but finishing as top scorer in 1978?

6 When Poland eliminated England in qualifying for the 1974 World Cup, who was the third team in the qualifying group who, just like the Poles, drew at Wembley?

7 Defeat at the hands of which unfancied side got Scotland's 1990 World Cup campaign off to a dreadful start?

8 Which much-capped midfield player was Celtic's only representative in the Scotland squad for the 1990 World Cup?

9 With which club were Zinedine Zidane and Didier Deschamps playing when they won the World Cup in 1998?

10 How many WCFTs did Johann Cruyff appear in?

And some harder or two-part questions for 2 points

11 Who were David Seaman's unused deputies at the 1998 World Cup?

12 Which 2 Premiership stars formed the Ivory Coast's central defence in the 2006 World Cup?

13 Allen Boksic, Robert Prosinecki, Davor Suker and Robert Jarni all played for which 2 nations in a World Cup?

14 Name the 3 sides to have contested 2 World Cup Finals and won neither.

15 Who scored the late, late penalty for Italy that eliminated Australia in the last 16 of the 2006 WCFT? Which Premiership defender unluckily gave away the spot-kick?

Questions 1-10, for 1 point each

1 Which country will host the 2010 World Cup?

2 What was the only occasion on which all 4 home nations qualified for a World Cup?

3 Which stadium hosted the 1994 World Cup Final in the USA?

4 Who beat American Samoa 31-0 in a World Cup qualifying match?

5 Rai, who played for Brazil in the 1994 World Cup, was the younger brother of which Brazilian superstar of the 1980s?

6 Who did Poland beat in the 3rd place play-off at the 1982 World Cup?

7 Who have won the European Championships but never won a match or scored a goal in a World Cup?

8 How many of their 13 matches in World Cups have Ireland won: is it 2, 4 or 6?

9 Who scored the opening goal of the 2002 World Cup against France?

10 Which Brazilian striker introduced the now over-used baby-rocking goal celebration in the 1994 WCFT?

And some harder or two-part questions for 2 points

11 Which country has had 2 players sent off in a World Cup Final, and in which year?

12 In a table of World Cup performances, based on 3 points for a win and 1 for a draw (inc matches resolved by penalty shoot-outs), who occupy the top 3 places?

13 Which 2 centre-backs were South Africa's only English-based players at the 1998 World Cup?

14 Who were the 2 Arsenal players in the 1998 Holland World Cup squad?

15 How many red cards were handed out in the 2006 WCFT? (1 pt for within 3)

Questions 1-10, for 1 point each

1   Which Peruvian star – by some distance that country's greatest player – scored 10 goals from midfield in World Cups?

2   Which England player was the oldest competitor at both the 1950 and 1954 World Cups?

3   Who scored for Turkey after 11 seconds of the 3rd place play-off at the 2002 World Cup, registering the finals' fastest goal?

4   Who administered the coup de grace to England's 2006 World Cup campaign when he scored Portugal's winning penalty?

5   Who was the youngest member of England's World Cup-winning side of 1966?

6   Which CONCACAF side made their only appearance in a World Cup in 1986, but lost all 3 games and failed to score?

7   Who eliminated Ireland in the second phase of the 1994 World Cup?

8   Which TV pundit played in the World Cup for Jamaica in 1998?

9   Which Italian defender, who would win 81 caps for the Azzurri, played in the 1982 World Cup Final, aged only 18?

10 Who scored a wonderful solo goal for Scotland as they almost redeemed themselves with a rousing victory against Holland in 1978?

And some harder or two-part questions for 2 points

11 Who scored Ireland's winner in a penalty shoot-out against Romania at the 1990 World Cup? Who made the save that made it possible?

12 Name 3 of the 4 members of England's World Cup squad from 1990 who were playing for Glasgow Rangers at the time.

13 Against which side did England play their first-ever World Cup game? Who scored their first goal in a 2-0 win?

14 Apart from substitute goalkeepers Nigel Martyn and David James, name 2 of the 3 players, all defenders, who made the 2002 WCFT squad but never got on the pitch?

15 Who became, in 1986, the first England player to be sent off in a World Cup? Who were the opposition that England failed to beat?

Questions 1-10, for 1 point each

1 What kind of animal was Winston, the England squad's mascot at the 1970 World Cup?

2 Which legend made his 3rd and final appearance in a World Cup for Colombia in 1998, aged 37?

3 Who was the Argentina captain sent off against England during a violent QF clash in 1966?

4 Who was voted Player of the Tournament at the 2002 World Cup, despite making the error that cost his team the opening goal in the Final?

5 After eliminating England with a dodgy goal and a wonder goal, who did Maradona bamboozle next in the 1986 World Cup?

6 In the 1974 World Cup failure to hammer which naïve African side cost Scotland a place in the QF?

7 In England's 1st-phase group at the 1990 World Cup, how many goals were scored in the 6 matches: was it 7, 9 or 12?

8 Who was captain of the Ireland team in the 1990 World Cup?

9 In which city did the first Final take place, in 1930?

10 Who scored inside a minute in England's first match at the 1982 WCFT, a 3-1 win over France?

And some harder or two-part questions for 2 points

11 What connected Australia, Holland, South Korea and Trinidad & Tobago at the 2006 World Cup?

12 Where were the Semi-Finals for the 1958 World Cup in Sweden held?

13 Which 2 European sides were eliminated when South Korea and USA surprisingly qualified from Group D for the knock-out phase of the 2002 World Cup?

14 England reached the QF in 1954 before going down 4-2 to a talented Uruguayan side. Which 2 1950s legends scored the England goals?

15 In a disgraceful and petulant display in the last 16 of the 2006 WCFT, which 2 sides had 2 men each dismissed as the Russian referee was forced to issue 16 yellow cards?

Answers on page 209

Questions 1–10, for 1 point each

1 Who was dubbed 'a clown' by Brian Clough on TV prior to an inspiring performance that saw England eliminated in qualifying for the 1974 World Cup?

2 How many of their 4 World Cup penalty shoot-outs have Italy won?

3 Which tiny country's side beat Luxembourg 4–0 in a World Cup qualifying match in 2004 to record their first-ever competitive victory?

4 Who was Scotland's manager during their farcical 1978 World Cup campaign?

5 Whose 2 goals clinched the 1954 World Cup Final for West Germany against Hungary?

6 Which Austrian striker scored twice as his side gained a satisfying, if meaningless, 3–2 win over West Germany in the 1978 World Cup?

7 Which other side, along with England, were beaten on penalties in the SF of the 1990 World Cup?

8 After England, which team had most English-based players in their squad for the 1998 World Cup: was it Jamaica, Norway, Scotland or USA?

9 Which 33-year-old Wimbledon player scored Jamaica's first WCFT goal?

10 Who was the acrobatic Brazilian forward, famous for his overhead kicks, who was top scorer at the 1938 WCFT?

And some harder or two-part questions for 2 points

11 Which 2 West Germany players played against England in the 1966 World Cup Final and then played in the winning team in 1974?

12 Which 2 AC Milan players were included in England's squad for the 1986 World Cup?

13 In the 1966 World Cup Final, the players wore squad numbers. Nine of the England team wore numbers between 1 and 11. Who wore 16 and 21 respectively?

14 Name the 3 Newcastle United players in England's 1998 World Cup squad.

15 Who eliminated a disappointing Brazil in the QF of the WCFT in 2006? Who scored the game's only goal?

113 **The Sun** Football Quiz - **Round 9**

Questions 1-10, for 1 point each

1. Who were the only previous winners not competing in the 2006 World Cup?

2. Joel Quiniou of France has registered most World Cup appearances in what role?

3. Which stadium hosted the 1982 World Cup Final in Spain?

4. Who failed to turn up for a World Cup qualifying match against Scotland in 1996, thus forfeiting the match?

5. Who, in 2002, became the oldest outfield player since Stanley Matthews to represent England in a World Cup?

6. Who was Italy's immaculate left-back when they won the 1982 World Cup?

7. When was the last time Scotland played in a World Cup?

8. How many goals have England scored in World Cups: is it 45, 74 or 110?

9. Which legend kept goal for the strongly fancied Soviet Union sides in 1962 and 1966?

10. Who settled the 1998 SF for Holland against Argentina by scoring a sublime goal in the 89th minute?

And some harder or two-part questions for 2 points

11. Who scored the German goals in the 1966 World Cup Final?

12. Who was the only member of Argentina's 1978 World Cup winning squad playing in Europe (with Valencia)? And how many of the 23-man squad for 2006 were playing in Europe?

13. Who beat Wales 1-0 in the 1958 World Cup QF? Which teenage sensation scored the goal?

14. Which two European nations made their debuts in a WCFT in 2002 and 2006 respectively? (This assumes Yugoslavia and Serbia & Montenegro are effectively the same country so don't count)

15. Which two cities hosted the 2006 World Cup SF?

Answers on page 209

Questions 1-10, for 1 point each

1 Who has made most appearances (17) for England in World Cups?

2 In how many World Cups did Diego Maradona appear?

3 Which Dutch star was sent off in a World Cup match for spitting at Rudi Voller of Germany, who was also sent off?

4 Saeed Owairan scored a sensational goal at the 1994 World Cup playing for which country against Belgium?

5 Which workhorse in the France World Cup-winning side had the unflattering nickname of 'the water-carrier'?

6 Which striker missed the 2006 World Cup after he was injured in a pre-tournament friendly for France against China?

7 Who scored England's goal when Maradona's double eliminated them from the 1986 World Cup?

8 A 3-0 defeat to which African side ended Scotland's participation in the 1998 World Cup?

9 Who are the only holders to be eliminated from the following WCFT without scoring a goal?

10 In 1954 an Asian side competed in the WCFT for the first time. Who beat Japan to claim the place?

And some harder or two-part questions for 2 points

11 Which 3 members of Ron Greenwood's 1982 World Cup team were provided by Ipswich Town?

12 Who scored Northern Ireland's winner in their outstanding win over hosts Spain at the 1982 World Cup? Which Irish player was unluckily sent off in the same game?

13 Which pair of brothers played for Holland in the 1998 World Cup?

14 Who were ordered to play their Euro 2008 home qualifiers behind closed doors after scenes of mayhem following their elimination in a play-off for a place in the 2006 WCFT? Who were their opponents that night?

15 Which 2 English-based members of Sweden's 2006 WCFT squad came to blows during training prior to the tournament?

Answers on page 209

115 Sun Football Quiz - **Round 11**

Questions 1–10, for 1 point each

1 Which southern city was the venue for England's group matches at the 1990 World Cup in Italy?

2 Which German player has played in the most matches in World Cups?

3 Who put a nightmare World Cup Final in 1998 behind him to score both goals in the Final of 2002?

4 Italy returned home after the 1966 World Cup to be greeted with a hail of rotten fruit after losing to which unfancied side?

5 Who was the left-footed, moustachioed dead-ball specialist in the Brazil side of 1970?

6 The inspirational playmaker Jozef Masopust led which team to the World Cup Final in 1962?

7 Who shocked holders Argentina in the opening game of the 1990 World Cup?

8 Which West Ham goalkeeper was Czechoslovakia's only English-based player at the 1990 World Cup?

9 Which club side, a great force in the 1980s, provided 12 members of the Soviet Union squad at the 1986 WCFT, including most of the first team?

10 Who managed England in the 1982 WCFT?

And some harder or two-part questions for 2 points

11 Who denied England qualification for the 1974 World Cup by beating them at home and drawing at Wembley? How many times have they beaten England in a competitive fixture since?

12 Which twins played in the 1978 World Cup Final for Holland?

13 Which 2 related players were both unused members of England's 1998 World Cup squad?

14 In 1986, which player, later voted European Footballer of the Year, became the only man to score a hat-trick in a WCFT match and end up on the losing side, as USSR lost 4–3 to which opponents?

15 Which member of the Holland squad at the 2006 WCFT was on Liverpool's books but subsequently left, and which other Dutch star joined them after the tournament?

Answers on page 209

Questions 1-10, for 1 point each

1. Which then-Chelsea player's last-minute goal against England in the 1998 World Cup left England needing to beat Colombia in their final group game?

2. Who was the veteran Italian goalkeeper who made 17 appearances in World Cups between 1974 and 1982, ending with a winner's medal in Spain?

3. Who lost their opening match of the 1982 World Cup 2-1 to Algeria?

4. Who captained Northern Ireland at the 1958 World Cup?

5. Which Dutch midfielder's shooting brought him 5 goals during the 1974 World Cup?

6. Who did Holland hammer 4-0 in a sensational display in the second phase of the 1974 World Cup?

7. Whose last-ditch winner saw England scrape past Belgium in the last 16 of the 1990 World Cup?

8. Who scored the Golden Goal that squeezed France past Paraguay in the last 16 of the 1998 World Cup?

9. Who became the first team to be eliminated from a WCFT without losing a match in 1974?

10. Who is the Republic of Ireland's leading scorer in WCFTs?

And some harder or two-part questions for 2 points

11. Who captained the Brazil side that won the 1994 World Cup Final? Who started the tournament as captain but didn't even make the Final team?

12. Which 2 home countries qualified from the same group for the 1982 World Cup, eliminating Sweden and Portugal?

13. How many players did Bayern Munich contribute to West Germany's World Cup Final team in 1974? (1 pt for one either way)

14. Which side came from 3-0 down to beat North Korea 5-3 in 1966, and who scored 4 of their 5 goals?

15. Had England won their penalty shoot-out against Portugal at the 2006 WCFT, which two players would have been suspended for the SF?

Questions 1-10, for 1 point each

1   Who is England's leading goalscorer, with 10, in World Cups?

2   The Battle of Santiago in 1962, probably the dirtiest match in World Cup history, was played between hosts Chile and which other side?

3   What was the fate of the unfortunate Andres Escobar after he scored an own-goal in Colombia's 1994 World Cup game against the USA?

4   Which Argentina striker scored hat-tricks at both the 1994 and 1998 World Cups?

5   Who was Italy's 40-year-old goalkeeper at the 1982 World Cup?

6   Which side qualified from the Asia/Oceania group for the 1982 World Cup?

7   England are preparing to apply to host the World Cup in which year?

8   Who was in his 4th World Cup squad for Scotland in 1998, a month before his 40th birthday?

9   Who refereed the 2002 World Cup Final?

10   Who succumbed 6-0 to Argentina in 1978, a match the hosts needed to win and score at least 4 times?

And some harder or two-part questions for 2 points

11   Which Brazilian was the first man to win a World Cup both as player and coach? And which German emulated him in 1990?

12   Who were the 3 members of Scotland's 1978 World Cup squad who had just won the league title with Nottingham Forest?

13   In World Cup terms, what links Ray Clemence, Joe Corrigan, Gary Bailey, Chris Woods (twice) and Dave Beasant?

14   Which Aston Villa striker scored both goals for Northern Ireland as they beat Czechoslovakia 2-1 to reach the QF in 1958? Which major footballing power did they eliminate in pre-WCFT qualifying?

15   Which attacking full-back scored 2 minutes from the end of extra time in Italy's SF with Germany at the 2006 WCFT? Who added the coup-de-grace in injury time?

Answers on page 210

Questions 1-10, for 1 point each

1 Which country was the first to host the World Cup for a second time?

2 In Scotland's disastrous 1978 World Cup campaign, defeat by Peru was followed by an unthinkable draw against which unrated opposition?

3 Who was the only member of Brazil's 2006 World Cup squad playing in the Premiership?

4 Which surname has appeared the most times in World Cup Finals: is it Taylor, Johansson, Gonzalez or Angel?

5 Why did Maradona miss Argentina's 1994 World Cup 2nd-round clash with Romania?

6 Who qualified for the 1986 World Cup from European Group 3 along with England?

7 Which side reached the 2nd phase of a World Cup for the first and (thus far) only time by beating Morocco and Belgium in 1994?

8 Who has won more games in World Cups: USA, Nigeria or Japan?

9 Which former Chelsea centre-forward holds the record for an England player's shortest WCFT career, appearing for 6 minutes against Poland in 1986?

10 Geoff Hurst was England's final hero in 1966, but whose 2 goals sank Portugal in the semis?

And some harder or two-part questions for 2 points

11 Which 2 great Italian players missed the first and last of their side's penalties in the shoot-out at the end of the 1994 World Cup Final against Brazil?

12 Which 2 of the top-seeded sides fell in the initial groups at the 2002 World Cup?

13 Which 2 sides qualified automatically as joint hosts for the 2002 WCFT?

14 Which pair of brothers played in the 1954 WCFT for West Germany?

15 Which country has received the most red cards (10) in World Cups? How many have England clocked up?

Questions 1–10, for 1 point each

1 What surname was shared by Nilton and Djalma, the two full-backs in the great Brazilian side of 1958?

2 Which Juventus player scored an outstanding hat-trick for Poland against Belgium in the 2nd phase of the 1982 World Cup?

3 Who scored twice for Argentina in the 1978 World Cup Final against Holland?

4 The opening match of the 1966, 1970, 1974 and 1978 World Cups had the same scoreline. What was it?

5 Which England World Cup winner would later go to the Finals as manager of Ireland?

6 In the 2006 World Cup Wayne Rooney was sent off for stamping on which other Premiership player?

7 Who scored 4 times as Spain beat Denmark 5–1 in the 2nd phase of the 1986 World Cup?

8 Who scored both of Italy's goals in the 2–1 win over Bulgaria that saw them reach the 1994 World Cup Final?

9 How many caps did Martin Peters and Geoff Hurst each have going into the 1966 World Cup Final: was it 3, 7 or 17?

10 Who was the Romanian playmaker with a sweet left foot who led his team to a fine 3–2 win over strongly fancied Argentina in 1994?

And some harder or two-part questions for 2 points

11 Which Dutch player scored the goal (from a free kick) that saw Graham Taylor's England fail to qualify for the 1994 World Cup? And why was Taylor furious with the referee?

12 Who coached South Korea when they reached the SF as hosts at the 2002 World Cup? And which side did he take to the 2006 World Cup?

13 Which 2 goalkeepers were the USA's only English-based players at the 1998 World Cup?

14 Who scored for the Republic of Ireland when they pulled off a shock 1–0 win over Italy in the 1994 WCFT? Who captained the side?

15 Name the 2 members of Germany's 2006 World Cup squad who were playing abroad (both in England)

Questions 1–10, for 1 point each

1 Who scored the only goal in Brazil's 1–0 win over England in the classic match at the 1970 World Cup?

2 Who scored his 9th World Cup goal in his 95th and final match for West Germany in the 1986 World Cup Final against Argentina?

3 Zidane scored twice for France in the 1998 World Cup Final; who scored their late 3rd goal?

4 Who scored 5 goals for Russia against Cameroon in a 1994 World Cup match?

5 Who scored Ireland's first-ever goal in a World Cup in a 1–1 draw against England in 1990?

6 Artur Boruc, Celtic's first-choice goalkeeper since 2005, played for which country in the 2006 World Cup?

7 Who scored Argentina's winning goal in the 1986 World Cup Final, after West Germany had clawed back a 2–0 deficit?

8 Who made his first serious impact on the world stage with a wonder goal for England against Argentina at the 1998 World Cup?

9 Who captained the brilliant Brazilians in 1970?

10 Which goalkeeper has kept the most clean sheets in WCFT history (10)?

And some harder or two-part questions for 2 points

11 Which England captain was discarded by Bobby Robson when he was appointed manager in 1982? Who replaced him as skipper for Robson's first game?

12 Who collapsed and died just as his Scotland side clinched qualification for the 1986 World Cup? And who took temporary charge of the team?

13 Which Aston Villa player was the only English-based member of Yugoslavia's last team to play in a World Cup, in 1998? For which country did he go on to win many more caps?

14 What was the venue for England's defeat on penalties by West Germany at the 1990 WCFT in Italy? Where was the other SF played, and why did many of the crowd favour Argentina?

15 How many of Sweden's squad for the 2006 WCFT were registered with English clubs? (1 pt if within 2)

Questions 1–10, for 1 point each

1. Which Premiership player scored the Senegal goal that saw reigning champions, France, beaten in the opening game of the 2002 World Cup?

2. Who recorded 2 of the World Cup's biggest wins, beating South Korea 9-0 in 1954 and El Salvador 10-1 in 1982?

3. Which country did Arsenal's Kolo Toure represent in the 2006 World Cup?

4. What is the most common score in World Cup matches?

5. Whose only 2 goals in an international career of over 120 matches (and counting) came in a World Cup SF?

6. Whose goal, which should have been disallowed for handball, was crucial in ensuring Scotland, and not Wales, qualified for the 1986 World Cup?

7. Which Romanian player scored twice in the 2nd-round match against Argentina at the World Cup in 1994, and earned a move to the Premiership soon after?

8. Who recorded their only win in a World Cup match when they beat Japan 2-1 in 1998?

9. Who presented the trophy to the winning Italian side in Rome in 1934?

10. Who beat Uruguay on penalties in a play-off to qualify for the 2006 WCFT, having lost to them at the same stage prior to the 2002 tournament?

And some harder or two-part questions for 2 points

11. Which 2 French players have been sent off in World Cup Finals?

12. At the 1998 World Cup in France which politically sensitive opponents were drawn in the same group as the USA? What was the score when the 2 met?

13. Which 2 players won the World Cup with Italy in 2006 and the Champions League with Milan the following year?

14. Which 3 players missed penalties in the shoot-out to decide the match between England and Argentina in 1998? (2 for England, 1 for Argentina)

15. Which predatory striker scored the winner as West Germany came from 2-0 down to beat England in the 1970 World Cup? Who was England's goalkeeper that day, and was blamed for the defeat?

Answers on page 210

Questions 1-10, for 1 point each

1 Who holds the record for most goals scored in a single World Cup, with 13 in 1958?

2 Which Brazilian striker scored twice in the 1958 World Cup Final and again in the 1962 Final?

3 Who scored for Cameroon in the 1994 World Cup against Russia, at the grand old age of 42?

4 Which English referee gave Croatia defender Josip Simic 3 yellow cards before sending him off in the 2006 World Cup?

5 Who was the manager of Ireland whose feud with Roy Keane filled the newspapers prior to the 2002 World Cup?

6 Who was the only Liverpool player in the England 1970 World Cup squad?

7 Which attacking full-back scored Brazil's winner from a free-kick in the World Cup QF against Holland?

8 What nationality was the referee who sent off Zidane in the 2006 World Cup Final?

9 Whose hat-trick saw Italy to a 3-2 win in a classic 1982 QF against Brazil?

10 Who captained England at the 1998 World Cup?

And some harder or two-part questions for 2 points

11 Apart from Geoff Hurst, who is the only other English player to score a hat-trick in a World Cup match? Who were the opponents?

12 Which 2 members of the Ireland squad at the 2002 World Cup were also in the 1990 squad?

13 In 1998, who beat Brazil in a group-phase game for the first time since 1966? And who scored that country's equaliser and earned the winning penalty?

14 Where did England play 4 of their 5 home qualifiers for the 2006 WCFT? And which other Premiership ground hosted the 5th, against Azerbaijan?

15 Who was the Argentine player involved in David Beckham's sending off in the 1998 World Cup? And who was the referee?

Questions 1-10, for 1 point each

1 Who overcame Helmut Rahn's 40-year-old record when he scored his 11th World Cup goal in 1994, a German record?

2 Which Northern Ireland star was the youngest to appear in a World Cup, aged 17 in 1982?

3 How many European teams have won the World Cup outside Europe?

4 The England team that beat Paraguay at the 1986 World Cup featured two players with which name?

5 Which was the only postwar World Cup in which Brazil failed to get beyond the group stage?

6 Where did England play their group matches at the 1982 World Cup in Spain?

7 Who was the German goalkeeper who faced the penalty shoot-out against England at the 1990 World Cup?

8 How many of their 23 matches in World Cups have Scotland won: is it 2, 4 or 8?

9 Who were the first team to win the World Cup 3 times, thereby getting to keep the original Jules Rimet Trophy?

10 What do Luis Monti, Jose Santamaria and Ferenc Puskas have in common in World Cup history?

And some harder or two-part questions for 2 points

11 Who recorded the biggest win at a World Cup for nearly 30 years when they beat Saudi Arabia 8-0 in 2002? Who scored a hat-trick?

12 When they went to the 1982 World Cup, with which clubs had Northern Ireland strikers Gerry Armstrong and Billy Hamilton just achieved promotion from the 2nd and 3rd tier respectively?

13 Which 3 Fulham players (2006–07 season) represented the USA in the 2006 World Cup?

14 Name the 4 African sides who competed in a WCFT for the first time in 2006?

15 Which two coaches led the sides out for the 2006 World Cup Final?

124 Sun Football Quiz - **Round 20**

Questions 1–10, for 1 point each

1 In the 1998 World Cup penalty shoot-out against England, who missed with Argentina's first penalty?

2 A member of which opposing side was sent off in the first minute of a World Cup match against Scotland, after a disgraceful foul on Gordon Strachan?

3 Graham Taylor resigned after England failed to qualify for the 1994 World Cup. Which Scotland manager also 'fell on his sword' for the same reason?

4 Who was Northern Ireland's manager when they reached the World Cup in 1982 and 1986?

5 Who was the former World Cup-winning captain who managed Argentina at the 1998 World Cup?

6 In the 1974 World Cup, how many goals had Holland conceded in 6 games prior to the Final?

7 Which Italian striker was leading scorer at the 1990 World Cup?

8 Who was Brazil's goalkeeper at the 1990, 1994 and 1998 World Cups?

9 How many of the 1998 Nigeria squad played league football in their own country?

10 Everyone remembers the Soviet (Azerbaijani) linesman, but what nationality was the referee in the 1966 World Cup Final?

And some harder or two-part questions for 2 points

11 Which English referee awarded a penalty to Holland in the 2nd minute of the 1974 World Cup Final? Who scored from the spot-kick?

12 Who was the only member of England's 1982 World Cup squad not playing in England? With which German club was he playing?

13 A surprise defeat at the hands of which side helped see England eliminated from the 1950 World Cup? What was the score?

14 Most knowledgeable football fans can name the England World Cup-winning team. Can you name the other 4 squad players who featured in the earlier group matches?

15 Whose 2 goals took Germany past Sweden in the 2006 WCFT? And whose late equaliser took them into a successful penalty shoot-out with Argentina in the QF?

Mixed Bag

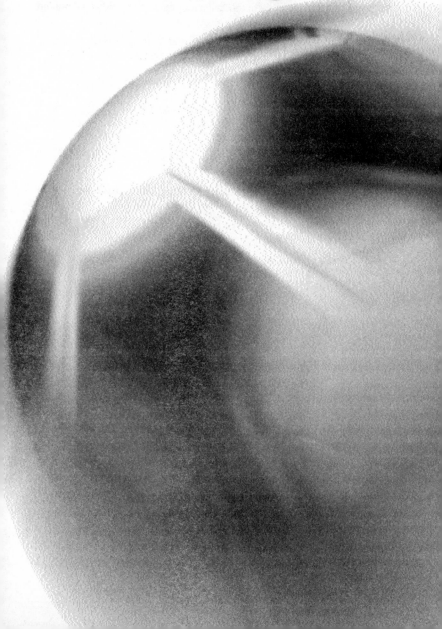

Questions 1-10, for 1 point each

1 What tear-stained piece of football memorabilia was sold at auction in 2004 for £28,680?

2 Former professional footballer Dave Whelan made a few million out of which chain of stores prior to buying Wigan Athletic?

3 Pop star Elton John was once chairman of which English club?

4 Which former Tottenham favourite stood down as Hartlepool United manager in 1991 after being diagnosed with a brain tumour, and sadly died 3 months later?

5 Who was the top flight's leading scorer in 1958-59, 1960-61, 1962-63, 1963-64 and 1968-69?

6 What first did Jacqui Oatley achieve on *Match of the Day* in April 2007?

7 In England football terms, what happened at the El Tequendama Hotel in Bogota, Colombia?

8 Who became Charlton's record signing, at £4.75m in 2001?

9 Who is the most recent international footballer to have also played first-class cricket?

10 Which referee, later head of the Premiership refereeing panel, took charge of the 1994 Champions League Final, when AC Milan destroyed Barcelona?

And some harder or two-part questions for 2 points

11 What age was Stanley Matthews when he retired from League football in 1965? (1 pt for 2 years either way)

12 In 1970 Leeds were on for the treble, but lost the lot. Who pipped them for the league title? Who beat them in the FA Cup Final? Who beat them in a European Cup SF?

13 Name the 6 overseas winners of the PFA Player's Player of the Year award (i.e. not from British Isles).

14 Which 2 2nd-tier clubs won the FA Cup in the 1970s?

15 Which 2 countries, bottom of the FIFA rankings, arranged an international match to coincide with the 2002 World Cup Final?

Questions 1-10, for 1 point each

1 Which town, his birthplace, has a memorial to Sir Stanley Matthews?

2 Of which club is Harrods' owner, Mohammed al-Fayed, the owner and chairman?

3 The death of which footballer and gentleman, aged 85, in February 2000, was marked by one-minute silences at every league ground in England?

4 Which league side play at the National Hockey Stadium?

5 Which of these sides has never dropped into the 4th tier of the league: Bolton Wanderers, Derby County, Sheffield United, Wolverhampton Wanderers?

6 Which legendary manager won the FA Amateur Cup in 1939 as a player with Bishop Auckland?

7 What, in 2006, connected Port Vale's Chris Birchall, West Ham's Shaka Hislop and Coventry's Stern John?

8 Who cost Newcastle £750,000 in 1991 when they bought him from Charlton and repaid them handsomely with over 300 consistent appearances?

9 Who won most caps for Italy: Gianfranco Zola, Luca Vialli or Roberto Di Matteo?

10 Who are Wiltshire's finest (actually, only) league club?

And some harder or two-part questions for 2 points

11 Which German goalkeeper earned (deserved) notoriety for a shocking tackle on Patrick Battiston of France in a 1982 WCFT SF? And who did he edge into 2nd place in a subsequent French poll to find the most unpopular man in history?

12 For which side did Temuri Ketsbaia play in an FA Cup Final? What nationality is Ketsbaia?

13 Manchester United hold the record for both the biggest home win and biggest away win since the start of the Premiership; who were the two opponents?

14 In which year and against which opposition did David Beckham make his England debut?

15 For whom did Derby receive £7m from Leeds in October 2001? Where was he playing in 2006-07?

Questions 1-10, for 1 point each

1 Which club side fielded 6 former England captains in its ranks in 1982?

2 Robbie Williams follows which lower-division side?

3 Which player's move from Newcastle to Arsenal in 1961 sparked a court case that changed footballer's rights forever?

4 Which music entrepreneur was the driver behind moving Wimbledon FC to Milton Keynes?

5 Which is the only one of these sides to have dropped into the 3rd tier of the league: Aston Villa, Chelsea, Leicester City, West Ham United

6 Who was manager of Aston Villa when they last won the league?

7 What was kept in a shoebox under the bed of FIFA official Dr Ottorino Barrassi during the Second World War?

8 Who cost Arsenal £6m in 2001, a fee which ended up being £500,000 per League game?

9 What did influential manager Herbert Chapman unilaterally introduce for his team in 1928, 10 years before it became mandatory?

10 Which Italian goalkeeper could lay claim to be Alex Ferguson's worst-ever signing?

And some harder or two-part questions for 2 points

11 Chelsea signing Jiri Jarosik spent most of the 2005–06 season on loan at which club? And who took him on a permanent deal in the summer of 2006?

12 Which 2 men have had 2 spells as manager of the Welsh national team?

13 Name the 4 sides to have won 3 consecutive league titles in England.

14 In which year did goal difference replace goal average? (1 pt for within 2 years)

15 Which Bradford City chairman admitted that signing an overseas star on £40k per week may have damaged his team's finances? Who was the star?

Questions 1–10, for 1 point each

1 Which charismatic manager persuaded Kevin Keegan to play for Southampton after his successful spell with Hamburg?

2 Comedians Lenny Henry and Frank Skinner follow which Midlands team?

3 Which Newcastle legend was known as 'Wor Jackie'?

4 Which ground was the 'temporary' home of Wimbledon FC for 10 years?

5 Who won the inaugural football league, winning 'The Double' in the process?

6 Which World Cup-winning star died of a heart attack whilst trying to put out a fire at his home in April, 2007?

7 Which nation won the 1999 Women's World Cup Final?

8 Who got most caps for England: Matthew Le Tissier, Andy Sinton or Geoff Thomas?

9 Who beat Oldham Athletic 13–4 in a Div 3 (North) match in 1934, the highest goals aggregate in an English league match?

10 Which famous club are known as 'The Old Lady'?

And some harder or two-part questions for 2 points

11 Birmingham City's MD, Karen Brady, is married to which international player? What nationality is he?

12 Rinus Israel won a European Cup with which club in 1970, and played in a World Cup Final for which country?

13 Who won the gold medals in men's and women's football at the 2004 Olympic Games in Athens?

14 Who resigned as FA Chief Executive in 2002? To which post did he go?

15 Who were the 2 wingers in Tommy Docherty's entertaining Manchester United side of the 1970s?

Answers on page 212

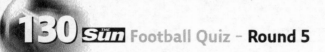

Questions 1-10, for 1 point each

1 Where did Leicester City play their home games prior to building The Walkers Stadium?

2 Chesney in *Coronation Street* has a dog named after which Manchester United star?

3 In which year did the Millennium Stadium open?

4 Which team were known as 'The Crazy Gang' due to their spirit of organised mayhem?

5 What was stolen from the shop of William Shillock, a shoemaker in Birmingham, in 1895?

6 Who took over as Chairman at Carlisle United in 1992 and promised top-flight football within a decade?

7 What connects Naranjito, Pique, Footix and Goleo VI?

8 Which club brought Des Walker back to England after an unsettled year with Sampdoria in Italy?

9 Which young Brazilian star was top scorer in the 2004 Copa America?

10 Which England player's injury problems earned him the affectionate nickname of 'Sick-note'?

And some harder or two-part questions for 2 points

11 Which 2 Blackburn players indulged in some fisticuffs during a Champions League match in Moscow in 1995?

12 Which London side won the Nationwide Conference with some ease in 2006-07? Which club, relegated from the league the previous season, were the runaway early leaders, but faded after Christmas?

13 How many caps did Gazza win? (1 pt for 3 either way)

14 Which 2 former England captains managed Exeter in the 1980s/90s?

15 Which 3 brothers played for Southampton in the same match in 1988?

Questions 1-10, for 1 point each

1 For which footballing incident is Tofik Bakhramov known?

2 Which former Premiership star competed on the BBC show *Strictly Come Dancing* in 2006?

3 Who started the 1999–2000 season by scoring own goals in successive matches for Leicester City?

4 In 1989, which striker became Wimbledon FC's first full international?

5 Who started life as Small Heath?

6 Who swapped Victoria for Britannia?

7 Which band penned England's 1990 World Cup anthem, 'World In Motion'?

8 Which Irish international became Millwall's record deal when they sold him to Liverpool for £2.3m in 1995?

9 Which side have won the German Bundesliga a record 19 times?

10 Who play Celta Vigo in a derby match?

And some harder or two-part questions for 2 points

11 Who threw a punch at Alan Shearer during a Newcastle club night out in Dublin? What happened afterwards?

12 How many of the 24 Conference clubs in 2006–07 have played league football? (1 pt for within 2)

13 Name the 2 Liverpool players to have won 8 league championship winners' medals.

14 Who were the first British club to contest a European Final, and in which competition?

15 Who had a chart hit with the anthem 'Nice One Cyril'? Who was Cyril?

Answers on page 212

Questions 1-10, for 1 point each

1 Which former England international has carved out a second successful sporting career as a racehorse trainer?

2 Which France and Chelsea defender was known as 'The Rock'?

3 Which other London club bought Martin Peters from West Ham for £200,000, a British record at the time?

4 Which former footballer became a presenter on the popular TV show, *Gladiators*?

5 Which legend died of a heart attack whilst watching Everton against Liverpool in 1980?

6 What did lower-division footballers Ted Hemsley, Phil Neale, Chris Balderstone and Arnie Sidebottom have in common?

7 Which team took to the field in 100° heat in Switzerland in 1954 wearing woollen long-sleeve shirts, and subsequently lost 7-0?

8 Which star of the US 1994 WCFT campaign earned a move to Italy for his performances and the nickname 'Jesus' for his appearance?

9 Who won the most caps for Argentina: Batistuta, Maradona or Kempes?

10 Who was fined £5,000 (far less than one day's wages), when the TV cameras showed he had feigned injury to get an opponent dismissed at the 2002 World Cup?

And some harder or two-part questions for 2 points

11 Who received an 11-match ban for pushing over a referee in 1998? Who was the ref?

12 How did Adams Park come to host a major SF in 2006-07? What was the result?

13 Name the 4 Irish (Northern or RoI) winners of the PFA Players' Player of the Year.

14 What is the name of the great Brazilian stadium in Rio? Which club play there?

15 Which 2 pairs of brothers played for Wales against Northern Ireland in 1955?

Questions 1-10, for 1 point each

1 Why did Tony Adams miss 8 weeks of the 1990-91 season?

2 Who led the PFA's campaign to scrap the maximum wage in the 1950s?

3 Who was made President of UEFA in January 2007?

4 In the Sky TV programme *Big Ron Manager,* Ron Atkinson was seen dispensing advice to the management team of which lower-division club?

5 Who has been President of FIFA since 1998?

6 Which Fulham star was the game's first £100-a-week player?

7 Which Reading forward was involved in the serious head injury to Chelsea goalkeeper Petr Cech in 2006-07?

8 What was the nickname of Andoni Goicoechea, the notoriously violent man-marker who ended Maradona's season (and almost his career) in 1983?

9 River Plate are the most successful side in the national league of which country?

10 Who was *Match of the Day*'s first commentator?

And some harder or two-part questions for 2 points

11 In 1998, which 2 players won the FA Cup, the Premiership and the World Cup?

12 Name the 3 Iceland internationals who have played for Bolton in the last decade.

13 'You've won it once. Now you've got to win it again.' Who? And when?

14 Which 2 sides ended England's interest in the 1954 and 1958 World Cups?

15 Which deputy chairman of Chelsea was killed in a helicopter accident? He was returning from a game against which club?

Questions 1-10, for 1 point each

1 What was the name of the healer in whom Glenn Hoddle put a large degree of misplaced faith whilst he was England manager?

2 Who took over as manager of Coventry City in 1961 and took them from the 3rd Division to the 1st?

3 Who was the Swedish president of UEFA from 1990 to January 2007?

4 Which club were forced to share Bath City's Twerton Park stadium for a number of years?

5 Which Frenchman was FIFA President from 1921 until 1954?

6 How were Sunderland promoted to the top flight in 1990, despite finishing only 6th in the 2nd tier and losing the play-off final to Swindon?

7 What connects Adebayor, Petit and Eboue, apart from the fact that they have all played for Arsenal?

8 Which Brazilian star of the 1950s and 60s was known as 'Little Bird'?

9 Who holds the record for league appearances for Celtic (with 486): is it Billy McNeill, Danny McGrain or Henrik Larsson?

10 Why did Ian Bishop wear the No.12 shirt for West Ham in a league game in 1993? (Squad numbers were not yet used for league games)

And some harder or two-part questions for 2 points

11 Which English club brought Eric Cantona to England, and who was the manager responsible?

12 Which 2 clubs do the following players have in common: Nicolas Anelka, Yuri Djorkaeff, Bruno N'Gotty, Jay-Jay Okocha?

13 What is the relationship between Brian Quinn and David Murray?

14 Who joined Chelsea for £10m in the January 2004 transfer window? Which club were selling?

15 Which club bought Portuguese international Paolo Futre, even though he was almost lame? Who was the manager at the time?

Questions 1-10, for 1 point each

1 Who was Manchester United's assistant manager in their successful season in 2006-07?

2 Who lasted just 48 days as manager of Wales in 1994?

3 Who was fired as a media pundit after making offensive remarks about Marcel Desailly on air?

4 Nigel Martyn became the first £1m goalkeeper when he moved from Bristol Rovers to which club?

5 Where are the headquarters of FIFA?

6 What connects Premiership stars Robbie Savage, Rob Hulse and Dean Ashton?

7 Former World Snooker champion turned presenter John Parrott is a passionate supporter of which Premiership side?

8 Why is a Coventry City fanzine called *Garry Mabbutt's Knee*?

9 Who made most league appearances for Liverpool: Jamie Carragher, Ian Callaghan or Emlyn Hughes?

10 Who once put on 109 in a partnership with Australian test star Matthew Hayden in a league cricket match?

And some harder or two-part questions for 2 points

11 Which 2 footballers duetted on the 1980s chart hit 'Diamond Lights'?

12 Everton didn't compete in the 1985-86 ECWC, despite being holders of the trophy; for what 2 reasons?

13 Who bought Crystal Palace from Ron Noades in 1998, but soon sent the club into liquidation; and who purchased the club from the administrators in 2000?

14 Wolfie Smith in the TV comedy series *Citizen Smith* was regularly seen sporting which club's colours? Who played Wolfie?

15 Which 2 sides took 5 games to settle an FA Cup SF in 1980?

Answers on page 213

136 Sun Football Quiz - **Round 11**

Questions 1-10, for 1 point each

1 A sculpture of which footballing legend stands outside the new Wembley Stadium?

2 Who is West Brom's all-time top scorer?

3 How many caps did Roy Keane win for Ireland: was it 49, 67 or 90?

4 Who play at the Spotland stadium?

5 Which famous manager took charge of the Great Britain soccer team at the 1948 Olympics?

6 Which league club play at Prenton Park?

7 Oasis frontman Noel Gallagher is often seen in the crowd watching which Premiership side?

8 What name do the South Africans give their national football team?

9 How many games did Chelsea lose in the Premiership in 2004-05?

10 Which Scottish international also represented his country at squash, volleyball and golf?

And some harder or two-part questions for 2 points

11 Which proud record did Peter Schmeichel maintain even whilst playing for the blue half of Manchester in 2002-03?

12 Who were the 3 overseas players in Aston Villa's League Cup-winning team in 1996?

13 Which former chairman installed his son as chairman of Oxford United, because legislation dictated that he could only own one club himself? And which club did he own?

14 Which North East non-league side attracted a 42,000 crowd for a 5th-round FA Cup match against Wrexham in 1978? What was the venue?

15 Name the 2 French players who have been top scorer in Serie A.

Questions 1–10, for 1 point each

1 With which club did Geoff Hurst have his single, largely unsuccesful, foray into management?

2 What was the general name given to the behind-the-scenes structure that brought Liverpool such continuity and success in the 1970s and 80s?

3 Which entrepreneur is the chairman of Middlesbrough FC?

4 Which ticket tout and former chairman of Barnet died of a heart attack aged 69 in 1999?

5 What momentous feat was sealed by goals from Bobby Smith and Terry Dyson in 1961?

6 Which team moved from Coldblow Lane to Zampa Road, but simply stuck 'New' in front of the name of their ground?

7 Who does Alex Ferguson sometimes refer to as 'Old Vinegar Face'?

8 What does the Bayern part of Bayern Munich mean?

9 How many times was Eric Cantona capped by France: was it 13, 30 or 45?

10 Which Ipswich goalkeeper holds the record for most penalties saved in a season? (8 out of 10)

And some harder or two-part questions for 2 points

11 Which 2 sides are known as 'The Old Firm'?

12 Who were the 2 sponsors of the League Cup between Littlewoods and Worthington?

13 Name the 3 Championship sides (2005–06) wearing shirts with yellow, gold or amber in them.

14 Which 2 Dutch stars reduced their side's chances in the 1978 WCFT by pulling out before the tournament?

15 Who was the assistant manager to Alex Ferguson when the club won the treble in 1999? Who did he replace?

Questions 1–10, for 1 point each

1 Nobby Stiles was manager of which club for 4 years (1977–1981) before retiring from the game altogether?

2 Which 24-year-old Belgian footballer's contract dispute changed the face of football's transfer system for ever in 1988?

3 Who was the sugar daddy whose funds ensured Blackburn Rovers' growth into a club of Premiership stature?

4 Which Northern Ireland international (88 caps) was the last youth signing by Sir Matt Busby for Manchester United?

5 What was the revised capacity of Wembley after safety work following the Hillsborough disaster: was it 75,000, 82,500 or 92,500?

6 Which England international cricketer made a handful of appearances for Scunthorpe United in the early 1980s?

7 Who was hospitalised by a disgraceful challenge from Ben Thatcher in August 2006?

8 Which Dutch international of recent years earned the nickname 'Pitbull' for his abrasive style of play?

9 Whose fondness for changing his line-up earned him the nickname 'Tinkerman'?

10 Gillespie Road underground station changed its name to what in the 1930s, at the request of the local football club?

And some harder or two-part questions for 2 points

11 Name 2 of the 3 clubs for whom England goalkeeper Gordon Banks played club football in England?

12 A 1970 World Cup qualifying tie between which 2 Central American states resulted in a mini-war with over 3,000 dead?

13 Which 2 teams won the double in the 19th century?

14 Who made a club record 583 League appearances for Charlton from 1934–56? In what position?

15 Alfredo Di Stefano made international appearances for Spain and which 2 South American countries?

Questions 1-10, for 1 point each

1 What is the abbreviated name of the controlling body for North American football?

2 A monument to which former great stands outside Elland Road, Leeds?

3 Which goalkeeper had spells at Peterborough, Birmingham City and QPR before a £1.3m 1990 transfer saw him join one of the top flight's giants?

4 St James's Park hosted Conference football in 2006-07. Explain.

5 Who won his Spurs but sold them before recruiting his Apprentice?

6 Who followed father John into the management seat at Bournemouth in 2006?

7 Which Blackburn striker has played international football for Grenada?

8 What is the nickname of the Cameroon national team?

9 Which self-styled wit was sacked by Sky after a tasteless pun about the similarity between the word 'tsunami' and 'Toon Army'?

10 The Pools Panel came into being during the great freeze of which year?

And some harder or two-part questions for 2 points

11 Why did Bhutan and Montserrat play each other on the day of the 2002 World Cup Final?

12 How many seasons did Wimbledon spend in the top flight before their relegation in 2000? (1 pt if within 2)

13 With which club did Raddy Antic play top-flight football in England? Which famous European club did he go on to manage?

14 From which club did Charlton buy Irish international goalkeeper Dean Kiely in 1999? Who did he play for in 2006-07?

15 What does UEFA stand for?

Answers on page 213

Questions 1-10, for 1 point each

1   What is 35cm high and weighs 3.8kg?

2   Who was appointed Director for Football Development at the FA in 2003?

3   Who scored a hat-trick on his debut in a 4-2 Southampton win over Arsenal?

4   Which Irish international was Aston Villa's most-capped player, winning 64 caps whilst with the club?

5   Whose attempt to look cool by turning up for the FA Cup Final in cream suits brought them well-deserved derision in the 1990s?

6   What is Chesterfield's nickname, taken from the town's unusual church?

7   As of the end of February 2007, who is Newcastle's most-capped current player?

8   Which Dutch international was convicted of manslaughter after a driving incident in which another driver was killed?

9   'I don't think of foreigners as being professionals in the same sense as us. They're not prepared to give everything ...' Who was singing the tired old xenophobic tune in 1973?

10 Who is Edson Arantes do Nascimento?

And some harder or two-part questions for 2 points

11 With which club did Tony Adams have a tricky introduction to management? And with which Premiership side was he working as a coach in 2006-07?

12 Who paid who £5m for Ade Akinbiyi in summer 2000?

13 Which territory's main club side are AC Ajaccio? In which league do they play?

14 Who won the 2nd division in 1920, having been robbed of a place in an expanded 1st division by a ballot that elected which side in their place?

15 What was the estimated attendance at the 1950 World Cup Final between Brazil and Uruguay? (1 pt if within 10,000)

Questions 1-10, for 1 point each

1 The entire squad of which Italian club side was wiped out in a 1949 air crash?

2 Who play at The Hawthorns?

3 Which High Court judge was behind a series of detailed recommendations for safety and social measures to improve football in the late 1980s?

4 Of which club was Dr Jozef Venglos a curious and disastrous choice as manager in 1990-91?

5 Which Frenchman was made European Footballer of the Year 3 years in succession in the 1980s?

6 Who won the non-league double of Conference title and FA Trophy in 1993, and won promotion to the league for the first time?

7 Who paid Bradford City £2m apiece for Des Hamilton (1997) and Andy O'Brien (2001)?

8 Which Birmingham City star player was required to wear an electronic tag after early release for a custodial sentence for drink-driving?

9 Who compared missing a crucial penalty to 'stepping off the edge of the world into silence'?

10 Which commentator died on the eve of England's 5-1 victory over Germany in 2001?

And some harder or two-part questions for 2 points

11 Which AC Milan striker was the first African to be named World Footballer of the Year? In which country would he later stand as President?

12 Name the 5 Premiership (2005-06) clubs who were amongst the 12 founder members of the Football League.

13 Who sent David Elleray a signed shirt when the referee retired, Elleray having sent him off 4 times in his career? What was Elleray's occupation?

14 Who became the first £1,000 player in 1905? He moved from Sunderland to which other club?

15 Who sang at the famous gala concert which closed the 1990 WCFT in Italy?

Questions 1-10, for 1 point each

1 Which footballing great made a surprise appearance, aged 50, for Garforth Town against Tadcaster in November 2004?

2 What was the name given to the ultra-defensive sweeper system introduced by Inter Milan in the 1960s?

3 A statute to which former icon stands outside Old Trafford?

4 Who play at the Underhill Stardium in Hertfordshire?

5 Since 1968, who is the only player based in England who has been voted European Footballer of the Year?

6 Who owns the Memorial Stadium, where Bristol Rovers have played their home games since 1996?

7 From which club did Sheffield Wednesday buy Paolo Di Canio in 1997?

8 Which Chelsea player, not exactly known for his ferocious tackling, was sent off twice in the 2005-06 Premiership season?

9 'It's a tremendous honour. I'm going to have a banana to celebrate.' Whose response to being voted Footballer of the Year?

10 What is Wendy Tome's claim to fame?

And some harder or two-part questions for 2 points

11 Which club brought Paolo Di Canio to Britain? Which was his final British club before returning to Italy?

12 Who was the first £100,000 player; who splashed the cash, and who pocketed it?

13 According to whose fans, who was so good they named him twice?

14 Which 2 future Liverpool players appeared against them for Newcastle in the 1974 FA Cup Final?

15 Which 2 London grounds were World Cup venues in 1966?

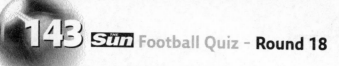

Questions 1–10, for 1 point each

1 What are Telstar, Questra and Tango Durlast?

2 Who is the only player to score 100 goals for both an English and a Scottish club?

3 Which former Arsenal and England star died of cancer in 2001, aged 33?

4 Who played for Birmingham City aged 16 years 7 months in September 1970?

5 Who lifted the 2006 World Cup?

6 Who was the larger-than-life character who managed Barnet when they won promotion to the league?

7 Which Irish international was Southampton's record outlay, at £4m in 2001?

8 Which megastar received a 2-year suspended sentence for shooting journalists with an air-gun?

9 Which TV celebrity was revealed to be having an affair with sexy Sven?

10 Which *Grandstand* presenter appeared on Wogan in a turquoise tracksuit claiming to be the son of God?

And some harder or two-part questions for 2 points

11 For which club did Stuart Pearce make over 400 league appearances? And who was the Coventry City manager who signed him from non-league Wealdstone?

12 In one of the 1990s' more bizarre deals, which club did Joey Beauchamp leave for West Ham; how many games did he play for the Hammers, and why did he leave?

13 The brothers Mark and Brian Stein notched up over 1,000 League games between them. Which of them scored more goals? Where were they born?

14 In 1951 Brentford cleared some of their debt by selling which 2 players, later to become far better known as managers?

15 In 1950 just one player in the WCFT, George Robledo, played in the English league. For which club? And for which country did he play?

Questions 1-10, for 1 point each

1 To which recently deceased great Brazilian sportsman did the 1994 squad dedicate their World Cup victory of that year?

2 Who was Ian Wright's rhyming strike partner at Crystal Palace?

3 Which Cameroon international collapsed and died during a match in France in 2003?

4 Explain this list:
Keane/Sutton/Cole/Bergkamp/Collymore/Shearer/Ferdinand/Van Nistelrooy/Veron/Ferdinand/Shevchenko.

5 Which Englishman was the first winner of the European Footballer of the Year award, in 1956?

6 Who paid Crewe Alexandra £3m for Dean Ashton in 2005?

7 Which Premiership manager's given first name is Llewellyn?

8 Who was the winger sent home from Scotland's 1978 World Cup camapign for taking banned substances?

9 Comedian and actor Alan Davies is a regular attendee at whose home games?

10 Which of these players has never been European Footballer of the Year: Denis Law, Kevin Keegan, Kenny Dalglish, Michael Owen?

And some harder or two-part questions for 2 points

11 In which year was Steven Gerrard born? (1 pt for 1 year either way)

12 Which 2 Newcastle players indulged in a bit of fisticuffs with each other and got red-carded in 2005?

13 Name the 3 sides with the best attendances in the Premiership in 2004-05.

14 Which 3 members of Don Revie's great Leeds side have all been manager of the club?

15 Who was the then-secretary at the FA with whom Sven-Goran Eriksson had a much-publicised affair? Which FA executive resigned after his own involvement with the same woman was revealed?

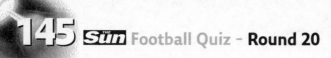

Questions 1-10, for 1 point each

1 Who play their home games at the venue for the 2006 World Cup Final?

2 From which other North-West side did Everton buy the legendary Dixie Dean?

3 Which current player is Northern Ireland's all-time leading scorer by a considerable distance?

4 Who was co-manager of Charlton alongside Alan Curbishley for 4 years in the 1990s?

5 For what is the 'Ballon d'Or' awarded?

6 Who bought Peter Crouch from Portsmouth for £4.5m in 2002?

7 Which pony-tailed defender became a bit of a cult hero at QPR and then Newcastle after his move from Hereford in 1990?

8 Who was jailed for passing on forged notes to the YTS boys at Wrexham?

9 Who sold David Beckham a Ford Escort, after Beckham first joined Manchester United?

10 Which other nation played their home games in England between 1972 and 1974?

And some harder or two-part questions for 2 points

11 In which year was Paul Gascoigne born? (1 pt for 1 year either way)

12 Which 2 Leeds United footballers were charged with GBH and affray in January 2000?

13 Which striker scored 14 goals for Mexico in qualification for the 2006 WCFT? Which English club did he join, becoming the first Mexican to play in the Premiership?

14 Which two survivors of the Munich air crash were part of of the 1968 European Cup-winning Manchester United team?

15 Which referee announced his retirement after receiving death threats in the wake of Chelsea's acrimonious Champions League encounter with which side in 2004-05?

Questions 1-10, for 1 point each

1 Which Argentina international moved from Paris St Germain to Manchester United in 2004?

2 In which country was French defender, Marcel Desailly, born?

3 In which ground do the vocal home support occupy the Holte End?

4 How much did Liverpool pay for Ian Rush in 1980: was it £15,000, £125,000 or £300,000?

5 Which German was the first winner of the FIFA World Player of the Year award in 1991?

6 In 1994-95, who were initially ejected from the FA Cup but reinstated after a lengthy legal dispute which saw the FA, unsurprisingly, capitulate?

7 Who is the high-profile chairman of Fulham?

8 Which former Arsenal player was jailed for a variety of offences including brothel-keeping and forgery?

9 What is the name of Wayne Rooney's girlfriend?

10 For which country did Enzi Francescoli win 122 caps in the 1980s and 90s?

And some harder or two-part questions for 2 points

11 What was remarkable about Jimmy Greaves' debuts for each of his 4 clubs and for England? What was especially remarkable about his Spurs' debut?

12 Who sent Wayne Rooney off in a Champions League match in September 2005 for sarcastically applauding a decision, and who were the opponents?

13 In 1988-89, which side were awarded 4 penalties in a game against Brighton (who also got 1), and how many did they successfully convert?

14 Who in 1986 was the last non-League side to win away against top-flight opposition in the FA Cup? Who were the victims?

15 Nick Hornby's book *Fever Pitch* chronicles his time watching which side? Who played Hornby's character in the film of the book?

Questions 1-10, for 1 point each

1 What was the nickname of 1970s Leeds star, Allan Clarke?

2 Which Liverpool star of the 1970s was known as 'Crazy Horse'?

3 Which stadium was the main venue for the 1948 Olympic Games?

4 Which City were wound up following dodgy financial dealings in 1919, but re-emerged the same year as a United?

5 Who was Wales' manager when they last beat England, in 1984?

6 Who was Secretary of the Football League from 1957-1979?

7 Who got Bolton into the Premiership in 1994-95 but left before the club started their first season?

8 Who was censured for dropping his shorts in a match against Coventry in 1979?

9 Sir Richard Attenborough was once a director of which football club?

10 Which town's women's team have been at the forefront of the women's game while their men's side have never reached the top flight?

And some harder or two-part questions for 2 points

11 Who did Southampton beat 3-2 in an emotional farewell to The Dell? Who scored the last-ever goal at the ground?

12 Which 3 Leicester City players were accused, and cleared, of assaulting 3 women in a La Manga hotel in 2004?

13 Who scored the Liverpool goals in their famous comeback against Milan in the 2005 Champions League Final?

14 Whose goal knocked Leicester out of the FA Cup in 2001 and sent which side to the semi-final?

15 In which year did David Beckham marry Victoria 'Posh Spice' Adams? What was their first child named?

Questions 1-10, for 1 point each

1   Which 1970s hard-man rejoiced in the nickname 'Chopper'?

2   Who is this? He won 7 league titles, 3 FA Cups, a Champions League and played 56 times for Ireland.

3   Who scored 4 as Arsenal routed Liverpool 6-3 at Anfield in the Carling Cup in January 2007?

4   Which World Cup winner also made a record number of appearances for Leeds United?

5   How many goals did Ian Rush score for Wales in his 73 internationals: was it 28, 36 or 44?

6   Who was West Ham's Scottish right-back of the 1980s with a reputation for taking (and scoring) fierce penalty kicks?

7   What is Matthew Simmons' claim to fame?

8   Who was once censured by the FA for using the lavatory reserved for the referee and his assistants?

9   Which actress was once married to Premiership striker Lee Chapman?

10 Which 2001 hit movie starred Parminder Nagra and Keira Knightley as footie-mad teenagers?

And some harder or two-part questions for 2 points

11 Which 2 top-flight goalkeepers were accused of match-fixing in the 1990s?

12 Vinnie Jones was booked after 4 seconds of an FA Cup tie playing for who against which of his former clubs?

13 Which 3 England players also had fathers who played for England? (In all cases the son has won more caps)

14 Which game in the 2002 World Cup produced a record 16 yellow cards and 1 red?

15 With which 2 clubs did Liam Brady begin and end his career?

Questions 1-10, for 1 point each

1 What connects Brazilian stars Gerson and Socrates with Osvaldo Ardiles and Johann Cruyff?

2 Hunter Davies' *The Glory Game*, a football classic, was a diary of the fortunes of which club during 1971-72?

3 Reading's Kevin Doyle and Shane Long were both bought from which Irish league club?

4 Who garnered a club record £11.5m fee for Emile Heskey when they sold him to Liverpool in 2000?

5 Who is Wales' most-capped outfield player?

6 Which Scottish striker won Europe's Golden Boot (top scorer in any league) award in 1993?

7 Which unfancied side became the first side to beat Bayern Munich in Munich when they did so in the UEFA Cup in 1993-94?

8 Antonio Rattin was sent off in the 1966 WCFT playing for which side against England?

9 Which professional footballer had a relationship with Ulrika Jonsson, which broke up after incidents of domestic violence?

10 What do Matt Holland, Alan Brazil and Mike England have in common?

And some harder or two-part questions for 2 points

11 In which year was Diego Maradona born? (1 pt for 2 years either way)

12 Who was sent off for spitting in a 1990 World Cup match between Germany and Holland, and who was the target who also got his marching orders?

13 Name the 3 sides with which Trevor Steven won League titles.

14 In 1959, who scored his 100th League goal in fewer games than any other player? For which club?

15 Which English side reached the semifinals of the 2001 Champions League, and who was the unlikely source of 6 goals in an impressive campaign?

150 SUN Football Quiz - **Round 25**

Questions 1–10, for 1 point each

1 Which Manchester United star was voted European Footballer of the Year in 1968?

2 Who was President of FIFA before Sepp Blatter?

3 Alexandre Gaydamak bought Portsmouth from which other wealthy businessman?

4 Who were first elected to the league in 1892 under the name Newton Heath?

5 Who was manager of Southampton when they reached the 2003 FA Cup Final?

6 Australian international Craig Moore played over 200 games in a decade for which Scottish club?

7 As well as football, Paul McGrath's autobiography, *Back from the Brink*, chronicles what episode in his life?

8 Who was sacked by BBC Five-Live after suggesting disgruntled fans should turn up at a referee's house on a radio phone-in?

9 What was the name of the wife frequently beaten up by folk-hero Paul Gascoigne?

10 Of which club was snooker player Steve Davis a director?

And some harder or two-part questions for 2 points

11 Who would contest a local derby between The Saints and Pompey?

12 Alf Ramsey won the Football League title as a player and a manager; with which 2 clubs?

13 Which 2 countries have won the Copa America 14 times, a joint record?

14 Which 2 countries played out a sham of a fixture with the result that they both qualified for the second phase in the 1982 WCFT and edged out Algeria?

15 Which classy defender was the first to win 100 caps for Denmark, and which 2 players have subsequently passed his total of 102 caps?

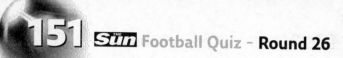

Questions 1-10, for 1 point each

1. What was the name of the racehorse over which Alex Ferguson had a long-running feud with John Magnier?

2. What was Mark Hughes' first job as a manager?

3. Who are known as 'The Owls'?

4. Which referee carries the nickname 'The Thing From Tring'?

5. Who knocked Liverpool out of both domestic cups in the space of 4 days in 2006-07?

6. Who was the Nigerian international who scored twice as Everton won the 1995 FA Cup SF against Tottenham 4-1?

7. For which country does Mark Viduka play international football?

8. Who was Liverpool manager when they last won promotion to the top flight in 1962?

9. Which US family took over Manchester United in 2005?

10. Who scored on his debut for Paraguay against Colombia in 1989, and why is that fact remarkable?

And some harder or two-part questions for 2 points

11. Whose 2 goals against the Faroe Islands in 2004 made him Ireland's all-time leading scorer? Whose record did he eclipse?

12. Which German great and former manager is chairman at Bayern Munich and who did he appoint as manager in summer 2004?

13. Name the 6 London clubs in the first Premiership season (1992-93).

14. Which Belgian striker suffered a career-ending broken leg in a clash with Richard Wright soon after arriving in England? For which club had he signed?

15. Which British player was known as 'El Toro' (The Bull) at Barcelona in the 1990s? What was his nickname in this country?

Answers on page 215

Questions 1-10, for 1 point each

1 What did pioneering English referee, Ken Aston, devise after encountering communication problems during international matches?

2 Where was the venue for the first official international between England and Scotland?

3 Which Southampton player was banned for 10 games for pushing referee Alan Wiley in 2005?

4 Vladimir Romanov is the controversial chairman of which SPL club?

5 Where were the majority of the FA Cup Finals before 1900 played?

6 Who was the Georgian international who became a cult figure at Manchester City in the 1990s?

7 How many goals did Wigan goalkeeper Mike Pollitt concede in the 2006 Carling Cup Final?

8 Who was manager of AS Monaco when they won the French title in 1988?

9 Former Everton chairman Sir John Moores was the power behind which business empire?

10 Which former Olympian tried to introduce a hopelessly under-researched and unworkable membership system in the early 1990s as Minister For Sport?

And some harder or two-part questions for 2 points

11 Who is the Chief Executive of Chelsea FC, and of which club was he previously Chief Executive?

12 Name the 4 men who managed Millwall in a turbulent 2005.

13 Who was Arsenal's leading scorer in their 1970–71 double-winning season, and with which club did he win further titles?

14 Which Yugoslav-born full-back made 167 appearances for Southampton in 2 spells? Who did he manage to a Scottish Cup Final success in 1994?

15 Who is this? He started with Cobh Ramblers before Brian Clough snapped him up; (2 pts if you already have the answer) he missed his chance of European success through suspension and missed the 2002 WCFT after a fit of pique.

Questions 1-10, for 1 point each

1 Which veteran goalkeeper was shown a red card for a professional foul after 13 seconds playing for Sheffield Wednesday in 2000?

2 Who signed Henrik Larsson twice, whilst manager at Feyenoord and then Celtic?

3 What colour shirts are the primary kit of Blackpool?

4 Tony Mowbray left which SPL club in 2006-07 to manage West Bromwich Albion?

5 League of Wales team The New Saints only acquired that name in 2006-07; they were once known as Llantsantffraid – under what name did they play from 1997-2006?

6 Gordon Strachan's first foray into management was as player-manager with which Midlands club?

7 At which ground were 33 people killed in a crush at an FA Cup QF in 1945-46?

8 For which club did Kevin Keegan leave Fulham?

9 Who are the only team to win the World Cup playing in red?

10 In which country might you watch Fluminense play Botafogo?

And some harder or two-part questions for 2 points

11 David Bentley spent 2004-05 on loan from Arsenal at which Premiership club? Which club bought him in 2006?

12 Who was the colourful coach who resigned as boss of QPR in 2005-06, and with which club does he now manage?

13 Who were the two wide players who fed the SAS in Blackburn's Premiership-winning side of 1993-94?

14 In 1959, what was notable about Hibs striker Joe Baker's international debut?

15 Who took over ownership of Aston Villa in 2006? Who was the former Chairman whose shares were bought out?

Questions 1-10, for 1 point each

1 Thierry Henry met his wife, Nicole Merry, whilst shooting adverts for which car?

2 Which Southampton legend missed only 1 penalty in over 50 attempts?

3 Which club has snooker magnate Barry Hearn as its chairman?

4 Linfield, Coleraine and Glentoran play in the top division of which league?

5 What event prompted Ferenc Puskas' move to Real Madrid and his compatriot Sador Kocsis' move to Barcelona?

6 Which Welsh international moved from Leeds to Juventus in 1957, more than doubling the British transfer record in the process?

7 In 1973-74, a pitch invasion by which side's supporters prompted the FA to order their cup tie against Nottingham Forest to be replayed?

8 Which side did Jack Charlton lead to the old Division 2 title in 1974?

9 Which country's national side were known as 'Das Wunderteam' due to their reputation between the wars?

10 Who, in 2005, became the first Russian side to lift a European trophy?

And some harder or two-part questions for 2 points

11 The official name of which Premiership club's ground is The Boleyn Ground? By what name is it usually known?

12 Who are the Holdsworth twins?

13 Which two sides has Tommy Hutchison scored for in an FA Cup Final?

14 In a 2001 friendly against Mexico, who became the first 3 players from the same club to score in an England international?

15 How many red and yellow cards did Tomas Repka accumulate in 164 league matches for West Ham (1 pt if within 5)

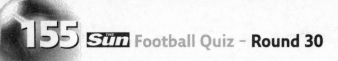

Questions 1–10, for 1 point each

1 Who did John Hartson kick in the head during a West Ham training session?

2 In 2005, who tried to sue Gary Lineker for defamation of character after Lineker wrote an unflattering newspaper piece about him?

3 Fat Boy Slim, Des Lynam and Jamie Theakston are all high-profile supporters of which league team?

4 Who has won more of the fixtures between Wales and Ireland?

5 In which country did the great Eusebio end his playing career?

6 Who was Aston Villa's record signing, bought from River Plate in Argentina for £9.5m?

7 Who was fired as manager of Manchester United in 1981 after failing to win a trophy in 4 years?

8 Who was coach of Juventus from 1977 to 1985, delivering the club's first European Cup and a host of other titles?

9 With which club did legendary Scottish playmaker Alex James win 4 league titles?

10 Under what name did Birmingham win Division 2 in 1893?

And some harder or two-part questions for 2 points

11 Which league side are known as 'The Saddlers'? What is the name of their ground?

12 Who was the son of Welsh international Ivor Jones, and with which club did he win the bulk of his 58 caps?

13 Name the 2 clubs with which Dave Mackay won League titles

14 Which 3rd-division team won at Chelsea and Sunderland en route to a 1976 FA Cup semi-final? Which future England manager was in the team?

15 Which 2 players scored in each World Cup from 1958 to 1970?

Questions 1-10, for 1 point each

1 Mike Flanagan and Derek Hales were sent off during a 1979 FA Cup tie. What was unusual?

2 What is the French football magazine regarded for many years as the best voice of the game in Europe?

3 For how much were Leyton Orient put up for sale after their chairman's business collapsed in 1995?

4 Who won the first of many league titles in 1901?

5 What pop-star nickname was George Best given by adoring Portuguese fans after his brilliant performance against Benfica in the European Cup in 1966?

6 Why did Dennis Bergkamp rarely feature in Arsenal's away games in Europe?

7 Who moved across Stanley Park for £1m in 1990?

8 Who led both Borussia Dortmund and Bayern Munich to Champions League success?

9 Which colourful England goalkeeper of the early years of the 20th century was 6'6' and weighed in at 22st?

10 Which former England captain had the nickname 'Captain Marvel'?

And some harder or two-part questions for 2 points

11 Which 3 regional leagues comprise Level 7 of the FA's structure for English league football?

12 Which father and son were manager and player in the 1991 FA Cup Final?

13 Who were the first club to use an artificial pitch, and was it in 1974, 1981 or 1989?

14 Keith Houchen won the FA Cup with which club? Years later he scored a last-minute winner against Arsenal playing for which club?

15 In which season was 3 points for a win introduced? (1 pt for within 2 years)

Questions 1–10, for 1 point each

1 Which Chelsea and Australia goalkeeper was suspended for 9 months in 2003 after testing positive for cocaine?

2 Which was Gary Lineker's first club, his home town?

3 Bournemouth's red and black kit, introduced in 1971, was based on which legendary Italian club?

4 Ted Drake's 42 goals in 1934–35 is still a record seasonal league tally for which club?

5 Manchester United's Champions League win over Bayern Munich came on the 90th anniversary of whose birth?

6 The Munich air crash in 1958 happened when Manchester United were flying back from which other European city?

7 Brian Clough became embroiled in bung accusations surrounding the purchase of which player?

8 For how many days was Steve Coppell manager of Manchester City in 1996: was it 8, 33 or 62?

9 Who were introduced in 1891, presumably to give the crowds someone to abuse other than the players?

10 What was the nickname of Ireland international Liam Brady?

And some harder or two-part questions for 2 points

11 Who play in the Kassam Stadium? What was the name of their old ground prior to 2001?

12 Which father and son notched up almost 20 league clubs and over 400 goals between them from 1959 to the end of the century, and which club was the only one common to both?

13 What is the address of the Football Association, and who is their current Chief Executive?

14 Which 2 clubs were nearly merged as Thames Valley Royals in the 1980s?

15 Which club were relegated from the top flight and declared bankrupt in 1982, and which former player led a consortium which spared the club financial disaster?

Questions 1-10, for 1 point each

1 Which Brazilian star became, in 2003, the first player to be voted FIFA World Player of the Year 3 times?

2 Who did Gary Lineker succeed as the principal presenter of *Match of the Day*?

3 By what more familiar name is Chesterfield's Recreation Ground better known?

4 Who was the 1st division's top scorer when his side, Everton, won the last league title before WWII in 1939?

5 Which player has scored most goals in a Manchester United career?

6 Who were banned from European competition after their supporters' behaviour during a tie with Ipswich Town in the 1973-74 UEFA Cup, thus missing the chance of entering the next season's European Cup as Italian champions?

7 How much did Liverpool pay Scunthorpe for Kevin Keegan in 1971: was it £35k, £75k or £275k?

8 Vanderlei Luxemburgo was sacked as coach of which famous club in 2005-06?

9 In what way did Ali Ben Nassar let England down in 1986?

10 Fans chanting 'Feed The Goat' is a celebration ritual greeting another goal from which striker?

And some harder or two-part questions for 2 points

11 For which club did Shaka Hislop make his league debut? For which country has he played in a WCFT?

12 Which pair of brothers played in the 1982 WCFT Final for West Germany?

13 Which 2nd Division derby attracted 55,003 in December 1976, and who was the main attraction?

14 Where did Kevin Keegan become manager in 1997? Who was his co-manager, later jettisoned?

15 Which two strikers swapped places at Birmingham and Crystal Palace in 2002, but ended up together at Palace in 2005-06?

Questions 1-10, for 1 point each

1 Which entepreneur had Reading's stadium named after him after providing most of the funds to build it?

2 What did ITV call their highlights package when they briefly won the franchise from *Match of the Day* at the start of the 21st century?

3 In the 1986–87 season, who were forced to play a league game at Hartlepool after they were locked out of their ground by the bailiffs?

4 Jimmy Dickinson was a long-serving player with which club?

5 Who were banned from European competition after their fans rioted at the 1975 European Cup Final?

6 Who were refused entry into the 1985–86 League Cup after unilaterally imposing a ban on away fans at their ground?

7 Who did Liverpool buy from Celtic as a replacement for Kevin Keegan?

8 Brothers Hakan and Murat Yakin have 93 caps (March 2006) between them for which country?

9 Who was sent off for the first time in his career by a show-pony referee in 1992, having gone 971 matches without a red card?

10 Which club celebrated 100 seasons of top-flight football in 2002–03?

And some harder or two-part questions for 2 points

11 Prior to Chelsea in 2007, which 2 sides have won both domestic cups in the same season?

12 Who was the youngest FA Cup Final captain in the 1969 Final between Manchester City and Leicester City? With which club did he win a league title a few years later?

13 Who was the first overseas player to win the PFA Player of the Year, and in which year?

14 Who are joint top scorers for Scotland, with 30?

15 Which 2 clubs have been in the top division in England since the end of WWII?

160 **sun** Football Quiz - **Round 35**

Questions 1–10, for 1 point each

1 Who upset the Chelsea management by undergoing surgery for an ankle injury without the club's prior agreement?

2 Who won promotion to the second tier when they beat Rotherham 3–1 on the last day of the season to hold off Blackpool?

3 Who scored the winner for West Ham in the last-day win at Manchester United that saw them avoid the drop in 2006–07?

4 Whose late goal settled the 2007 FA Cup Final?

5 Whose long-expected move from Bayern Munich to the Premiership was confirmed at the end of the 2006–07 season?

6 Who was SPL top scorer in 2006–07?

7 Who lost the first (home) leg of their 2006–07 third tier play-off SF 2–0, but won a remarkable second leg 5–2 to reach the Final?

8 Which well-travelled striker was the second tier's top scorer in 2006–07 with unfashionable Colchester?

9 Who was the leading Premiership scorer in 2006–07 outside the top two teams?

10 Who came on at half-time in the 2007 FA Cup Final only to be substituted himself in extra-time?

And some harder or two-part questions for 2 points

11 Who resigned as manager of Newcastle just before the end of the 2006–07 season? And who was confirmed as his replacement?

12 Which 3 sides clinched the available UEFA Cup spots by finishing 5th, 6th and 7th at the end of the Premiership season in 2006–07?

13 Who was appointed Torquay manager for just 10 minutes in a bizarre turn of events at the 2006–07 season's end? Which former club employee and manager led the consortium that took over the club?

14 Which 3 sides clinched automatic promotion from the third tier of the league in 2006–07?

15 Who, in 2007, became the first side since Real Madrid in 1986 to win the UEFA Cup 2 years in succession? Which of their countrymen did they beat in the Final?

Questions 1-10, for 1 point each

1 Who scored the winner for Wigan as they won 2-1 at Sheffield United on the last day of the 2006-07 season to avoid dropping out of the Premiership?

2 Who won the second tier manager of the season award after taking his side from the bottom of the table to be winners of the title at the end of 2006-07?

3 Who was the Premier League Chief Executive who came under fire over the ruling that saw West Ham avoid a points deduction for breaking the league's transfer regulations?

4 Who was voted Premiership Manager of the Year for 2006-07 even though his side didn't even get into Europe?

5 Who refereed the 2007 FA Cup Final?

6 Who won Serie B, Italy's second division, in 2006-7?

7 Who was the only one of the 22 starters in the 2007 FA Cup Final who had played in a previous FA Cup Final for a different club?

8 Who finished 13 points ahead of Shrewsbury in the third tier in 2006-07, but still lost to the Shropshire club in the play-offs?

9 Who was arrested for bringing a dog into Britain without the necessary quarantine in 2007?

10 How many live domestic football matches will the BBC be able to show in 2007-08?

And some harder or two-part questions for 2 points

11 Who scored 3 times as West Brom beat local rivals Wolves to reach the 2007 second tier Play-Off Final?

12 Which 2 managers resigned less than a week after their clubs had met in the last game of the Premiership season?

13 Who scored the equalising goal for Bolton against Chelsea on the 28th April that realistically sealed the fate of the Premiership in 2006-07? Against which side did Manchester United win 4-2 after being 0-2 down on the same day?

14 Who secured league status for the first time in their history at the end of the 2006-07 season? Which relatively recent league side did they beat in the play-off Final?

15 Who won the German Bundesliga in 2006-07? Which side failed to qualify for the Champions League for the first time in over a decade?

Answers on page 217

Name the
Team

In this quiz you have to name the team specified. The figures in brackets indicate the number of players you need to identify to earn 1/2/3 points respectively. If 11 players are asked for, the first 11 names given will be taken.

1 The Arsenal side (inc 3 subs) that lost the 2006 Champions League Final to Barcelona. (7-8/9-11/ 12+)

2 The Celtic side that won the 1967 European Cup Final. (4-5/6-7/ 8+)

3 The England team that beat Scotland 9-3 at Wembley in 1961. (3/4-5/6+)

4 The Leeds side (inc 1 sub) who played both legs of the 1971 Fairs Cup Final against Juventus. (4-5/6-7/8+)

5 The Manchester United side (inc 2 subs) that beat Chelsea 4-0 in the 1994 FA Cup Final. (4-5/6-7/8+)

6 The Scotland team that beat Holland 3-2 in the 1978 WCFT, but to no avail. (4-5/6/7+)

7 The West Germany side that won the 1974 World Cup Final. (3-4/5-6/7+)

8 The Reading side (inc 3 subs) that clinched promotion to the Premiership with a 1-1 draw at Leicester on 25 March 2006. (4-5/6-8/9+)

9 The Brazil side (starting line-up), maybe the greatest ever seen, that won the 1970 World Cup Final against Italy. (4-5/6-7/8+)

10 The Blackburn side (starting line-up) that lost the 2007 FA Cup SF to Chelsea. (4-5/6-7/ 8+)

1 The England starting line-up against Poland in 1973, the match that saw them fail to qualify for the 1974 WCFT. (3-4/5-6/7+)

2 The Everton team that won the FA Cup Final against Watford in 1984. (4-5/6-7/8+)

3 The Leicester City side (inc 2 subs) that beat Tranmere in the 2000 League Cup Final. (4-5/6-7/ 8+)

4 The AC Milan starting 11 that destroyed Steaua Bucharest 4-0 in the 1989 European Cup Final. (4/5-6/7+)

5 The Northern Ireland starting line-up when they beat Spain 1-0 in the 1982 WCFT. (3-4/5/6+)

6 The Sheffield Wednesday starting line-up in the FA Cup Final replay against Arsenal in 1993. (4/5-6/7+)

7 The Aston Villa side (inc 3 subs) that lost the 2000 FA Cup Final to Chelsea. (5-6/7-8/9+)

8 The Wigan Athletic side (starting 11) that lost the 2006 Carling Cup Final to Manchester United. (5-6/7-8/9+)

9 The Manchester City side (inc 1 sub) that won the ECWC Final against Gornik Zabrze in 1970. (3-4/5-6/7+)

10 The France side (inc 3 subs) who won the Euro 2000 Final against Italy. (7-8/9-10/11+)

1   The Aberdeen side (inc 1 sub) that won the ECWC Final in 1983. (3-4/5-6/7+)

2   The Chelsea side (inc 1 sub) that won the 1970 FA Cup Final replay against Leeds. (4-5/6-7/8+)

3   The Everton team that lost the FA Cup Final in 1968. (3-4/5-6/7+)

4   The starting line-up when Leeds beat Deportivo La Coruna 3-0 in the 2001 Champions League QF. (4-5/6-7/8+)

5   The Manchester United starting line-up for the majestic 7-1 win against Roma in the 2007 Champions League QF. (4-5/6-8/9+)

6   The Scotland team that beat World Champions England 3-2 in 1967. (3-4/5/6+)

7   Name the 10 players to have been sent off playing for England. (5-6/7-8/9-10)

8   The Arsenal team that beat Liverpool 2-1 in the 1987 League Cup Final. (4/5-6/7+)

9   The Tottenham side (inc 1 sub) that broke a 16-year hoodoo by beating Chelsea in a league match in November 2006. (5-6/7-9/10+)

10 The France side (starting line-up) that beat Brazil in a fabulous World Cup match in 1986. (4/5-6/7+)

1   The Aston Villa side that won the 1994 League Cup Final against Manchester United. (3-4/5-6/7+)

2   The England starting line-up for the 'turnip' match in the 1992 European Championship against Sweden. (3-4/5-6/7+)

3   The Ipswich Town side which played in both legs of their UEFA Cup win in 1981. (4-5/6/7+)

4   The Liverpool 12 who played in both legs of the 1976 UEFA Cup Final against Bruges. (4-5/6-7/8+)

5   The Nottingham Forest side that won the 1990 League Cup Final. (4-5/6/7+)

6   The Tottenham side that won the FA Cup as part of the Double in 1961. (3-4/5-6/7+)

7   The Middlesbrough side (inc 2 subs) that lost the 2006 UEFA Cup Final to Sevilla. (6-7/8-10/11+)

8   The Ajax side (inc 2 subs) that won the 1995 European Cup Final 1-0 against Milan. All but 3 have played in England or Scotland since. (6-7/8-9/10+)

9   The Norwich side that beat Bayern Munich in the UEFA Cup in 1975. (4-5/6-7/8+)

10   The Italy side (inc. subs) that won the 2006 World Cup Final against France. (5-7/8-9/10+)

Answers on page 219

1 The Ajax team that completed a hat-trick of European Cup Final wins for the club in 1975, beating Juventus 1–0. (3-4/5-6/7+)

2 In 2007 Bolton fielded a team in a Cup replay against Arsenal featuring players from 13 different nations. Identify as many of the countries as possible, and name the country that had 2 players. (6-7/8-9/10+)

3 The England starting line-up for the opening match of their 1986 WCFT campaign against France. (3-4/5-6/7+)

4 The Ireland team that beat Holland 2–1 in a World Cup qualifier in 1980. (3-4/5/6+)

5 The Liverpool line-up (inc 3 subs) for the 5–4 UEFA Cup Final win against Alaves. (7-8/9-10/11+)

6 The Nottingham Forest side that won the club's first European Cup in 1979. (4-5/6-7/8+)

7 The Wales team that beat England 1–0 in the final series of Home Internationals in 1984. (3-4/5/6+)

8 The Chelsea starting line-up when they clinched their first Premiership title at Bolton in April 2005. (5-6/7-8/9+)

9 The Wimbledon side (inc 2 subs) that won the 1988 FA Cup Final against Liverpool. (3-4/5-6/7+)

10 The Newcastle team (starting line-up) that beat Manchester United 5–0 in a Premiership match in October 1996. (4-5/6-7/8+)

1 The Crystal Palace side (inc 2 subs) that drew the FA Cup Final 3-3 with Manchester United in 1990. (3-4/5-6/7+)

2 The England starting line-up when they beat Holland 4-1 at Euro 96. (4-5/6-7/8+)

3 The Ireland team that beat Northern Ireland 3-0 in Dublin en route to qualification for the 1994 WCFT. (4-5 for 1 pt, 6+ for 2 pts)

4 The Liverpool side that started the 1985 European Cup Final, the night of the Heysel tragedy. (5-6 /7-8/9+)

5 The FC Porto side (starting XI) that beat Monaco 3-0 in the 2004 Champions League Final. (3/4-5/6+)

6 The Arsenal side (inc 1 sub) that won the FA Cup as part of the Double in 1971. (4-5/6-7/8+)

7 The West Ham side (inc 3 subs) for the 2006 FA Cup Final against Liverpool. (6-7/8-10/11+)

8 The Portsmouth side (inc 2 subs) that beat Manchester United in April, 2007. (5-6/7-9/10+)

9 The Brazil side (starting line-up) that lost to Italy in a brilliant match in the 1982 World Cup. (3-4/5-6/7+)

10 The Wales team that beat Italy in 2002. (4-5/6-7/8+)

True or False?

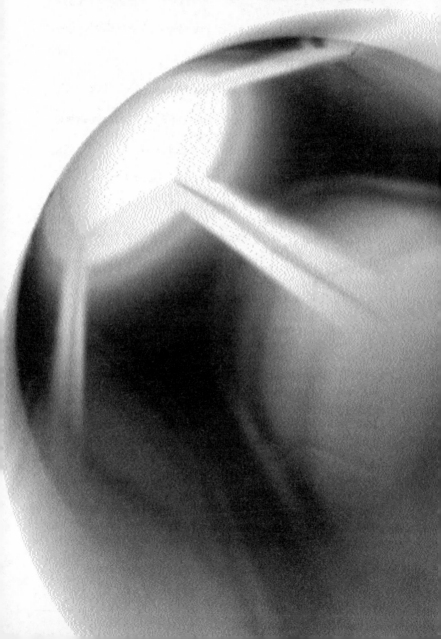

In this quiz you have to look at each statement in the lists that follow and decide if it is true or false.

1. Liverpool's Xabi Alonso's father also played in the World Cup for Spain.

2. Wales have never qualified for a WCFT.

3. Pele played in all 3 of Brazil's World Cup Finals in 1958, 1962 and 1970.

4. The two North East grounds used in the 1966 WCFT group matches were St James's Park and Ayresome Park.

5. The Parc des Princes hosted the 1998 World Cup Final.

6. There was no pre-qualifying for the WCFT until after WWII.

7. Northern Ireland qualified for the 1958 WCFT from a group of 3 which included Italy and Portugal.

8. None of the home nations won their qualifying group and reached the 1966 WCFT tournaments.

9. Jimmy Nicholl and his brother Chris both played in the 1982 WCFT for Northern Ireland.

10. At the 1978 World Cup, not a single player appeared who had played in that year's FA Cup Final.

11. Arsenal scored in every one of their Premiership games in their unbeaten 2003–04 season.

12. In 2004–05 not a single member of Liverpool's Champions League-winning squad managed 10 league goals.

13. Manchester United's record outlay on a player is higher than the highest fee they have received.

14. Michael Owen is the only player to score over 20 Premiership goals in 5 successive seasons.

15. In 2002–03 3 players outscored the entire Sunderland team in the Premiership.

16. Dennis Wise was once sent off playing for England against Norway.

17. Alex Ferguson is the only manager to win both English and Scottish leagues.

18. Brian Clough never won the FA Cup as a player or as a manager.

19. Bobby Moore never won a domestic trophy.

20. In 2003–04, Celtic beat Rangers on all 5 occasions they met.

1 Ajax are the only Dutch side to have won the European Cup.

2 Kevin Keegan inspired Hamburg to their first victory in the European Cup.

3 Newcastle have never won a European trophy.

4 Since the start of the SPL in 1998–99, Celtic and Rangers have occupied the top 2 spots in the league every year.

5 Angus McAngus, Rob Roy and Hamish Moncrieff-McCracken have all played in the Scottish FA Cup Final.

6 Bristol City manager Gary Johnson was manager of the Latvian national team for 3 years.

7 Cambridge United fell out of the league in 2005 because they were deducted 10 points for going into administration.

8 Barnet's record league win, 7–0 over Blackpool in November 2000, included a goal by former England striker Tony Cottee.

9 Portsmouth have never won the league.

10 Terry Venables never played for England.

11 Aberdeen centre-halves Alex McLeish and Willie Miller won over 100 caps between them.

12 After many years at Preston, Tom Finney accepted a lucrative offer to end his career with Padova in Italy's Serie B.

13 Matthew Le Tissier once scored a goal in the FA Cup against Barnsley with a 25-yard overhead kick.

14 Billy Bonds played his entire career with West Ham.

15 Northern Ireland manager, Lawrie Sanchez, is English and never played for Northern Ireland.

16 No side from the former East Germany ever reached the final of a European competition.

17 Gordon Strachan won Championship medals as a player in both Scotland and England.

18 Merthyr Tydfil once beat Italian side Atalanta in the ECWC.

19 No player has ever won an international cap at Colchester United.

20 Juventus play in black & white because they were inspired by Newcastle United.

Answers on page 221

1. Turkey have never scored against England in 10 internationals.

2. When Manchester United won the FA Cup in 1998–99, they eliminated Liverpool, Chelsea and Arsenal on the way to the final.

3. The 1878 FA Cup Final was refereed by one Mr S.R. Bastard.

4. Percy de Paravicini, Cuthbert J. Ottaway and Toodles Woodhouse have all played in an FA Cup Final.

5. Since 1900 there has never been an FA Cup Final between two West Midlands sides.

6. Matt Busby won an FA Cup-winner's medal playing for Manchester City.

7. Bobby Charlton never won an FA Cup winner's medal.

8. When they met in the 1965 FA Cup Final, Liverpool and Leeds United were both looking for their first win in the competition.

9. The 1989 disaster at Hillsborough could easily have happened the previous season as it hosted an FA Cup SF between the same two teams.

10. The same season Crystal Palace beat Liverpool in a memorable FA Cup SF (1989–90), they had also won 2–0 at Anfield in the league.

11. For all his success in the FA Cup as a player, Mark Hughes never won a league title-winner's medal.

12. Bobby Robson has never won a domestic trophy as a club manager in England.

13. Everton's hard-working midfielder Lee Carsley has never played international football.

14. Birmingham City have never won a major domestic trophy.

15. None of Chelsea's FA Cup Final team from 2000 was still playing for the club in 2006–07.

16. Bob Paisley and Bill Shankly were on the Liverpool playing staff together.

17. Yuri Djorkaeff's father played for France in the 1966 World Cup in England.

18. Denis Compton's brother, Leslie, remains England's oldest post-war debutant.

19. Former FA executive Mark Palios played professional football for Tranmere Rovers.

20. Tom Taylor of Staffordshire developed and marketed a streaker and a policeman to chase her for Subbuteo addicts.

1. Dynamo Kiev have won the Ukrainian league every year in the last 10 years.

2. Arsène Wenger's academic reputation is misleading, as his only degree was an honorary award from the University of Hertfordshire.

3. Aston Villa beat 2 German sides on their way to winning the 1982 European Cup.

4. Scunthorpe United's promotion in 2006–07 meant the club would play in the 2nd tier for the first time in their history.

5. Prior to 2007, and excepting the ill-fated Heysel final, Liverpool had won every major European club final they had contested.

6. Only Liverpool and Manchester United amongst English clubs have a 'full set' of European trophies: European Cup, ECWC and UEFA Cup.

7. Austria once beat Switzerland 7-5 in a World Cup QF.

8. The players involved in Zidane's dismissal in the 2006 World Cup Final also scored the game's 2 goals.

9. Martin Keown once captained England.

10. When Manchester United won the first Premiership title, none of Arsenal, Liverpool or Chelsea were in the top 5.

11. An army regiment once won the FA Cup.

12. TV pundit Chris Kamara was convicted of grievous bodily harm during a League match.

13. Former Arsenal legend Joe Mercer managed Chelsea to their only League title in 1955.

14. Liverpool never won the FA Cup under Bob Paisley.

15. Bradford City won the FA Cup in 1911, the year a new cup, manufactured in Bradford, was used.

16. The Home Internationals in 1949–50 and 1953–54 doubled as World Cup qualifiers.

17. Eric Cantona once described French manager, Henri Michel, on air, as 'a sack of s***'?

18. Jack and Bobby Charlton's mother, Cissie, was the sister of Jackie Milburn.

19. Stuart Pearce, Chris Waddle and Gareth Southgate featured in a humorous advert about missed penalties, promoting Domino's Pizza.

20. Of the 181 games he played whilst officially a Chelsea player, Mikael Forssell played less than a quarter of them for the club.

Answers on page 222

Quotes & Tours

Questions 1-10, for 1 point each

1 'We've been playing for an hour and it's just occurred to me that we're drawing 0-0 with a mountain top.' Ian Archer, in despair at Scotland's efforts against which opposition?

2 The welfare of which disastrous signing was once stated to be a lower priority than eating an out-of-date yoghurt by Southampton manager, Gordon Strachan?

3 'Davor has a left leg and a nose in the box.' Whose appraisal of a new signing?

4 'The world in which we live is boring. If you're different, you're considered crazy.' Which crazy person?

5 'Someone asked me last week if I missed the Villa. I said, "No, I live in one."' Who enjoyed the Italian lifestyle?

6 'It's like a .... the ref's shirt pocket. Every time there's a tackle, up pops a yellow card.' What's the missing word in this Keggy Keegle belter?

7 'You can spend £2m and then find the player cannot trap the ball.' Which ex-England manager bemoans inflation in 2001?

8 'What's so great about reality? My reality stank. I was ready for a bender.' Whose words in his candid autobiography?

9 'I'm going to sue Alan Hansen as he used to make me head all the balls.' Which of Hansen's former defensive partners?

10 'I've had more clubs than Jack Nicklaus.' Which well-travelled manager?

And some harder or two-part questions for 2 points

11 'I can't believe it, I can't believe it. Football. Bloody hell.' Whose reaction to what?

12 'We needed someone with deeper pockets than I've got.' Which outgoing mogul on which arriviste?

13 'I thought Christians were supposed to forgive people their sins, but that doesn't seem to be the case with me.' Who is getting a little bitter about which England manager?

14 'We lived the dream.' Whose platitude after nearly ruining which club?

15 'The last time I drove down here, I was in a tank liberating Italy.' Whose words at which event in 1977?

Questions 1-10, for 1 point each

1 'You get bunches of players like you do bananas, though that is a bad comparison.' Who unleashed this pearl of wisdom in the commentary box?

2 'Do that again son, and I'll break your legs.' Who reportedly said this to George Best after the Irishman cheekily nutmegged him?

3 'The World Cup is a truly international event!' Who enlightened TV audiences with this gem?

4 'Beckham is more of a pop star than a footballer.' Was the opinion of which former great?

5 'Was I the fifth Beatle? Not really.' Who?

6 'Newcastle girls are all dogs. England is full of them.' Which charming club chairman?

7 'I ... have managed to get myself painted as a living saint for keeping my promise to myself.' Whose words, and what was the saintly act?

8 'Argentina won't be at Euro 2004 because they're from South America.' Which tactical genius offered this geography lesson?

9 'I've never even heard of Senegal.' Who came clean during ITV's coverage of the 2002 World Cup?

10 'As we went out on the pitch he handed me a piece of paper. It was the evening menu for the Liverpool Royal Infirmary.' Jimmy Greaves reminisces about which hard-man?

And some harder or two-part questions for 2 points

11 'There should be a law against him. He knows what's happening 20 minutes before anyone else.' Which Scottish manager praising which Englishman?

12 'He wears a No.10 jersey. I thought it was his position but it turns out to be his IQ.' Whose unkind appraisal of who?

13 ' A medal from ...... and a kiss from ......, and with no disrespect to either, you wish it could have been the other way round!' Who did Vinnie Jones want to swap places after Wimbledon's FA Cup triumph?

14 'Jesus was a normal run-of-the-mill sort of guy who had a genuine gift, just as ... has.' Whose words, and with whom is he making comparison?

15 'If we see them on their coach on the way home we'll give them a wave.' Whose remarks after which match in 2002?

Questions 1-10, for 1 point each

1 'I wouldn't say I was the best manager in the business, but I was in the top one.' Whose assessment of his own career?

2 'Please don't call me arrogant, but I'm European champion and I think I'm a special one.' Who's so special?

3 'With the foreign players it's more difficult. Most of them don't even bother with the golf, they don't want to go racing. They don't even drink.' Which manager shows his lack of understanding of 'abroad'?

4 'He can make big men hide in corridors to avoid him.' Which manager is Martin O'Neill talking about?

5 'Our performance today would not have been the best-looking bird, but at least we got her in the taxi.' Whose unusual précis of which club's 3-0 win over Chesterfield?

6 'Sacking a manager is as big an event in my life as drinking a glass of beer.' Which Spanish club president made this obnoxious statement?

7 'Swan Lake on turf.' Whose fabulous description of which classic game?

8 'There's only two teams in Liverpool. Liverpool and Liverpool Reserves.' Whose dismissal of Everton?

9 'Why didn't you just belt it, son?' Whose mother in 1996?

10 'England did nothing in that World Cup, so why were they bringing books out? "We got beat in the quarter-finals. I played like s***. Here's my book".' Who was unimpressed by the glut of post-World Cup books?

And some harder or two-part questions for 2 points

11 'They'll be dancing in the streets of Raith tonight.' Who said this and what is the flaw in his thinking?

12 'He's the worst finisher since Devon Loch.' Who on who?

13 'We will win the European Cup. European football is full of cowards and we'll terrorise them.' Which cocky 1970s manager about to get his come-uppance, and with which club?

14 'Most people imagine us as an evil-looking bunch of characters with black capes and handlebar moustaches.' Who, on being a member of which notoriously dirty side?

15 'This is a bloody awful job but it's not going to turn me into a bloody awful person.' Which manager? Which job?

Answers on page 222

In 1983 England arranged a pointless 3-match 'Test' series in Australia against the Socceroos. Seven players made their debuts: Mark Barham, John Gregory, Nick Pickering, Nigel Spink, Danny Thomas, Paul Walsh and Steve Williams. Can you answer the following questions?

Questions 1-10, for 1 point each

1 Which of the 7 won just a solitary cap, for 37 minutes as a substitute in the final game?

2 Who was the England manager on that tour?

3 Which of the 7 has managed in the Premiership?

4 Which of the 7 scored for England, notching the winner in a 1–0 win in the 2nd game?

5 With which club was Mark Barham playing?

6 Which of the 7 moved to Liverpool the following year?

7 Who was the Sunderland player?

8 Which of the 7 had played in the 1982 FA Cup Final under Terry Venables?

9 The 7 won 14 caps on the tour; how many more did they win in total: 0, 9 or 21?

10 Which England winger went on the tour with only 1 cap and won the 2nd, 3rd and 4th of his 79 in total?

And some harder or two-part questions for 2 points

11 What was the centre-back pairing on the tour, both from the same club, once run by the England manager?

12 Apart from the answer to (4) above, which Italy-based player scored England's other goal? Which Italian club?

13 Which 17-year-old made his England debut against the same opponents 20 years later? For which club was he playing?

14 Which of the 7 won a European Cup-winner's medal? For which side?

15 Who moved to Spurs for £250,000 later that month? From which club?

Extra Hard

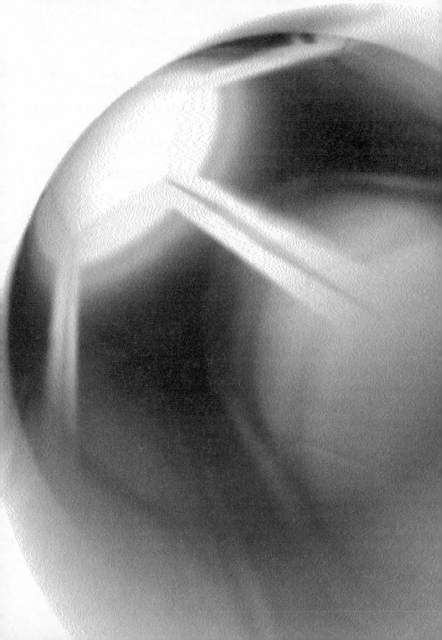

Here are some mean questions – definitely not for the faint-hearted!

Questions 1–7, for 1 point each

1 Whose dodgy dealings at Rotherham, Bournemouth and Southend led to a life ban from involvement in football?

2 Which veteran moved from Everton to Arsenal after WWII and stayed long enough to win 2 further league titles in 1948 and 1953?

3 Who scored 4 times in Spurs' record league victory, 9–0 against Bristol Rovers in 1977?

4 Which experienced international joined Crystal Palace from Hertha Berlin in 2004?

5 What disfigurement did Charlie George suffer in 1980?

6 Jim Standen, West Ham's goalkeeper in the 1964 FA Cup Final, also won what other sporting trophy later that summer?

7 Which European Cup-winning striker was bought by Liverpool in the summer of 1997?

And some harder or two-part questions for 2 points

8 Who scored a last-gasp winner for Arsenal to clinch the 1979 FA Cup Final 3–2? Who was in goal for Manchester United?

9 1978 and 1979 saw black players capped for the first time by England, Wales and Ireland: name the 3 players.

10 Who beat Leicester 4–3 in the play-offs to clinch a place in the Premiership in 1992–93? Which Welsh international scored the winner from the penalty spot?

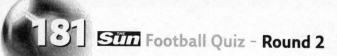

Questions 1–7, for 1 point each

1 Who rode a motorcycle through a hotel window after a knees-up in Spain in 1991?

2 Which giant striker was named Stockport County's Player of the Century at a gala dinner in 2002?

3 Which West Ham legend was the top flight's top scorer in 1929–30 with 41?

4 Who managed Argentina in 1966, and Atletico Madrid in the 1974 European Cup against Celtic, both teams noted for calculated brutality?

5 Who first appeared on the cover of boy's comic *Tiger* in 1954?

6 Ken Richardson was chairman of which club when he was sent to prison for attempting to set fire to the stadium as part of an insurance scam?

7 Which (former) chairman of Blackpool FC was given a 6-year jail sentence in the 1990s?

And some harder or two-part questions for 2 points

8 Who won the FA Cup 3 times in the 1920s, and which England international scored in 2 of the Finals?

9 Which Russian striker became the 1st player to score 5 times in a World Cup match in 1994, and who were on the receiving end?

10 Who led Swansea City to promotion in his 1st full season as manager in 2004–05, and with which club did he win his 31 caps with Wales?

Questions 1-7, for 1 point each

1 Who was manager of Stockport County when they achieved their highest-ever League finish (8th in the 2nd tier)?

2 Which English club did goalkeeper Robert (Rab) Douglas join from Celtic in 2005?

3 Who was the manager of the brilliant Milan side of the late 1980s/early 90s?

4 Which redoubtable coach served Auxerre for nigh on 40 years, winning the French league for the first time in the club's history and reaching the latter stages of the Champions League?

5 *Tales from the Boot Camp* was an entertaining autobiography from which seasoned campaigner?

6 Who were the 1st club to benefit from automatic promotion from the Conference, at the expense of Lincoln City?

7 For which club did TV chef Gordon Ramsay sign as a teenager?

And some harder or two-part questions for 2 points

8 The San Siro stadium is found in which city? After which great player from the city does its official name come?

9 Name the 3 Italian sides playing in Serie A in 2006-07 not based on the Italian mainland.

10 Which 2 sides from the same city were drawn against each other in the QF of the UEFA Cup in 2005-06?

Answers on page 223

Questions 1-7, for 1 point each

1 Which Chelsea defender went to the High Court to claim damages for a tackle from Dean Saunders that ended his career?

2 Which former Southampton youngster was QPR's top scorer in 2006-07?

3 Who was the last Scottish player (prior to 2007) to earn a European Cup-winner's medal?

4 Stewart Imlach was the father referred to in *My Father and Other Working Class Heroes* (William Hill Sports Book of the Year, 2005). Which club did he play for in an FA Cup Final, and for which country did he appear in the 1958 WCFT?

5 Which Arsenal player missed the final penalty in the shoot-out for the 1980 ECWC Final?

6 Ayr United's record transfer remains the sale of which player to Liverpool in 1981?

7 Who was the Mexican goalkeeper who appeared in a series of lurid outfits, all of which he designed himself?

And some harder or two-part questions for 2 points

8 Which Yorkshire club fell out of the league in 1970, went into liquidation in 1974 and were re-formed in 1988? Who took their place in the league?

9 Name the 3 winners of the European Cup to play in all-white shirts.

10 Port Vale's joint record signings, wingers Jon McCarthy and Gareth Ainsworth, were bought for £500,000 from which clubs?

Questions 1–7, for 1 point each

1 Who was both an FA Cup winner and PFA Footballer of the Year in 1995?

2 Who is the Port Vale goalkeeper who broke into the side as a 20-year-old and has since played over 200 league games for the club?

3 Which QPR striker scored all 4 goals as Ireland beat Turkey 4–0 in a European Championship qualifier in 1975?

4 In 2007, Histon (formerly Histon Institute) reached promotion to the Conference National after a succession of promotions. In 2007–08 they will enjoy a local derby against which other Conference side?

5 Why did Albert Stubbins' 226 goals in 7 seasons not make much of an impact?

6 Which Nottingham Forest striker made his debut for Ghana in October 2006?

7 Which early-20th century legend remains Sunderland's top league goalscorer?

And some harder or two-part questions for 2 points

8 Well-travelled striker Jamie Cureton had an outstanding 2006–07, scoring over 20 league goals in the 2nd tier for newly promoted Colchester. For which other 2 league clubs has he scored 50 or more league goals?

9 Which former Soviet Republic appeared in their 1st major tournament in Euro 2004, and who was their leading scorer?

10 Which 2 players scored hat-tricks as Swansea beat Hartlepool 8–0 to record their highest-ever league win in 1978? (Both would play for Wales.)

Questions 1-7, for 1 point each

1 Newcastle won the FA Cup 3 times in the 1950s, but lost in 1957 to which Third Division (South) team from London?

2 Which former Portsmouth and Gillingham stalwart was still a regular in the Brighton first team in 2006-07, aged 37?

3 Who scored with an unstoppable shot for Scotland against Brazil at the World Cup in 1982, before Brazil roused themselves to win 4-1?

4 Why did Sweden play Yugoslavia at Wembley in the summer of 1948?

5 Which Irish full-back was captain of the Manchester United team that won the league under Matt Busby in 1952?

6 Who managed England's women's team to the World Cup to be held in September 2007?

7 Who captained Arsenal throughout their purple patch in the 1930s?

And some harder or two-part questions for 2 points

8 Which former East German international was European Footballer of the Year in 2006? With which club did he win the European Cup?

9 Which 3 unfancied sides eliminated Chelsea from the UEFA Cup in 2000-01, 2001-02 and 2002-03?

10 Name the 3 clubs denied promotion to the league in 1994, 95 and 96 because of inadequate facilities. (Two of them made it in a later year.)

Questions 1-7, for 1 point each

1 Which future FA executive played for Tranmere Rovers in their famous 1-0 FA Cup win over Arsenal in 1973?

2 Which Spanish-born player made over 200 appearances for Scunthorpe United, and scored the play-off goal that finally saw them leave the bottom flight?

3 Which qualifiers from the Asian sector made their World Cup debut in England's group in 1982, earning some respect and a draw against Czechoslovakia?

4 Which Manchester-based Welsh winger was head of the players' union when they forced the FA to acknowledge their presence in 1908?

5 Whose late goal spared Ireland's blushes as they beat San Marino only 2-1 in a Euro 2008 qualifier in February 2007?

6 Which seasoned international and dead-ball specialist moved from Italian club Reggina to Celtic in 2005?

7 Who retired in 2000 having won 225 caps for the USA?

And some harder or two-part questions for 2 points

8 Which 2 English-based players scored the goals in the 2-legged play-off against Bahrain that saw Trinidad & Tobago qualify for the 2006 World Cup?

9 Which two Highland League sides joined the Scottish league in 2000 after the breakaway of the SPL?

10 In the 1967 FA Charity Shield, which goalkeeper scored with a long clearance? Which other keeper was embarrassed?

Answers on page 224

Questions 1-7, for 1 point each

1   Which Plymouth legend scored the winning goal when they beat a strong West Brom side on their way to the FA Cup SF in 1983-84?

2   Who were promoted from the Conference in 2003 and promoted again the following year?

3   Who enjoyed his birthday, his wedding anniversary and celebrated his England debut with a goal on 11th June 1970?

4   Which former Manchester City and England goalkeeper died in the Munich air crash, whilst working as a journalist?

5   Which former player turned writer co-wrote Roy Keane's controversial autobiography?

6   Who had their best-ever season when they won promotion to the 2nd tier for the first time and reached the League Cup SF in 1996-97?

7   What happened after Kenyon-Slaney scored England's first-ever international goal, way back in Queen Victoria's time?

And some harder or two-part questions for 2 points

8   In which year was Canada's sole appearance in a WCFT, and how many goals did they score?

9   Who scored a hat-trick for Rangers in the Scottish Cup Final against Hearts (5-1) in 1996? And who was the previous player to manage the feat, for Celtic, in 1972?

10   With which 2 North East clubs has Tommy Miller appeared either side of his 4 years at Ipswich?

Questions 1-7, for 1 point each

1 In 1991 a Tim Buzaglo hat-trick for which Isthmian League club ensured a remarkable victory over 2nd tier West Bromwich Albion?

2 Brian Yeo is the all-time top scorer for which South-East club?

3 Which England goalkeeper made the most league appearances for Bolton Wanderers (1956-1970)?

4 Which talented 1950s centre-forward, whose career was ruined by injury, is now chairman of Sheffield United?

5 Who was the Greek Cypriot entrepreneur who took over Millwall in 1997?

6 Which Premiership star also has an Islamic name, Abdul Salam Bilal?

7 Whose idea was the first England-Scotland international?

And some harder or two-part questions for 2 points

8 Which 2 members of Australia's 2006 World Cup squad had played in England in 2005-06, but not in the Premiership?

9 If you watched Les Girondins play Les Verts in France, which two sides would be playing?

10 Which 2 lower-division clubs played home to the prodigious but wayward talents of cult hero Robin Friday?

Questions 1-7, for 1 point each

1 Terry Bly scored twice as which 3rd-tier side caused a major upset by beating Manchester United 3-0 in the 3rd round of the FA Cup in 1958-59?

2 Which former player led Leyton Orient out of the bottom tier of the league as manager in 2005-06?

3 Who formed the central midfield partnership with Tim Sherwood for most of Blackburn's Premiership-winning season?

4 What trophy did Bristol City win in 1934, when they beat Tranmere Rovers 3-0 in the final?

5 Who was awarded £900,000 in damages after his career was ruined by a tackle from Huddersfield's Kevin Gray?

6 Who scored the goal in the 2004 play-off final that secured Crystal Palace's place in the Premiership?

7 What career path did World Cup winner Ray Wilson pursue after retiring from the game?

And some harder or two-part questions for 2 points

8 Who eliminated England from the 1962 World Cup, with a 3-1 victory in the QF? Which Italian-based striker scored England's goal?

9 Name the 4 European club sides that Bobby Robson has managed.

10 Which British-based player is Trinidad & Tobago's leading scorer? For which club did he sign in January 2007?

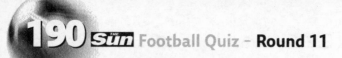

Questions 1-7, for 1 point each

1 Which other top-division side needed a replay to put out Hereford in the round after the non-leaguers memorably eliminated Newcastle?

2 Who was manager of Cheltenham Town as they rose into the league and eventually the 3rd tier?

3 Which former England defender was manager of Chester City when they regained their league status in 2004, only to leave days before the new season began?

4 What was significant about Fabio Liverani's debut for Italy in April 2001?

5 David Sheepshanks is the high-profile chairman of which club?

6 Which 16-year-old was Arsenal's youngest-ever debutant when he appeared in a League Cup match?

7 What connects Steve Coppell, Ian Dowie, Brian McClair and Shaka Hislop?

And some harder or two-part questions for 2 points

8 Who were the only 2 men to captain England on more than 20 occasions before WWII?

9 Which 2 continental sides were home for Welsh striker Dean Saunders for a season each during his itinerant career?

10 Who set a world record for 'keepy uppy' in 1997, and who was their spouse at the time?

Questions 1-7, for 1 point each

1 Which promising striker scored the only goal as Southampton beat local rivals Portsmouth in the 1983-84 FA Cup?

2 Which former playing stalwart took over as manager of Stockport County in 2006?

3 Who was Chelsea manager at the start of the first Premiership season in 1992?

4 Who scored 4 hat-tricks for Blackpool in 1977-78, the last one on the day he was presented with a special trophy for scoring 3?

5 Which England international led the Chelsea forward-line when they won their first league title in 1955?

6 Which Preston winger so impressed Bill Shankly in a 1961-62 FA Cup tie against Liverpool that he signed him the following summer?

7 Who mixed a long first-class cricket career with keeping goal for West Brom and Aston Villa in the late 1960s and 70s?

And some harder or two-part questions for 2 points

8 Which current Northern Ireland international had a father and a grandfather who also played for their country, and which club does he play for?

9 Who scored 28 league goals for QPR in Division 2 in 1979-80? Who paid over £1m for him at the end of the season?

10 Which inside-forward won the league title with Sunderland in 1936 and the FA Cup with Derby 10 years later? And which club did he lead into the 2nd division as player-manager in 1959?

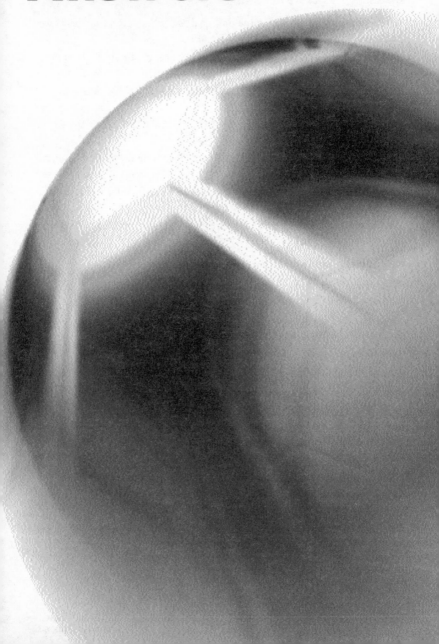

Answers

193 **Sun** Football Quiz – **Answers**

1 Preston **2** Northampton Town **3** Brighton & HA **4** John Gregory
5 Scunthorpe United **6** Crewe Alexandra **7** Walsall **8** Bristol Rovers
9 Peter Thorne **10** Manchester City **11** Swindon Town; they were
immediately demoted for financial irregularities **12** Birmingham City;
Ireland **13** 1986–87 **14** Leyton Orient; Leicester City **15** Burnley
& Wolves

1 West Ham United **2** Steve Ogrizovic **3** Ade Akinbiyi **4** Neil Harris **5**
Carlisle United **6** Bradford City **7** Hereford United **8** Trevor Benjamin
9 Shaun Goater **10** Steve Bull **11** Bremner, Cowans, Morley, Mortimer
12 Canadian; Tranmere Rovers **13** Mike Newell & David Speedie **14**
Gordon Banks; Stoke City **15** Tony Mowbray; Bryan Robson

1 Blackpool **2** Bolton Wanderers **3** Bristol City **4** Kevin Blackwell
5 Millwall **6** Carlisle United **7** Brian Clough **8** Sam Allardyce
9 Malcolm Macdonald **10** Brian Clough **11** Gary Sprake; David Harvey
12 Dean Windass; Bradford City **13** Reading; Bolton Wanderers
14 James Hayter; Wrexham **15** Wolves; Leeds United

1 Jan Molby **2** The Hatters **3** Preston North End **4** Southend United
5 Bristol City **6** Port Vale **7** Paul Merson **8** Alan Buckley **9** Colchester
United **10** Tottenham Hotspur **11** (Mike) Flanagan & (Clive) Allen
12 Grant & Gary – both played for Nottingham Forest **13** Reading;
Sunderland **14** Stockport County; Cardiff City **15** Norwich, West Ham,
Watford

1 Preston North End **2** Terry Paine **3** Michael Kightly **4** John Sheridan
5 John Aldridge **6** Gillingham **7** Hull City **8** Paul Ince **9** Roger Hunt
10 Leeds United **11** Phil Thompson, Mark Lawrenson, Gary Gillespie
12 Tony Cascarino & Teddy Sheringham **13** Middlesbrough;
Tottenham **14** Stockport County; Wolves **15** Michael Chopra;
Barnsley

1 Manchester United **2** Len Shackleton **3** Southampton **4** Rotherham
United **5** Bob Latchford **6** Dean Court **7** Brett Angell **8** Brian Flynn
9 Wilf Mannion **10** Frank Worthington **11** Alan Hansen & Phil Neal
12 Dennis Wise; Steve Claridge; Colin Lee; Dave Tuttle **13** George
Graham; Manchester United **14** Boston United; Dagenham
& Redbridge **15** Michael Ricketts; Middlesbrough

194 *Sun* Football Quiz – **Answers**

PAGE 12

1 Kenny Dalglish **2** Ipswich Town **3** Carlisle United **4** Yeovil Town **5** Nottingham Forest **6** Brighton & HA **7** Joe Kinnear **8** Bury **9** Ipswich Town **10** Francis Lee **11** Ian Rush; Roger Hunt **12** Swansea City; The Liberty Stadium **13** Joe Mercer; Malcolm Allison **14** Lee Hughes; Coventry City **15** Wolves; Southampton

PAGE 13

1 Andy Gray **2** Joe Payne **3** Kevin Gallen **4** Blackpool **5** Blackpool **6** Chesterfield **7** Gateshead **8** Torquay United **9** David Moyes **10** Newcastle **11** Nottingham Forest; Arsenal **12** Ted MacDougall & Phil Boyer **13** Graham Taylor; Wolves **14** Arsenal; David Jack **15** Colin Calderwood; Northampton Town

PAGE 14

1 Ted Drake **2** Blackburn Rovers **3** Preston North End **4** Steve Brooker **5** Oldham Athletic **6** Huddersfield Town **7** John Trollope **8** Oxford had replaced Accrington Stanley when they resigned from the league in 1962 **9** Kidderminster **10** Huddersfield Town **11** Denis Law; Manchester City **12** Colin Todd; David Wetherall **13** Howard Kendall & Colin Harvey **14** Ron Davies; George Best **15** Kenny Jackett; Roberto Martinez

PAGE 15

1 Cliff Bastin **2** Sunderland **3** Bournemouth **4** Hull City **5** Mark Kennedy **6** Dario Gradi **7** Hartlepool United **8** Mansfield Town **9** David Johnson **10** Huddersfield Town **11** Terry Neill; 1 **12** Tottenham Hotspur; Brentford **13** Ipswich Town; Nottingham Forest **14** 1888–89 **15** Brentford; Ron Noades

PAGE 16

1 Tommy Lawton **2** Lee Chapman **3** Barnsley **4** Cheltenham Town **5** Doncaster Rovers **6** Brentford **7** Jimmy Sirrel **8** Guy Whittingham **9** Martin Chivers **10** Marco Gabbiadini **11** Brian Clough & Jock Stein **12** Dario Gradi & Dave Bassett **13** Sammy Nelson & Pat Rice; Northern Ireland **14** Johnny Giles; 1 **15** Millwall; 2

PAGE 17

1 Michael Thomas **2** Aston Villa **3** Burnley **4** Dean Wilkins **5** Carlisle United **6** Cheltenham Town (they came up from the Southern League) **7** Shrewsbury Town **8** Simon Garner **9** Mick Channon **10** Mick Quinn **11** Frans Thijssen & Arnold Muhren **12** Graham Turner; he is also the club's Chairman **13** Derby County; Bolton Wanderers **14** Steve Bull; West Bromwich Albion **15** Kevin Keegan & Ray Clemence

---

195 The Sun Football Quiz - **Answers**

1 Billy Bremner **2** Dominic Matteo **3** Cardiff City **4** Kevin Blackwell
5 Bristol City **6** Port Vale **7** Matty Fryatt **8** Barnet **9** Crystal Palace
10 John Charles **11** Bob Latchford; Birmingham City **12** Notts
County; Neil Warnock **13** Marek Saganowski; Grzegorz Rasiak **14** Stan
Cullis; Billy Wright **15** Oxford United; Tranmere Rovers

1 Millwall **2** David Fairclough **3** Stockport County **4** Swansea City
5 Swansea City **6** Bournemouth **7** Bradford City **8** Ian Holloway of
Plymouth **9** Preston North End **10** Reading **11** Millwall; Chelsea
12 Clive Mendonca; Grimsby Town **13** Hartlepool & Walsall **14** Bill
Nicholson; Danny Blanchflower **15** Gareth Ainsworth; QPR

1 Hull City **2** Manchester City **3** Wolverhampton Wanderers **4** Simon
Charlton **5** Tranmere Rovers **6** Leyton Orient **7** Darren Huckerby
8 Wrexham **9** Mal Donaghy **10** Stuart Pearson **11** Peter Bonetti &
Ron Harris **12** Nathan Ellington & Jason Roberts **13** Steve Bruce sold
Alex; Ireland **14** Charlton Athletic; Michael Gray **15** Birmingham City;
Sunderland

1 Frank McAvennie **2** Nottingham Forest **3** Blackpool **4** Wycombe
Wanderers **5** Joe Royle **6** 1972 **7** Swindon Town **8** Sammy McIlroy
9 Leicester City **10** Manchester United **11** Jeff Astle & Tony Brown
12 Stuart Elliott; Northern Ireland **13** Mike Newell (Luton Town)
14 Chester City; Wrexham **15** Walsall; Portuguese

1 Derek Dougan **2** 3 **3** Colchester United **4** Jason McAteer **5** Swansea
City **6** Harry Redknapp **7** Brian Little **8** Bristol Rovers **9** Wimbledon
10 Kerry Dixon **11** Kevin Doyle & Dave Kitson **12** Micky Adams; Craig
Levein **13** Bristol Rovers; Yeovil Town **14** Carlisle United is the answer
to both parts **15** Dion Dublin & Darren Huckerby

1 West Ham United **2** Billy Bonds **3** Barry Hayles **4** Leicester City
5 Blackpool **6** Chesterfield **7** Peterborough United **8** Ipswich Town
9 Goalkeeper **10** Blackburn Rovers **11** Trevor Francis; Birmingham
City **12** Crystal Palace; Aston Villa; Middlesbrough **13** Yeovil Town;
2 years older **14** Sheffield United; Leeds United **15** MK Dons (formerly
Wimbledon) & Swindon Town

196 Sun Football Quiz – **Answers**

1 Huddersfield Town **2** Crystal Palace **3** Ipswich Town **4** Northampton Town **5** Carlisle United **6** Brentford **7** Shrewsbury Town **8** Blackpool **9** Luther Blissett **10** Burnley **11** Danny Gabbidon & James Collins **12** Marlon Harewood & Teddy Sheringham **13** Mark Robins; also Rotherham **14** Howard Kendall; Kevin Ratcliffe **15** Geoff Hurst; Trevor Brooking

1 Glasgow Rangers **2** Wycombe Wanderers **3** Dwight Yorke **4** Billy Sharp **5** Bristol City **6** John Rudge **7** Walsall **8** Rotherham United **9** Grimsby Town **10** Wolverhampton Wanderers **11** Stephen McPhail; Peter Whittingham **12** Roy Carroll; Manchester United **13** Simon Grayson; Colin Hendry **14** Arsenal & Manchester United **15** Tony Ford; Grimsby Town

1 Andrei Shevchenko **2** William Gallas **3** Gilberto Silva **4** Jimmy Floyd Hasselbaink **5** Linvoy Primus **6** Leeds United **7** Matt Taylor (Portsmouth) **8** Andy Johnson for Crystal Palace in 2004–05 **9** Jurgen Klinsmann **10** Chelsea **11** Uruguay; Tottenham Hotspur **12** Swindon Town & MK Dons (formerly Wimbledon) **1 3 8 14** Arsenal, Aston Villa, Chelsea, Everton, Liverpool, Manchester United, Tottenham Hotspur **15** Roy Evans; because of the farcical appointment of Gerard Houllier as joint-manager

1 Fulham **2** Robert Earnshaw **3** Philippe Albert **4** Francis Jeffers **5** Sami Hyypia (81 for Finland) **6** Millwall **7** John Hartson **8** George Burley (Ipswich Town) in 2001 **9** Gareth Bale **10** Matthew Etherington **11** Dennis Bergkamp & Nicolas Anelka **12** Danny Mills, Trevor Sinclair & Darius Vassell **13** Iain Dowie replaced Alan Curbishley and was replaced by Les Reed; Alan Pardew then took over, and was replaced at West Ham by Curbishley **14** Norway, Blackburn Rovers, Manchester United (twice) **15** Colin Todd & Roy McFarland

1 Bradford City **2** Bruce Rioch **3** Faustino Asprilla **4** Richard Wright **5** Steve Finnan **6** Richard Dunne **7** They conceded 100 goals **8** Manchester United **9** Giovanni Van Bronckhorst **10** Chris Armstrong **11** Liverpool & Newcastle **12** Henri Camara & Kevin Kilbane **13** John Carew; Ashley Young **14** Radhi Jaidi, Abdoulaye Faye, El-Hadji Diouf & Jay-Jay Okocha **15** Alan Hansen; Newcastle United

1 Matt Le Tissier **2** West Ham United **3** Michael Carrick **4** Northern Ireland **5** Graeme Murty **6** Portsmouth **7** Jan-Age Fjortoft **8** Aaron Lennon **9** Michael Essien **10** Andrei Kanchelskis **11** James Milner (then Leeds); James Vaughan (Everton) **12** Frank Clark, Stuart Pearce & Dave Bassett **13** Fulham; Tomas Kuszczak **14** Alain Perrin (Portsmouth); Iain Dowie (Charlton) **15** Attilio Lombardo; Terry Venables

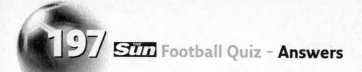

197 **Sun** Football Quiz - **Answers**

PAGE 31

1 Swiss **2** Crystal Palace **3** Paul Ince **4** Dean Ashton **5** Wolves **6** Charlton Athletic **7** Arsenal **8** 7th **9** 1992–93 **10** Trinidad & Tobago **11** Brad Friedel (Blackburn), Marcus Hahnemann (Reading), Tim Howard (Everton) **12** Sam Allardyce (Bolton); Glenn Roeder (Newcastle); Paul Jewell (Wigan) **13** Michael Ball; Manchester City **14** QPR, Tottenham, Newcastle, West Ham, Leicester, Bolton **15** Tony Adams; Dennis Bergkamp

PAGE 32

1 Rio Ferdinand **2** Lucas Neill **3** Dean Richards **4** Alan Shearer at Blackburn **5** Andy Johnson **6** Ipswich Town **7** West Bromwich Albion **8** Chris Armstrong **9** Juninho **10** Jackie Milburn **11** Andrew Cole, Thierry Henry & Kevin Phillips **12** Caleb Folan; West Ham United **13** 8th **14** Chris Coleman, Gareth Southgate, Aidy Boothroyd **15** Leeds United; Tottenham

PAGE 33

1 Mike Walker **2** Tottenham **3** Glenn Hoddle **4** Tottenham **5** Leeds United **6** Calum Davenport **7** David James **8** Massimo Maccarone **9** Sol Campbell **10** Howard Wilkinson **11** Paolo Ferreira; Ricardo Carvalho; Tiago; Maniche **12** Frank Lampard, Eidur Gudjohnsen & Didier Drogba **13** 15 **14** George Graham & Kenny Dalglish **15** Martin O'Neill; Peter Taylor

PAGE 34

1 Paul McGrath **2** Hidetoshi Nakata **3** Newcastle United **4** Neville Southall **5** Steed Malbranque **6** Reading **7** Patrick Vieira **8** Les Ferdinand **9** West Bromwich Albion **10** Kevin Keegan **11** Norwich City, Coventry City, Newcastle United, Celtic, Blackburn Rovers **12** Bolton Wanderers & Manchester City **13** Frank Lampard & Eidur Gudjohnsen **14** Fulham, Blackburn & Bolton (promoted 2001) **15** Ruud Van Nistelrooy & Juan Sebastian Veron

PAGE 35

1 Southampton **2** Aston Villa **3** West Ham United **4** Ole-Gunnar Solskjaer **5** 1 **6** Luis Boa Morte **7** Nwankwo Kanu **8** John Gregory **9** Robbie Fowler **10** 1 **11** Justin Hoyte & Theo Walcott **12** Chris Sutton, Dion Dublin & Michael Owen **13** Terry Venables, Peter Reid, Eddie Gray **14** Mark Stein, Ruud Van Nistelrooy **15** Tony Adams & Lee Dixon

PAGE 36

1 Ossie Ardiles **2** Real Madrid **3** Christian Gross **4** Aston Villa **5** Aston Villa **6** Adrian Boothroyd **7** Sylvain Wiltord **8** Andrew Cole **9** Chris Sutton **10** Chelsea **11** Robert Pires & Pascal Cygan **12** Barnsley, Bolton Wanderers & Crystal Palace **13** Norwich City, Blackburn Rovers, Chelsea, Birmingham City **14** Alan Shearer, Kevin Phillips, Thierry Henry **15** Peter Reid, Howard Wilkinson & Mick McCarthy

198 **Sun** Football Quiz - **Answers**

PAGE 37

1 Uwe Rosler **2** Barnsley, Swindon Town, Wolves **3** Manchester United **4** Glenn Hoddle **5** Emmanuel Pogatetz **6** Emre Belozoglu **7** 2nd in 1992-93, the first season **8** Blackburn Rovers **9** Nathan Ellington **10** 12th **11** Michael Duberry; Leeds United **12** Graeme Stuart; Wimbledon **13** Bryan Robson, Martin Jol **14** £21m **15** Glen Roeder; Trevor Brooking

PAGE 38

1 George Graham **2** Peter Schmeichel **3** David O'Leary **4** Aston Villa **5** 3 **6** Middlesbrough **7** Georgi Hristov **8** Everton **9** Brian McBride (USA) **10** Mikael Forssell **11** Alain Perrin; Joe Jordan **12** Frank Lampard, Steven Gerrard & Thierry Henry **13** Tony Yeboah, Eintracht Frankfurt in Germany**14** Portsmouth; Oldham Athletic's Boundary Park **15** Frank Arnesen; Chelsea

PAGE 39

1 Ray Harford **2** Old Trafford **3** Gareth Southgate **4** Matthew Upson **5** Franck Queudrue **6** 1 **7** Frank Lampard **8** Aston Villa **9** Peter Beagrie **10** Crystal Palace **11** Sean Davis, Pedro Mendes & Noe Pamarot **12** 17th **13** Luc Nilis, Ruud Van Nistelrooy **14** Joe Kinnear; Dean Holdsworth **15** Gordon Strachan; Paul Sturrock

PAGE 40

1 Oldham Athletic **2** Milan Baros **3** Wayne Rooney **4** Sammy Lee **5** Simon Davies **6** Joey Barton **7** Ledley King **8** Paul Robinson **9** Davor Suker **10** Eric Cantona **11** Mark Viduka & Ayegbeni Yakubu **12** Lawrie Sanchez; manager of Northern Ireland **13** David Pleat, Jacques Santini, Martin Jol **14** Exeter City; Manchester City **15** FC Porto & Valencia

PAGE 41

1 Gary Speed **2** 26 **3** Aston Villa **4** John Obi Mikel **5** Vincenzo Montella **6** Nottingham Forest **7** Manchester United **8** Blackburn Rovers **9** Slavisa Jokanovic **10** Brad Friedel **11** Lee Hendrie; Gavin McCann; Chris Sutton **12** Blackburn Rovers; Coventry City **13** Bradford City, Nottingham Forest, Oldham Athletic **14** David Platt & Dennis Bergkamp **15** Everton

PAGE 42

1 Marlon King **2** Ruud Van Nistelrooy **3** Tim Flowers **4** Mark Gonzalez **5** Predictably, his former club Aston Villa **6** Paul Jewell **7** Keith Gillespie **8** Eidur Gudjohnsen **9** Dion Dublin **10** Mick Quinn **11** Jimmy Bullard; Wigan Athletic **12** Steve Coppell, Stuart Pearce, Gareth Southgate, Sammy Lee **13** Wimbledon, Neil Sullivan **14** Warren Barton & Les Ferdinand **15** Christian Gross; Alan Sugar

1 Charlie George **2** Peter Shilton **3** Burnley **4** Lord Arthur Kinnaird **5** Oxford United **6** Ryan Giggs **7** Jimmy Greenhoff **8** Wolverhampton Wanderers **9** Roberto Di Matteo **10** Paul Scholes **11** Tranmere Rovers; Paul Rideout **12** Manchester United; Brighton & HA **13** Glenn Hoddle; Terry Fenwick **14** 6 (Les 1, Clive 2, Paul 3) **15** Blackburn Rovers & Watford

1 None **2** Hereford United **3** Norman Whiteside **4** Chris Kelly **5** Fulham **6** Peter Osgood **7** Ipswich Town **8** Cardiff City **9** Ronnie Rosenthal **10** Exeter City **11** Manchester City; Joey Barton **12** Trevor Sinclair; QPR **13** Howard Kendall; Everton **14** Paul Walsh; Mark Hughes **15** Manchester United; they were pressured by the FA into entering a meaningless World Club Championship

1 Manchester City **2** Gary Mabbutt **3** Mickey Thomas **4** Mark Hughes **5** Leyton Orient **6** 1–0. Enthralling stuff! **7** Blyth Spartans **8** Ian Rush **9** Bolton Wanderers **10** Cristiano Ronaldo **11** Bolton & West Ham **12** Wimbledon; Chelsea; Millwall **13** Aston Villa & West Brom **14** Martin Buchan; Aberdeen **15** 1995; Littlewood's

1 Everton **2** Bristol City **3** The Wanderers **4** Newcastle United **5** Chelsea **6** John Motson **7** It was a header, and Brooking was known as a conspicuously poor header of the ball **8** Ray Clemence **9** Roy Keane **10** EON **11** Colchester United; Ray Crawford **12** Dave Beasant; John Aldridge **13** David Webb; Old Trafford **14** Portsmouth; Darren Anderton **15** Plymouth Argyle; Watford

1 Walsall **2** He played much of the game with a broken neck **3** Blackburn Rovers **4** It was from the penalty spot **5** Nottingham Forest **6** Allan Clarke **7** Willie Young **8** Stuart McCall **9** Michael Owen **10** Leyton Orient **11** Wimbledon beating Liverpool in 1988 **12** Wycombe Wanderers; Lawrie Sanchez **13** Bolton Wanderers & Blackburn Rovers **14** Arsenal & Spurs; Sheffield United & Wednesday **15** Man United 11, Chelsea 3

1 Nat Lofthouse **2** Alan Pardew **3** It was won by Cardiff City **4** West Bromwich Albion in 1968 **5** Jeff Astle **6** Sunderland in 1973 **7** Tommy Hutchison **8** Pat Van Den Hauwe **9** Gianfranco Zola **10** He became the youngest player to appear in an FA Cup Final **11** Ryan Giggs; Peter Schmeichel **12** Bury; Chester City **13** Bolton (lost 4–3 in 1958), Crystal Palace (drew 3–3 and lost replay in 1990) & West Ham (drew 3–3 and lost on penalties in 2006) **14** Nicolas Anelka & Marc Overmars **15** Ruud Gullit; Arsène Wenger

200 **sun** Football Quiz - **Answers**

1 Jim Montgomery **2** Nottingham Forest **3** None **4** Yeovil Town
5 Arsenal (71 & 79) **6** Dave Watson **7** Jimmy Case **8** Paul Gascoigne
9 John Terry **10** Djibril Cissé **11** Andy Gray & Graeme Sharp **12** Jose
Antonio Reyes; Rob Styles **13** Bob Stokoe; Newcastle **14** Arsenal
& Sheffield United **15** Ian Rush; 5, also a record

1 Jackie Milburn **2** Margate **3** Eric Cantona **4** Newcastle United **5** He
was the first Cup Final substitute **6** 1974 **7** 1984 **8** Gary Charles
9 Freddie Ljungberg **10** Michael Ballack **11** Stan Mortensen; 4–3
12 Portsmouth in 1939, Derby County in 1946 **13** Alan Taylor;
Fulham **14** Roy Keane; Nelson Vivas **15** Sheffield Wednesday; Ian
Wright

1 Sutton United **2** Bobby Gould **3** Eric Cantona **4** 1960 **5** Leicester
City **6** Alan Mullery **7** Brighton & HA **8** Gary Lineker **9** Chelsea
10 Coventry City **11** Ricky Villa; Garth Crooks **12** Newcastle,
Tottenham (twice), Arsenal **13** Crystal Palace; Malcolm Allison
14 2000; Dennis Wise **15** Tommy Docherty; Southampton

1 Nigel Clough **2** Bury **3** Wimbledon **4** Barnsley, twice **5** Watford
6 Tommy Docherty **7** Watford **8** Tony Adams **9** Portsmouth
10 Solomon Kalou **11** Tottenham Hotspur; Chelsea **12** Manchester
United, Newcastle United (twice) **13** Jim McCalliog & Peter Osgood
14 Steve McManaman; 4–2 to United **15** Mike Trebilock; Harry
Catterick

1 Swedes 2 Turnips 1 **2** Yugoslavia **3** Ricardo **4** Sol Campbell **5** France
in 1984 **6** Greece **7** England **8** Marco Van Basten **9** Gary Lineker **10**
Clive Thomas **11** Alain Giresse, Jean Tigana, Luis Fernandez **12** Poland
& Ukraine **13** Denmark; Bobby Robson **14** Holland, Anfield **15**
Portugal, Michel Platini

1 Belgium **2** Spain **3** David Beckham **4** Mike Riley **5** Celtic's Gary
Caldwell **6** Spain **7** None **8** Laurent Blanc **9** Paul Scholes **10** Andy
Roxburgh **11** Portugal & Romania **12** Austria & Switzerland
13 Wales; Yugoslavia **14** West Germany (Euro 72, WC 74); France
(WC 98, Euro 2000) **15** Yugoslavia; Alan Mullery

201 **The Sun** Football Quiz - **Answers**

1 France **2** Czechoslovakia **3** Francesco Totti **4** Jacques Santini **5** Ally McCoist **6** Germany **7** France (1984, 2000) **8** Swiss **9** Gheorghe Hagi **10** David Platt **11** Stelios Giannakopoulos; Bolton **12** Michael Owen & Ashley Cole **13** Holland, England, Spain, Denmark **14** Estonia & Andorra **15** Graham Taylor, Alan Smith

1 Helder Postiga **2** None of them were in the squad **3** Henrik Larsson **4** Otto Rehhagel **5** Michel Platini **6** Gareth Southgate **7** Holland **8** Once, in 1988 **9** David Trezeguet **10** Phil Neville **11** Alan Shearer & Teddy Sheringham **12** Cyprus; Richard Dunne **13** USSR, France **14** Paul Gascoigne; Gary McAllister **15** Gaizka Mendieta; Raul

1 1992–93, **2** AC Milan **3** Palermo **4** Liverpool (vs Roma in 1984) **5** Hibernian **6** Swedish **7** Kaka **8** Colin Hendry **9** Cesare Maldini **10** Pierluigi Collina **11** Ruud Gullit, Frank Rijkaard & Marco Van Basten **12** Costinha; Paul Scholes **13** Nottingham Forest & Rangers **14** Red Star Belgrade & Olympique Marseille **15** Ajax, Real Madrid & AC Milan

1 Johann Cruyff **2** Paul Scholes **3** Gary Shaw **4** Karl-Heinz Riedle **5** Arthur Ellis **6** Tommy Gemmell **7** West Ham United **8** Andrew Cole **9** Deportivo La Coruna **10** Brussels **11** Alex Ferguson; Real Madrid **12** Nuno Valente; Porto **13** Liverpool & Aberdeen **14** AC Milan; Paolo Maldini **15** United won both: 1–0 in Glasgow, 3–0 in Manchester

1 Raul **2** Feyenoord **3** Everton **4** AC Milan **5** Juan Schiaffino **6** Panathinaikos **7** Michel Platini **8** Bodo Illgner **9** Ruud Van Nistelrooy **10** Peter Schmeichel **11** Dwight Yorke & Andrew Cole **12** Didier Drogba & Asier Del Horno **13** Laurie Cunningham & Steve McManaman **14** Gianluca Vialli; Fabrizio Ravanelli **15** Arsenal & Chelsea

1 Real Madrid **2** Dida **3** Denis Law **4** Glasgow Rangers **5** Stade de Reims **6** Internazionale; the game against Borussia Moenchengladbach was ordered to be replayed after Inter's Roberto Boninsegna was hit by a drinks can and had to be replaced **7** 2001-02 **8** Peter Schmeichel **9** John Terry **10** Rangers **11** Ferenc Puskas & Alfredo Di Stefano **12** Sevilla; 4–0 **13** Galatasaray; Arsenal **14** Barcelona & Bayern Munich **15** AS Monaco & Liverpool

202 *Sun* Football Quiz - **Answers**

1 Hampden Park **2** Chelsea **3** PSV Eindhoven **4** Rob Rensenbrink **5** Birmingham City **6** Juventus **7** In memory of the victims of the Hillsborough disaster, which had taken place 4 days earlier **8** Andrei Shevchenko **9** AC Milan **10** Mark Hughes **11** FC Porto; Henrik Larsson **12** CSKA Moscow; Sporting Lisbon **13** Faustino Asprilla; Colombia **14** Juventus; Filippo Inzaghi **15** Djimi Traore; Jerzy Dudek

1 Nottingham Forest **2** Rapid Vienna **3** FC Basle **4** Alan Smith **5** Norwich City **6** Bayern Munich **7** Sven-Goran Eriksson **8** Tore-Andre Flo **9** Michael Essien **10** Paris St Germain **11** Paolo Maldini; his father Cesare Maldini also captained Milan to victory **12** Dado Prso; Croatia **13** Blackburn Rovers & Liverpool **14** Real Madrid & Valencia **15** Wolves & Tottenham

1 Bayern Munich **2** Bobby Moncur **3** Tottenham Hotspur **4** Real Zaragoza **5** Eusebio **6** Jimmy Armfield **7** Fabien Barthez **8** Nicolas Anelka **9** AZ Alkmaar **10** Villa Park **11** Alaves, 5–4 **12** Joey Jones & Steve Heighway **13** Dundee United; AS Roma **14** Bayern Munich beat Real twice in the 2nd group phase, but lost 2–0 in Madrid in the SF and could only win 2–1 at home **15** Rotterdam, Feyenoord

1 Bayern Munich **2** Gianluca Vialli **3** Luis Garcia **4** Glasgow Rangers **5** Internazionale **6** St Etienne **7** Milan refused to resume the game after a delay for floodlight failure; they were losing **8** Valencia **9** Intertoto Cup **10** 5 **11** Trevor Francis & John Robertson **12** Steaua Bucharest & Red Star Belgrade **13** Manchester United; no-one, Liverpool were made to serve an additional year's ban **14** Arsenal, Manchester United & Leeds United **15** Villareal; Diego Forlan

1 25 years **2** Nigel Spink **3** Hernan Crespo **4** Leeds United **5** Benfica **6** Borussia Moenchengladbach **7** Chris Waddle **8** Bayer Leverkusen **9** Kolo Toure **10** Gianfranco Zola **11** Ferenc Puskas; 5–3 to Benfica **12** Kanu & Finidi George **13** Steaua Bucharest & Barcelona **14** Barry Town; FC Porto **15** Tottenham Hotspur; Sevilla

1 Jordi Cruyff **2** Ryan Giggs **3** Andrei Shevchenko **4** Leeds United **5** Ajax **6** Real Madrid **7** Jean-Pierre Papin **8** Newcastle United **9** Jens Lehmann **10** Lazio **11** Marseille; Rafael Benitez **12** Danny Granville; Michael Duberry; Steve Clarke; Eddie Newton; Dennis Wise **13** Gheorghe Hagi & Marius Lacatus **14** Iker Casillas; Zinedine Zidane **15** Real Madrid; Peter Osgood

---

Answers for pages 64-69

203 **Sun** Football Quiz - **Answers**

1 Frank Rijkaard **2** Bayer Leverkusen **3** AC Milan **4** Sheffield United
5 Real Madrid **6** Graeme Souness **7** Gianluigi Lentini **8** AC Milan; in
2003 they drew 0-0 and 1-1 with Inter – the clubs share the San Siro
stadium **9** Monaco **10** Dynamo Tbilisi **11** John-Arne Riise & Craig
Bellamy **12** Dundee United; IFK Gothenburg **13** Olympique Marseille;
Bernard Tapie **14** Valencia; FC Basle **15** Manchester City; Chelsea

1 Fenerbahce of Turkey, **2** Deportivo La Coruna **3** Benfica **4** Swansea
City **5** AC Milan **6** Tony Barton **7** Filippo Inzaghi **8** Dida **9** Didier
Deschamps **10** Parma **11** Nicolas Anelka; Ivan Campo; Fernando
Hierro **12** Dino & Roberto Baggio **13** Galatasaray; Eric Cantona
14 Ronaldo; David Beckham **15** Borussia Moenchengladbach & FC
Brugge

1 Budapest **2** Argentina **3** Borussia Monchengladbach
4 Internazionale **5** Ronaldo **6** Dino Zoff **7** Stilian Petrov **8** Djibril Cisse
9 Saint Etienne **10** Hungary **11** Franz Beckenbauer & Gerd Muller
12 Cagliari; Luigi Riva **13** Allan Simonsen; Borussia
Moenchengladbach **14** Ernst Happel; Austria **15** Fredi Kanoute; Mali

1 Hungary **2** Estonia (a Baltic state) **3** Jurgen Klinsmann **4** Roger Milla
5 Karl-Heinz Rummenigge **6** 35 **7** USA **8** Barcelona **9** Internazionale
10 Arsène Wenger **11** Craig Johnston & Harry Kewell **12** Ajax & AC
Milan **13** Rivaldo, Ronaldo (twice) & Ronaldinho **14** AS Monaco;
Emmanuel Adebayor **15** Brazil; FC Porto

1 Mozambique **2** AC Milan **3** Raymond Kopa **4** 68 **5** Latvia **6** Spain
7 Ajax **8** Bermuda **9** Turin (Torino) **10** Trondheim **11** Croatia (his
parents' birthplace); Scotland (with Celtic) **12** PSV Eindhoven; Park
Ji-sung **13** Eusebio & Luis Figo **14** Kanu; Celestine Babayaro **15**
Phillip Cocu; Barcelona

1 Internazionale **2** Gabriel Batistuta **3** Chelsea **4** Lazio **5** Belgium
6 France **7** Julius Aghahowa **8** Tomas Repka **9** Florence (Firenze)
10 Peru **11** Spartak Moscow; Serbia **12** Lev Yashin; he always wore a
black shirt **13** Olympique de Lyons; Gerard Houllier **14** Paolo Maldini;
Fabio Cannavaro **15** Jaap Stam; Ajax

204 ***Sun*** Football Quiz – **Answers**

1 Olympique Marseille **2** Gabriel Batistuta **3** Torino **4** Internazionale **5** Mateja Kezman **6** Tiago **7** Dennis Rommedahl **8** Argentina **9** Northern Ireland **10** Brazil **11** East & West Germany **12** Spain & Japan **13** Deportivo La Coruna; Roy Makaay **14** Hugo Sanchez; Real Madrid **15** Canada; Bayern Munich

1 Dynamo Kiev **2** Enzo Bearzot **3** Liverpool **4** Santos **5** West Germany **6** Dutch **7** 9 **8** Tomas Ravelli **9** Rosenborg (Trondheim) **10** Javier Zanetti **11** Pavel Nedved; Juventus **12** Ryan Nelsen; Blackburn Rovers **13** Geneva & Zurich **14** None **15** Adrian Mutu; Fiorentina

1 Olympique Marseille **2** Juventus **3** All started with points deducted as a result of the corruption scandal **4** New York Cosmos **5** Sergei Rebrov **6** Real Sociedad **7** Aleksandr Hleb **8** Internazionale **9** Lisbon (Lisboa) **10** Jonathon Woodgate **11** Brian & Michael Laudrup **12** Carlos Tevez & Javier Mascherano **13** Jacques Santini; Lyon **14** Sampdoria; Benfica **15** Luis Boa Morte; Arsenal

1 Roberto Baggio **2** 0 **3** Sweden **4** Juventus **5** Hristo Stoichkov **6** Mohammed Sissoko **7** Espanyol **8** Barcelona **9** South Africa **10** Lazio **11** Sweden; AC Milan **12** Nicklas Bendtner; Denmark **13** Didier Deschamps; Fabio Capello **14** Marco Tardelli **15** Zbigniew Boniek; Juventus

1 Jose Chilavert **2** Jari Litmanen **3** John Aldridge **4** Raul **5** AS Roma **6** Borussia Dortmund **7** Mallorca **8** Roy Wegerle **9** Dynamo Kiev **10** Bucharest (Bucuresti) **11** Kevin Keegan; Hamburg SV **12** Roy Hodgson; Finland **13** Jean-Marie Pfaff; Oliver Kahn **14** Brentford; Charlton Athletic **15** Ilie Dumitrescu & Gica Popescu

1 Helmut Schoen **2** Lazio **3** Rio de Janeiro **4** Sardinia **5** Giovanni Trapattoni **6** Bulgaria **7** Israel **8** J-League (Japan) **9** Fenerbahce **10** Sami Kuffour **11** Cruyff & Neeskens **12** Hossam Ghaly & Mido **13** Ukraine; Dynamo Kiev **14** Pascal Chimbonda; Wigan Athletic **15** Ottmar Hitzfeld; Borussia Dortmund

---

Answers for pages 77-82

1 Ajax Amsterdam **2** Barcelona **3** Napoli **4** Olympiakos (Athens)
5 Senegal **6** Teemu Tainio **7** USA **8** Roberto Di Matteo **9** Uruguay
10 Real Madrid **11** Luca Toni; he played in the World Cup Final **12** Tal
Ben Haim & Idan Tal **13** Villareal; Uruguay **14** Aaron Mokoena &
Benni McCarthy **15** Gregory Coupet; Lyon

1 Ajax Amsterdam **2** Montevideo, Uruguay **3** Barcelona **4** Roberto
Carlos **5** Patrick Vieira **6** Obafemi Martins **7** They all played in the old
East German league before unification **8** Holland **9** Helenio Herrera
10 Alessandro Del Piero **11** Thuram & Zambrotta **12** Steve Marlet;
Jean Tigana **13** Claudio Gentile **14** Rinus Michels, Johann Cruyff, Louis
Van Gaal, Frank Rijkaard **15** Ruud Gullit; Frank Rijkaard; Marco Van
Basten

1 Hungary **2** Lazio **3** Andoni Goicochea **4** Bobby Robson **5** Christian
Vieri **6** Goalkeeper Mark Schwarzer **7** Estonia **8** Anderlecht **9** Malta
10 Poland **11** Sevilla; Real Madrid **12** Stefan Schwarz & Anders
Limpar **13** Gheorghe Hagi **14** Schalke 04, VFB Stuttgart, Werder
Bremen **15** L.A. Galaxy; Alexei Lalas

1 Aston Villa, **2** Wigan Athletic **3** Tottenham **4** David Johnson **5** Kevin
Keegan **6** 11 **7** 1962 **8** Laurie Cunningham **9** Bobby Charlton **10** Zat
Knight **11** Glasgow, 1872 **12** David Platt, Des Walker, Trevor Francis
13 1984 **14** Roy McFarland, Colin Todd, Peter Shilton, Mark Wright
15 Germany; Dietmar Hamman

1 Colin Bell, **2** Hungarians **3** Channon, 46 **4** David Platt **5** Emile
Heskey **6** Viv Anderson **7** Stan Mortensen **8** Malcolm Macdonald
9 Steve Bull **10** Trevor Francis **11** Steve Foster, Mick Harford, Ricky
Hill, Brian Stein **12** Francis Jeffers; Australia won 3-1 **13** Brian
Clough; Don Revie **14** Phil Parkes, Jimmy Rimmer, Nigel Spink
15 David Beckham; Aki Rihilati

1 Martin Peters **2** Michael Owen **3** Andrew Cole **4** Peter Crouch (11 in
2006) **5** None **6** 9 **7** Owen Hargreaves **8** Scotland **9** 9 **10** Earl
Barrett **11** San Marino, Ian Wright **12** Iceland; Heidar Helguson
13 Ben Foster; Manchester United **14** David Beckham, Steve
McManaman, Michael Owen & Laurie Cunningham **15** Malaysia; Gary
Lineker

206 **Sun** Football Quiz – **Answers**

1 C.B.Fry **2** Malcolm Macdonald **3** Substitute **4** Micah Richards **5** Alan Thompson **6** 2 **7** Norway **8** David Healy **9** Gary Lineker **10** Romania scored and won **11** Steve Guppy, Port Vale **12** Kenny Sansom; West Brom **13** Derby County, Bolton Wanderers **14** Chris Kirkland; Wigan Athletic **15** Bryan Robson; John Barnes

1 Jimmy Greaves, **2** Kevin Keegan **3** Italy **4** Trevor Brooking **5** Steve Howey **6** Brighton **7** United Arab Emirates **8** Steve Bloomer **9** Alarmingly, Mariner with 35 **10** Stan Mortensen **11** They were in England's 1966 World Cup squad but never took the field **12** Terry Butcher & Russell Osman **13** Nigel Martyn, Danny Mills, Rio Ferdinand, Robbie Fowler **14** Ireland, Dublin **15** John Barnes, Mark Hateley

1 Lofthouse (33 to 63) **2** Bryan Robson **3** Paul Ince **4** Tommy Lawton **5** Ian Callaghan **6** Michael Ricketts **7** Bobby Robson **8** 57 **9** Gareth Southgate **10** Kenny Sansom **11** England! – he was sportingly 'loaned' to Wales as a sub **12** David Beckham, Teddy Sheringham **13** Ray Wilkins & Mark Hateley **14** Gerry Francis, Stewart Kennedy **15** Trevor Francis & Tony Woodcock

1 62 **2** Craven Cottage **3** Umbro **4** Saudi Arabia **5** 3 **6** Terry Venables **7** Bryan Robson **8** Switzerland beat England twice, in 1938 and 1981 **9** Wolverhampton Wanderers **10** Nat Lofthouse **11** Jimmy Greaves, Frank Haffey **12** Chris Powell & Luke Young **13** Leicester City, Stoke City, Nottingham Forest, Southampton, Derby County **14** Paul Scholes, Don Hutchison **15** Alan Hudson; once more

1 Peter Crouch **2** Arsenal **3** Tom Finney **4** Chris Waddle **5** 1 **6** Arsenal **7** Scotland **8** Hong Kong **9** Jimmy Armfield **10** Kerry Dixon **11** 45 (v 41) **12** Gary and Phil Neville **13** Tottenham Hotspur; back at Tottenham **14** 2; none **15** None. Phelan was Irish, Ratcliffe Welsh and Earle played for Jamaica. Stein was uncapped.

1 Bobby Robson **2** Keown, 43 **3** The Lightning Seeds **4** Beckham, 58 **5** Alan Smith **6** Nat Lofthouse **7** Nobby Stiles **8** Manchester City **9** Stanley Matthews **10** Tom Finney **11** Steve Bull, in 1989 **12** Right-back; Tottenham Hotspur **13** 18 (Worthington 9, Bowles 5, McKenzie 0, Osgood 4) **14** Michael Owen; Geneva **15** 2nd (England) & 6th

1 Billy Wright **2** 8 **3** Darius Vassell **4** Jimmy Greaves **5** Ben Foster **6** Joe Mercer **7** Aston Villa **8** Tony Adams **9** 2 **10** Dion Dublin, in 1997 **11** Graeme Le Saux & Matt Le Tissier **12** Stuart Pearce & Des Walker **13** Warren Barton & John Fashanu **14** Howard Wilkinson; Peter Taylor **15** Walter Winterbottom; 16 years

1 52 **2** Ibrox **3** Celtic's European Cup win of 1967 **4** Jim Leighton (91 caps) **5** Aberdeen **6** Partick Thistle **7** Livingstone **8** Kris Boyd **9** Aberdeen **10** 3 (Aitken, McStay & Cooper) **11** Gordon Strachan & Jim Leighton **12** Steve Clarke; Jose Mourinho's assistant **13** John McGinlay; Duncan Shearer **14** Nacho Novo; Raith Rovers **15** 4; Jock Wallace

1 Queens Park **2** Jimmy Johnstone **3** Billy Liddell **4** Mo Johnston **5** Jimmy McGrory **6** Inverness Caledonian Thistle **7** Meadowbank Thistle **8** Hughie Gallagher **9** Livingstone **10** Pierre Van Hooijdonk **11** Peter Lorimer; Eddie Gray **12** Hearts & Motherwell **13** Paul Le Guen; Lyon **14** Willie Miller & Alex McLeish **15** Dick Advocaat; coach of Dutch national team

1 Hibernian **2** Brian Laudrup **3** The Lisbon Lions **4** Gordon Strachan **5** Pat Bonner (his 80 caps were for Ireland) **6** Stranraer **7** Alan Thompson **8** Bobby Collins **9** Kris Boyd **10** Jock Stein **11** Walter Smith; Ally McCoist **12** They gave 'Well a 2–1 win over Celtic and handed the title to Rangers **13** Richard Gough; Tottenham **14** Paolo Di Canio & Jorge Cadete **15** Billy Davies (Derby), George Burley (Southampton), Peter Grant (Norwich)

1 Graeme Souness **2** Dundee United **3** Hearts **4** Hearts **5** Darren Fletcher **6** St Johnstone **7** Hearts **8** Dumbarton **9** Mark Viduka **10** St Mirren **11** Chris Sutton; Chelsea **12** Hibernian & Kilmarnock **13** John Greig **14** 26 **15** Berti Vogts; Kuwait

1 Partick Thistle **2** 20 **3** Alex McLeish **4** Neil Sullivan **5** John Robertson **6** Dunfermline **7** Paul Telfer **8** Airdrie **9** Partick Thistle **10** Dunfermline **11** Alan Thompson & Alan Stubbs **12** Thomas Gravesen; Everton **13** Dundee United; Everton **14** Wim Jansen; Henrik Larsson **15** Kenny Dalglish & George Graham

1 Duncan Ferguson, **2** Alex James **3** Davie Cooper **4** Tore-Andre Flo
5 Gretna **6** Raith Rovers **7** Ugo Ehiogu **8** Motherwell in 1994–95
9 Jock Stein **10** Willie Maley **11** Hearts & Hibernian **12** Dundee
United & Aberdeen **13** St Johnstone; Vennegoor of Hesselink **14** Billy
McNeill; David Hay **15** Darren Fletcher & Christian Dailly

1 Jairzinho of Brazil, in 1970 **2** Bobby Moore **3** His team lost (6–5)
4 Argentina **5** Zinedine Zidane **6** Willie Donachie **7** Romario
8 Ukraine **9** Paolo Maldini **10** USA, 1994 **11** Rigobert Song; he
became the first player to be sent off in two different WCFTs **12** Davor
Suker; Croatia **13** Juan Schaffino; Brazil **14** Francky Van Der Elst and
Enzo Scifo **15** Lothar Matthaus; Andreas Brehme

1 Billy Wright, **2** Grzegorz Lato **3** Rudi Voller **4** Tunisia **5** Danny Mills
6 Owen Hargreaves **7** France **8** Italy **9** Faroe Islands **10** USSR
11 Kevin Keegan & Trevor Brooking **12** Bulgaria; France **13** Jamaica;
Ricardo Gardner **14** Northern Ireland & Wales **15** Ecuador; Reading

1 Poland, **2** Berti Vogts **3** Laurent Blanc **4** Franz Beckenbauer
5 Marco Materazzi **6** 6 **7** 5th **8** Jorge Valdano **9** Graham Taylor
10 Oprah Winfrey **11** USA, China **12** Croatia, 3–0 **13** Michael Owen
(3), Steven Gerrard, Emile Heskey **14** Celtic (Boruc, Zurawski);
Southampton (Rasiak, Kosowski) **15** Chris Waddle; Gary Lineker

1 Gary Lineker **2** Mexico **3** Ronaldinho **4** Golden Boot **5** Mario
Kempes **6** Wales **7** Costa Rica **8** Paul McStay **9** Juventus **10** 1, 1974
11 Nigel Martyn & Tim Flowers **12** Kolo Toure (Arsenal) & Abdoulaye
Meite (Bolton) **13** Yugoslavia & Croatia **14** Czechoslovakia (34, 62),
Holland (74, 78), Hungary (38, 54) **15** Francesco Totti; Lucas Neill

1 South Africa, **2** 1958 **3** Rose Bowl, Pasadena **4** Australia **5** Socrates
6 France **7** Greece **8** 2 **9** Papa Bouba Diop **10** Bebeto **11** Argentina;
1990 **12** Brazil, Germany (inc West Germany) & Italy **13** Lucas
Radebe (Leeds) & Mark Fish (Bolton) **14** Dennis Bergkamp & Marc
Overmars **15** 28

1 Teofilo Cubillas **2** Stanley Matthews **3** Hakan Sukur (it masked the fact that he had a dreadful tournament) **4** Cristiano Ronaldo **5** Alan Ball **6** Canada **7** Holland **8** Robbie Earle **9** Guiseppe Bergomi **10** Archie Gemmill **11** David O'Leary; Packy Bonner **12** Chris Woods, Gary Stevens, Trevor Steven, Terry Butcher **13** Chile; Stan Mortensen **14** Gareth Southgate, Martin Keown, Wes Brown **15** Ray Wilkins; Morocco

1 A bulldog **2** Carlos Valderrama **3** Antonio Rattin **4** Oliver Kahn **5** Belgium **6** Zaire, they only won 2-0 **7** 7 **8** Mick McCarthy **9** Montevideo (Uruguay) **10** Bryan Robson **11** Dutch coaches **12** Gothenburg & Stockholm **13** Poland & Portugal **14** Tom Finney and Nat Lofthouse **15** Portugal & Holland

1 Jan Tomaszewski **2** Just 1, the 2006 Final **3** Liechtenstein **4** Ally McLeod **5** Helmut Rahn **6** Hans Krankl **7** Italy **8** Norway (11) **9** Robbie Earle **10** Leonidas **11** Franz Beckenbauer & Wolfgang Overath **12** Mark Hateley & Ray Wilkins **13** Martin Peters & Roger Hunt **14** Alan Shearer, David Batty, Rob Lee **15** France; Thierry Henry

1 Uruguay **2** Referee **3** Bernabeu, Madrid **4** Estonia **5** Teddy Sheringham **6** Antonio Cabrini **7** 1998 **8** 74 **9** Lev Yashin **10** Denis Bergkamp **11** Haller & Weber **12** Mario Kempes; 20 **13** Brazil; Pele **14** Slovenia, Ukraine **15** Munich & Berlin

1 Peter Shilton **2** 4 **3** Frank Rijkaard **4** Saudi Arabia **5** Didier Deschamps **6** Djibril Cissé **7** Gary Lineker **8** Morocco **9** France in 2002 **10** South Korea **11** Terry Butcher, Mick Mills, Paul Mariner **12** Gerry Armstrong; Mal Donaghy **13** Frank & Ronald De Boer **14** Turkey, Switzerland **15** Freddie Ljungberg & Olof Mellberg

1 Cagliari, on Sicily **2** Lothar Matthaus **3** Ronaldo **4** North Korea **5** Rivelino **6** Czechoslovakia **7** Cameroon **8** Ludek Miklosko **9** Dynamo Kiev **10** Ron Greenwood **11** Poland; none **12** Willy & Rene Van Der Kerkhof **13** Les & Rio Ferdinand **14** Igor Belanov; Belgium **15** Jan Kromkamp; Dirk Kuyt

210 **The Sun** Football Quiz - **Answers**

1 Dan Petrescu **2** Dino Zoff **3** West Germany **4** Danny Blanchflower **5** Johan Neeskens **6** Argentina **7** David Platt **8** Laurent Blanc **9** Scotland **10** Robbie Keane with 3 in 2002. No other player has scored more than 1 **11** Dunga; Rai **12** Scotland & Northern Ireland **13** 6 **14** Portugal; Eusebio **15** Wayne Rooney (red card); John Terry (2nd yellow)

1 Gary Lineker **2** Italy **3** He was shot and killed **4** Gabriel Batistuta **5** Dino Zoff **6** New Zealand **7** 2018 **8** Jim Leighton **9** Pierluigi Collina **10** Peru **11** Mario Zagallo; Franz Beckenbauer **12** Archie Gemmill, John Robertson & Kenny Burns **13** They all travelled to World Cups but never played because of Peter Shilton **14** Peter McParland; Italy **15** Fabio Grosso; Alessandro Del Piero

1 Mexico **2** Iran **3** Gilberto Silva **4** Gonzalez or Gonzales **5** He was banned after failing a drug test **6** Northern Ireland **7** Saudi Arabia **8** USA (6) **9** Kerry Dixon **10** Bobby Charlton **11** Franco Baresi & Roberto Baggio **12** Argentina & France **13** Japan and South Korea **14** Fritz & Otto Walter **15** Argentina; 3

1 Santos, **2** Zbigniew Boniek **3** Mario Kempes **4** 0-0 **5** Jack Charlton **6** Ricardo Carvalho **7** Emilio Butragueno **8** Roberto Baggio **9** 7 **10** Gheorghe Hagi **11** Ronald Koeman; Koeman should have been sent off earlier, and the ref ordered the free kick to be retaken **12** Guus Hiddink; Australia **13** Kasey Keller & Brad Friedel **14** Ray Houghton; Andy Townsend **15** Jens Lehmann (Arsenal) & Robert Huth (Chelsea)

1 Jairzinho **2** Karl-Heinz Rummenigge **3** Emmanuel Petit **4** Oleg Salenko **5** Kevin Sheedy **6** Poland **7** Jorge Burruchaga **8** Michael Owen **9** Carlos Alberto **10** Peter Shilton **11** Kevin Keegan; Ray Wilkins **12** Jock Stein; Alex Ferguson **13** Savo Milosevic; Serbia **14** Turin (Torino); Naples, Maradona played for Napoli, and had just led them to their first (and only) Serie A title **15** 2

1 Papa Bouba Diop **2** Hungary **3** Ivory Coast **4** 1-0 **5** Lilian Thuram **6** Joe Jordan **7** Ilie Dumitrescu **8** Jamaica **9** Benito Mussolini **10** Australia **11** Desailly & Zidane **12** Iran; Iran won 2-1 **13** Andrea Pirlo; Gennaro Gattuso **14** Paul Ince, Hernan Crespo, David Batty **15** Gerd Muller; Peter Bonetti

1 Just Fontaine, **2** Vava **3** Roger Milla **4** Graham Poll **5** Mick McCarthy **6** Emlyn Hughes **7** Branco **8** Argentinian (Hector Elizondo) **9** Paolo Rossi **10** Alan Shearer **11** Gary Lineker; Poland in 1986 **12** Niall Quinn & Steve Staunton **13** Norway; Tore Andre Flo **14** Old Trafford, Manchester; St James's Park, Newcastle **15** Diego Simeone; Kim Milton Nielsen

1 Jurgen Klinsmann **2** Norman Whiteside **3** None **4** Gary Stevens **5** 1966 **6** Bilbao **7** Bodo Illgner **8** 4 **9** Brazil (in 1970) **10** They have all played in a WCFT for two different countries (Ita/Arg; Uru/Spa; Hun/Spa respectively) **11** Germany; Miroslav Klose **12** Watford & Burnley **13** Brian McBride, Carlos Bocanegra & Clint Dempsey **14** Cote d'Ivoire, Togo, Angola, Ghana **15** Marcello Lippi & Raymond Domenech

1 Hernan Crespo **2** Uruguay **3** Andy Roxburgh **4** Billy Bingham **5** Daniel Passarella **6** 1 **7** Toto Schillaci **8** Claudio Taffarel **9** None **10** Swiss **11** Jack Taylor; Johann Neeskens **12** Tony Woodcock; Cologne **13** USA; 1–0 **14** Ian Callaghan, John Connolly, Jimmy Greaves, Terry Paine **15** Lukas Podolski; Miroslav Klose

1 Gazza's shirt from the 1990 WC SF **2** JJB Sports **3** Watford **4** Cyril Knowles **5** Jimmy Greaves **6** First female commentator on the programme **7** Bobby Moore was arrested in 1970, and accused of stealing a bracelet from a store in the hotel lobby **8** Jason Euell **9** Scotland goalkeeper, Andy Goram **10** Philip Don **11** 50 **12** Everton; Chelsea; Celtic **13** Cantona, Bergkamp, Ginola, Van Nistelrooy, Henry (twice), Ronaldo **14** Southampton (1976) and Sunderland (1973) **15** Montserrat and Bhutan

1 Stoke **2** Fulham **3** Sir Stanley Matthews **4** Milton Keynes Dons **5** Derby County **6** Bob Paisley **7** They all played for Trinidad & Tobago in the 2006 World Cup **8** Rob Lee **9** Vialli (59). Zola got 35, Di Matteo 34 **10** Swindon Town **11** Harald Schumacher; Hitler **12** Newcastle United; Georgian **13** 9–0 v Ipswich (h), 8–1 v Nottm Forest (a) **14** 1996; Moldova **15** Seth Johnson; back at Derby

1 Southampton **2** Port Vale **3** George Eastham **4** Pete Winkleman **5** Aston Villa **6** Ron Saunders **7** The World Cup **8** Richard Wright **9** Numbered shirts **10** Massimo Taibi **11** Birmingham City; Celtic **12** Mike Smith & John Toshack **13** Arsenal, Huddersfield Town, Liverpool, Manchester United **14** 1976 **15** Geoffrey Richmond; Benito Carbone

212 *Sun* Football Quiz - **Answers**

1 Lawrie McMenemy **2** West Brom **3** Jackie Milburn **4** Selhurst Park
5 Preston North End **6** Alan Ball **7** USA **8** Andy Sinton (12). Thomas
got 9 and Le Tissier 8 **9** Tranmere Rovers **10** Juventus **11** Paul
Peschisolido; Canadian **12** Feyenoord; Holland **13** Argentina & USA
14 Adam Crozier; Chief Exec of the Royal Mail **15** Steve Coppell &
Gordon Hill

1 Filbert Street **2** (Peter) Schmeichel **3** 1999 **4** Wimbledon **5** The FA
Cup **6** Michael Knighton **7** They have all been World Cup mascots
8 Sheffield Wednesday **9** Adriano **10** Darren Anderton **11** David Batty
& Graeme Le Saux **12** Dagenham & Redbridge; Oxford United **13** 57
14 Alan Ball & Gerry Francis **15** Danny, Rodney & Ray Wallace

1 He was the linesman who ruled that Geoff Hurst's shot had crossed
the line in the 1966 WCF **2** Peter Schmeichel **3** Frank Sinclair **4** John
Fashanu **5** Birmingham City **6** Stoke City (old and new ground) **7** New
Order **8** Mark Kennedy **9** Bayern Munich **10** Deportivo La Coruna
11 Keith Gillespie; he missed and Shearer laid him out **12** 9 **13** Alan
Hansen & Phil Neal **14** Birmingham City in the Fairs Cup in 1960
15 Tottenham (as 'The Cockerel Chorus'); full-back Cyril Knowles

1 Mick Channon **2** Marcel Desailly **3** Tottenham Hotspur **4** John
Fashanu **5** Dixie Dean **6** They all played first-class cricket **7** Scotland
8 Alexei Lalas **9** Maradona (91), Batistuta (78), Kempes only 43
10 Rivaldo **11** Paolo Di Canio; Paul Alcock **12** Wycombe reached the
Carling Cup SF. They drew 1–1 with Chelsea **13** Pat Jennings, Liam
Brady, Paul McGrath, Roy Keane **14** Maracana; Fluminense **15** John
& Mel Charles, Ivor & Len Allchurch

1 He was jailed for drink-driving **2** Jimmy Hill **3** Michel Platini
4 Peterborough United **5** Sepp Blatter **6** Johnny Haynes **7** Stephen
Hunt **8** The Butcher of Bilbao **9** Argentina **10** Kenneth Wolstenholme
11 Patrick Vieira & Emmanuel Petit **12** Gudni Bergsson; Eidur
Gudjohnsen; Arnur Gunnlaugsson **13** Alf Ramsey, just before extra
time in the 1966 World Cup Final **14** Uruguay; Soviet Union **15**
Matthew Harding; Bolton

1 Eileen Drewery **2** Jimmy Hill **3** Lennart Johansson **4** Bristol Rovers
5 Jules Rimet **6** Swindon were demoted for financial irregularities **7** They
are all called Emmanuel **8** Garrincha **9** Billy McNeill **10** As a mark of
respect for Bobby Moore, who had just died, the No.6 shirt wasn't used
11 Leeds United; Howard Wilkinson **12** Bolton Wanderers & Paris St
Germain **13** They are chairman of Celtic and Rangers, respectively
14 Scott Parker; Charlton **15** West Ham United; Harry Redknapp

213 *The Sun* Football Quiz - **Answers**

1 Carlos Queiroz **2** John Toshack **3** Ron Atkinson **4** Crystal Palace
5 Zurich **6** All started with Crewe **7** Everton **8** The own goal which won
Coventry the 1987 FA Cup went in off the aforementioned appendage
9 Ian Callaghan **10** Gary Neville **11** Glenn Hoddle & Chris Waddle **12**
They won the title in 1985 as well so would have played in the European
Cup, but by then the post-Heysel ban was in place **13** Mark Goldberg;
Simon Jordan **14** Fulham; Robert Lindsay **15** Arsenal & Liverpool

1 Bobby Moore, **2** Tony Brown **3** 67 **4** Rochdale **5** Matt Busby
6 Tranmere Rovers **7** Manchester City **8** Bafana Bafana **9** 1 **10** Alan
Hansen **11** Never on the losing side in a Manchester derby
12 Bosnich (Aus), Milosevic (Yug) & Yorke (T&T) **13** Robert Maxwell;
Derby County **14** Blyth Spartans; St James's Park **15** Platini &
Trezeguet

1 Chelsea **2** 'The Boot Room' **3** Steve Gibson **4** Stan Flashman
5 Spurs' League and FA Cup double, the first in the 20th century
6 Millwall **7** Arsène Wenger **8** Bavarian, referring to the region of
Germany in which Munich lies **9** 45 **10** Paul Cooper **11** Celtic &
Rangers **12** Rumbelows & Coca-Cola **13** Hull City, Norwich City,
Wolves **14** Johann Cruyfff & Win Van Hanegem **15** Steve McLaren;
Brian Kidd

1 Preston **2** Jean-Marc Bosman **3** Jack Walker **4** Sammy McIlroy
5 82,500 **6** Ian Botham **7** Pedro Mendes of Portsmouth **8** Edgar
Davids **9** Claudio Ranieri **10** Arsenal **11** Chesterfield, Leicester City,
Stoke City **12** El Salvador & Honduras **13** Preston NE & Aston Villa
14 Sam Bartram **15** Argentina & Colombia

1 CONCACAF **2** Billy Bremner **3** David Seaman **4** It is the name of the
home of Exeter City as well as Newcastle **5** Alan Sugar **6** Kevin Bond
7 Jason Roberts **8** Indomitable Lions **9** Rodney Marsh **10** 1963
11 They were officially the 2 worst sides in FIFA's rankings (202 &
203) **12** 14 **13** Luton Town; Real Madrid **14** Bury; West Brom
15 Union of European Football Associations

1 The Jules Rimet Trophy (the original World Cup) **2** Trevor Brooking
3 Alan Shearer **4** Steve Staunton **5** Liverpool **6** Spireites (after the
famous crooked spire) **7** Michael Owen **8** Patrick Kluivert **9** Bobby
Charlton **10** Pele **11** Wycombe Wanderers; Portsmouth **12** Leicester
paid Wolves **13** Corsica; French **14** Tottenham Hotspur; Arsenal
15 205,000

1 Torino **2** West Brom **3** Lord Justice Taylor **4** Aston Villa **5** Michel Platini **6** Wycombe Wanderers **7** Newcastle United **8** Jermaine Pennant **9** Chris Waddle **10** Brian Moore **11** George Weah; Liberia **12** Aston Villa, Blackburn, Bolton, Everton, West Brom **13** Roy Keane; schoolteacher (at Harrow) **14** Alf Common; Middlesbrough **15** The 'Three Tenors', Domingo, Carreras & Pavarotti

1 Socrates **2** Catenaccio **3** Sir Matt Busby **4** Barnet **5** Michael Owen in 2001 **6** Bristol RUFC **7** Celtic **8** Arjen Robben **9** Gordon Strachan **10** She was the first female to referee a league match in the UK **11** Celtic; Charlton Athletic **12** Denis Law (1962), Manchester United, Torino **13** Bolton; Jay-Jay Okocha **14** Alan Kennedy & Terry McDermott **15** Wembley & White City

1 Types of football **2** Kenny Dalglish **3** David Rocastle **4** Trevor Francis **5** Fabio Cannavaro **6** Barry Fry **7** Rory Delap **8** Diego Maradona **9** Ulrika Jonsson **10** David Icke **11** Nottingham Forest; Bobby Gould **12** Oxford United; none; he was homesick, so returned to Swindon **13** Mark (197 in 524); Brian got 153 in 522. They were born in Cape Town, SA **14** Jimmy Hill & Ron Greenwood **15** Newcastle United; Chile

1 Ayrton Senna **2** Mark Bright **3** Marc-Vivien Foe **4** English transfer record **5** Stanley Matthews **6** Norwich City **7** Alan Curbishley **8** Willie Johnston **9** Arsenal **10** Kenny Dalglish **11** 1980 **12** Lee Bowyer & Kieron Dyer **13** Manchester United, Newcastle, Manchester City **14** Billy Bremner, Eddie Gray and Allan Clarke **15** Faria Alam; Mark Palios

1 Hertha Berlin **2** Tranmere Rovers **3** David Healy **4** Steve Gritt **5** The European Footballer of the Year **6** Aston Villa **7** Darren Peacock **8** Mickey Thomas **9** Ryan Giggs **10** Northern Ireland; it was the height of 'the troubles' **11** 1967 **12** Lee Bowyer, Jonathon Woodgate **13** Jared Borgetti; Bolton **14** Bobby Charlton & Bill Foulkes **15** Anders Frisk; Barcelona

1 Gabriel Heinze **2** Ghana **3** Villa Park **4** 300,000 **5** Lothar Matthaus **6** Tottenham Hotspur **7** Mohammed al-Fayed **8** Peter Storey **9** Coleen McLoughlin **10** Uruguay **11** He scored in all of them; he scored a hat-trick **12** Kim Milton Nielsen; Villareal **13** Crystal Palace; 1 **14** Altrincham (2–1 at Birmingham) **15** Arsenal; Colin Firth

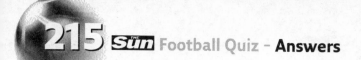

215 **Sun** Football Quiz - **Answers**

1 'Sniffer' **2** Emlyn Hughes **3** Wembley **4** Leeds **5** Mike England
6 Alan Hardaker **7** Bruce Rioch **8** Sammy Nelson of Arsenal **9** Chelsea
10 Doncaster (Belles) **11** Arsenal; Matt Le Tissier **12** Keith Gillespie,
Paul Dickov, Frank Sinclair **13** Steven Gerrard, Vladimir Smicer and
Xabi Alonso **14** Roy Essandoh; Wycombe Wanderers **15** 1999;
Brooklyn

1 Ron Harris **2** Dennis Irwin **3** Julio Baptista **4** Jack Charlton **5** 28
6 Ray Stewart **7** He was the supporter kung-fu'd by Eric Cantona
8 Robbie Savage **9** Leslie Ash **10** *Bend It Like Beckham* **11** Bruce
Grobelaar & Hans Segers **12** Chelsea; Sheffield United **13** George
Eastham jnr, Nigel Clough, Frank Lampard jnr **14** Germany v
Cameroon **15** Arsenal & West Ham

1 They were all heavy smokers **2** Tottenham Hotspur **3** Cork City
4 Leicester City **5** Gary Speed **6** Ally McCoist **7** Norwich City
8 Argentina **9** Stan Collymore **10** They have all played international
football against the country of their surname **11** 1960 **12** Frank
Rijkaard; Rudi Voller **13** Everton, Rangers, Olympique Marseille
14 Brian Clough (Middlesbrough) **15** Leeds United; Lee Bowyer

1 George Best **2** Joao Havelange **3** Milan Mandaric **4** Manchester
United **5** Gordon Strachan **6** Rangers **7** His fight against alcoholism
8 Danny Baker **9** Sheryl **10** Leyton Orient **11** Southampton &
Portsmouth **12** Tottenham in 1951; Ipswich Town in 1962
13 Argentina & Uruguay **14** West Germany & Austria **15** Morten
Olsen; Peter Schmeichel & Michael Laudrup

1 Rock of Gibraltar **2** Wales **3** Sheffield Wednesday **4** Graham Poll
5 Arsenal **6** Daniel Amokachi **7** Australia **8** Bill Shankly **9** The Glazers
10 Jose Luis Chilavert. He is a goalkeeper **11** Robbie Keane; Niall
Quinn **12** Franz Beckenbauer; Felix Magath **13** Arsenal, Chelsea,
Crystal Palace, QPR, Tottenham, Wimbledon **14** Luc Nilis; Aston Villa
15 Mark Hughes; Sparky

1 Yellow & red cards **2** Kennington Oval **3** David Prutton **4** Heart of
Midlothian **5** Kennington Oval **6** Georghiou Kinkladze **7** None; he was
injured and replaced by John Filan after 14 minutes **8** Arsène Wenger
9 Littlewoods **10** Colin Moynihan **11** Peter Kenyon; Manchester
United **12** Dennis Wise, Steve Claridge, Colin Lee, Dave Tuttle **13** Ray
Kennedy, Liverpool **14** Ivan Golac; Dundee United **15** Roy Keane

216 *The Sun* Football Quiz - **Answers**

PAGE 153
1 Kevin Pressman **2** Wim Jansen **3** Tangerine **4** Hibernian **5** Total Network Solutions **6** Coventry City **7** Burnden Park **8** No club; he left to become England manager **9** England in 1966 **10** Brazil **11** Norwich City; Blackburn Rovers **12** Ian Holloway; Plymouth Argyle **13** Stuart Ripley; Jason Wilcox **14** He became the first player at a Scottish club to win an England cap **15** Randy Lerner; Doug Ellis

PAGE 154
1 Renault Clio **2** Matt Le Tissier **3** Leyton Orient **4** Northern Ireland **5** The Soviet invasion of Hungary **6** John Charles **7** Newcastle United **8** Middlesbrough **9** Austria **10** CSKA Moscow (Dynamo Kiev are Ukrainian, Dynamo Tbilisi are from Georgia) **11** West Ham United; Upton Park **12** Dean & David **13** He scored at both ends for Manchester City and Tottenham (an own goal) in 1981 **14** Paul Scholes, David Beckham, Teddy Sheringham **15** 44

PAGE 155
1 Eyal Berkovic **2** Harry Kewell **3** Brighton & HA **4** Wales **5** USA **6** Juan Pablo Angel **7** Dave Sexton **8** Giovanni Trapattoni **9** Arsenal **10** Small Heath **11** Walsall; Bescot Stadium **12** Cliff Jones; Tottenham Hotspur **13** Tottenham (1961), Derby County (1972) **14** Crystal Palace; Peter Taylor **15** Pele & Uwe Seeler

PAGE 156
1 They were sent off for fighting, but both played for Charlton **2** *L'Equipe* **3** £5 **4** Liverpool **5** El Beatle **6** He is afraid of flying **7** Peter Beardsley **8** Ottmar Hitzfeld **9** Bill 'Fatty' Foulke **10** Bryan Robson **11** Northern Premier (Unibond); Southern League, Isthmian League (Ryman) **12** Brian Clough & Nigel Clough **13** Queens Park Rangers; 1981 **14** Coventry City; York City **15** 1981–82

PAGE 157
1 Mark Bosnich **2** Leicester City **3** AC Milan **4** Arsenal **5** Matt Busby **6** Belgrade **7** Teddy Sheringham **8** 33 **9** Linesmen **10** Chippy **11** Oxford United; The Manor Ground **12** Tony & Mark Hateley; Coventry City **13** 16 Lancaster Gate; Brian Barwick **14** Oxford United & Reading **15** Wolves; Derek Dougan

PAGE 158
1 Ronaldo **2** Des Lynam **3** Saltergate **4** Tommy Lawton **5** Bobby Charlton **6** Lazio **7** £35k **8** Real Madrid **9** He allowed Maradona's 'Hand of God' goal to stand **10** Shaun Goater **11** Reading; Trinidad & Tobago **12** Karl-Heinz and Bernd Forster **13** Chelsea v Fulham; George Best **14** Fulham; Ray Wilkins **15** Andy Johnson; Clinton Morrison

217 **Sun** Football Quiz - **Answers**

PAGE 159
1 John Madejski **2** *The Premiership* **3** Middlesbrough **4** Portsmouth **5** Leeds United **6** Luton Town **7** Kenny Dalglish **8** Switzerland **9** Peter Shilton **10** Everton **11** Arsenal & Liverpool **12** David Nish; Derby County **13** Frans Thijssen; 1981 **14** Denis Law & Kenny Dalglish **15** Arsenal & Everton

PAGE 160
1 Michael Ballack **2** Bristol City **3** Carlos Tevez **4** Didier Drogba **5** Owen Hargreaves **6** Kris Boyd of Rangers **7** Yeovil (against Nottingham Forest) **8** Jamie Cureton **9** Benni McCarthy (15 for Blackburn), **10** Arjen Robben **11** Glenn Roeder; Sam Allardyce **12** Tottenham, Everton & Bolton **13** Leroy Rosenior; Colin Lee **14** Hartlepool United; Walsall; Swindon Town **15** Sevilla; Espanyol

PAGE 161
1 David Unsworth **2** Roy Keane **3** Richard Scudamore **4** Steve Coppell **5** Steve Bennett **6** Juventus, after their demotion for their part in the bribery scandal **7** Wayne Bridge (Southampton, 2003) **8** Milton Keynes Dons **9** Jose Mourinho **10** None; ITV have won the rights to screen live FA Cup matches **11** Kevin Phillips **12** Neil Warnock & Paul Jewell **13** Kevin Davies; Everton **14** Morecambe; Exeter City **15** VFB Stuttgart; Bayern Munich

PAGE 163
1 Lehmann, Eboue, Toure, Campbell, Cole, Hleb (Reyes), Fabregas (Flamini), Silva, Ljungberg, Pires (Almunia), Henry **2** Simpson, Craig, Gemmell, Murdoch, McNeill, Clark, Johnstone, Wallace, Chalmers, Auld, Lennox **3** Springett, Armfield, McNeil, Robson, Swan, Flowers, Douglas, Greaves, Smith, Haynes, Charlton **4** Sprake; Reaney; Cooper, Bremner, Charlton, Hunter, Lorimer, Clarke, Jones, Giles, Madeley; S: Bates **5** Schmeichel, Parker, Irwin (Sharpe), Bruce, Kanchelskis (McClair), Pallister, Cantona, Ince, Keane, Hughes, Giggs **6** Rough, Kennedy, Donachie, Buchan, Forsyth, Rioch, Gemmill, Souness, Hartford, Dalglish, Jordan **7** Maier, Vogts, Schwarzenbeck, Beckenbauer, Breitner, Overath, Hoeness, Bonhof, Grabowski, Muller, Holzenbein **8** Hahnemann, Murty, Sonko, Ingimarsson, Shorey, Oster (Long), Harper, Gunnarsson (Sidwell), Convey (Hunt), Kitson, Doyle **9** Felix, Carlos Alberto, Piazza, Everaldo, Brito, Jairzinho, Clodoaldo, Gerson, Rivaldo, Pele, Tostao **10** Friedel, Mokoena, Nelsen, Samba, Warnock, Bentley, Dunn, Emerton, Pedersen, McCarthy, Roberts

218 *Sun* Football Quiz - **Answers**

1 Shilton, Madeley, Hughes, Bell, McFarland, Hunter, Currie, Channon, Chivers, Clarke (Allan), Peters **2** Southall, Stevens, Bailey, Ratcliffe, Mountfield, Reid, Steven, Heath, Sharp, Gray, Richardson **3** Flowers, Sinclair, Taggart, Elliott, Guppy, Oakes (Impey), Lennon, Izzett, Savage, Cottee (Marshall), Heskey **4** Galli, Tassotti, Costacurta, Baresi, Maldini, Colombo, Rijkaard, Ancelotti, Donadoni, Gullit, Van Basten **5** Jennings, Jimmy Nicholl, Donaghy, Chris Nicholl, McLelland, McCreery, O'Neill, McIlroy, Armstrong, Hamilton, Whiteside **6** Woods, Nilsson, Worthington, Harkes, Palmer, Warhurst, Wilson, Waddle, Hirst, Bright, Sheridan **7** James, Delaney, Ehiogu, Southgate, Barry, Alan Wright (Hendrie), Boateng, Merson, Ian Taylor (Stone), Carbone (Joachim), Dublin **8** Pollitt, Chimbonda, Henchox, De Zeeuw, Baines, Bullard, Kavanagh, Scharner, Teale, Camara, Roberts **9** Corrigan, Book, Booth, Heslop, Pardoe, Doyle (Bowyer), Oakes Towers, Bell, Lee, Young **10** Barthez, Thuram, Blanc, Desailly, Lizarazu (Pires), Deschamps, Vieira, Djorkaeff (Trezeguet), Zidane, Dugarry (Wiltord), Henry

1 Leighton, Rougvie, Miller, McLeish, McMaster, Cooper, Strachan, Weir, McGhee, Black (Hewett), Simpson **2** Bonetti, Harris, McReadie, Hollins, Dempsey, Webb, Baldwin, Cooke, Osgood (Hinton), Hutchinson, Houseman **3** West, Wright, Wilson, Kendall, Labone, Harvey, Husband, Ball, Royle, Hurst, Morrissey **4** Martyn, Mills, Ferdinand, Matteo, Harte, Bowyer, Dacourt, Batty, Kewell, Smith, Viduka **5** Van Der Sar, O'Shea, Brown, Ferdinand, Heinze, Fletcher, Carrick, Giggs, Ronaldo, Rooney, Smith **6** Simpson, Gemmell, McReadie, Greig, McKinnon, Baxter, Wallace, Bremner, McCalliog, Law, Lennox **7** Mullery, Ball, Cherry, Wilkins, Beckham (twice), Ince, Scholes, Batty, Smith (Alan), Rooney **8** Lukic, Anderson, Sansom, Williams (Steve), O'Leary, Adams, Rocastle, Davis, Quinn, Nicholas, Hayes **9** Robinson, Chimbonda, King, Dawson, Assou-Ekotto, Lennon, Jenas, Zokora, Ghaly, Berbatov, Keane (Defoe) **10** Bats, Amoros, Bossis, Tusseau, Battiston, Tigana, Giresse, Platini, Fernandez, Rocheteau, Stopyra

---

Answers for pages 164-165

219 The **Sun** Football Quiz - **Answers**

1 Bosnich, Barrett, Staunton, Teale, McGrath, Richardson, Daley, Townsend, Saunders, Atkinson, Fenton **2** Woods, Keown, Pearce, Batty, Palmer, Walker, Daley, Webb, Platt, Lineker, Sinton **3** Cooper, Burley, Mills, Thijssen, Osman, Butcher, Wark, Muhren, Mariner, Brazil, Gates **4** Clemence, Neal, Smith, Thompson, Hughes, Case, Kennedy (Ray), Callaghan, Heighway, Keegan, Toshack, Fairclough **5** Sutton, Laws, Pearce, Chettle, Walker, Crosby, Parker (Garry), Hodge, Carr, Clough, Jemson **6** Brown, Baker, Henry, Blanchflower, Norman, Mackay, Jones, White, Smith, Allen, Dyson **7** Schwarzer, Parnaby, Rigott, Southgate, Queudrue, Boateng, Morrison (Maccarone), Rochemback, Downing, Viduka (Cattermole), Hasselbaink **8** Van Der Sar, Reiziger, Blind, Rijkaard, F De Boer, Seedorf (Kanu), Davids, Litmanen (Kluivert), George, R De Boer, Overmars **9** Gunn, Culverhouse, Butterworth, Prior, Newman, Bowen, Fox, Goss, Crook, Sutton, Robins **10** Buffon, Zambrotta, Cannavaro, Materazzi, Grosso, Camoranesi (Iaquinta), Perrotta (Del Piero), Gattuso, Pirlo, Totti, Toni

1 Stuy, Suurbier, Hulshoff, Blankenburg, Krol, Rep, Haan, Neeskens, Keizer, G Muhren, Cruyff **2** Finland (Jaaskelainen), Spain (Campo), Ivory Coast (Meite), Jamaica (Gardner), Wales (Speed), England (Nolan), Iran (Teymourian), Greece (Stelios), Senegal (Diouf), France (Anelka), Portugal (Vaz Te), Denmark (Pedersen), Israel (Ben Haim and Tal) **3** Shilton, Mills, Sansom, Thompson, Butcher, Wilkins, Coppell, Francis (Trevor), Mariner, Rix, Robson **4** Peyton, Langan, Hughton, Piers O'Leary, David O'Leary, Lawrenson, Grealish, Daly, Stapleton, Brady, Givens **5** Westerveld, Babbel, Hyppia, Henchoz (Smicer), Carragher, Gerrard, Hamann, McAllister, Murphy, Owen (Berger), Heskey (Fowler) **6** Shilton, Anderson, Clark, McGovern, Lloyd, Burns, Francis, Bowyer, Birtles, Woodcock, Robertson **7** Southall, Dave Phillips, Joey Jones, Robbie James, Hopkins, Ratcliffe, Alan Davies, Gordon Davies, Rush, Hughes, Thomas **8** Cech, Geremi, Terry, Ricardo Carvalho, Gallas, Tiago, Makelele, Jarosik, Lampard, Gudjohnsen, Drogba **9** Beasant, Goodyear, Young, Thorn, Phelan, Wise, Sanchez, Jones, Gibson (Scales), Cork (Cunningham), Fashanu **10** Srnicek, Watson, Peacock, Albert, Beresford, Batty, Lee, Beardsley, Ginola, Shearer, Ferdinand

1 Martyn, Pemberton, Shaw, Gray (Madden), O'Reilly, Thorn, Barber (Wright), Thomas, Bright, Salako, Pardew **2** Seaman, Gary Neville, Pearce, Ince, Adams, Southgate, Anderton, Gascoigne, Shearer, Sheringham, McManaman **3** Bonner, Irwin, Phelan, Keane, Moran, McGrath, Houghton, Townsend, Quinn, Coyne, Staunton **4** Grobbelaar, Neal, Beglin, Lawrenson, Hansen, Nicol, Dalglish, Whelan, Wark, Rush, Walsh **5** Vitor Baia, Paulo Ferreira, Jorge Costa, Carvalho, Nuno Valente, Pedro Mendes, Costinha, Maniche, Deco, Carlos Alberto, Derlei **6** Wilson, Rice, McNabb, Storey (Kelly), McLintock, Simpson, Armstrong, Graham, Radford, Kennedy, George **7** Hislop, Scaloni, Ferdinand, Gabbidon, Konchesky, Benayoun, Fletcher (Dailly), Reo-Coker, Etherington (Sheringham), Ashton (Zamora), Harewood **8** James, Lauren, Primus, Stefanovic, Traore, O'Neill, Davis, Hughes, Taylor, Mwaruwari (Lua Lua), Kanu (Kranjcar) **9** Waldir Peres, Leandro, Luizinho, Junior, Oscar, Cerezo, Socrates, Falcao, Eder, Zico, Serginho **10** Paul Jones, Delaney, Melville, Gabbidon, Speed, Pembridge, Savage, Davies, Giggs, Bellamy, Hartson

1 True; he played in 1982 **2** False; they reached the 1958 Finals after beating Israel in a play-off **3** False; he was injured in the opening game of the 1962 tournament **4** False; It was Roker Park and Ayresome **5** False; it was the more modern Stade de France **6** False; only the first tournament in 1930 didn't have pre-qualifying **7** True; they beat both at home and drew away in Portugal **8** True; England qualified as hosts **9** False; they did both play but they aren't related **10** True; Ipswich & Arsenal were unrepresented **11** False; it was 2001–02 when they scored in every game. They had four 0-0 draws in 2003–04 **12** True; Baros was top scorer with 9 **13** True; Ferdinand and Rooney both cost more than the £25m Real Madrid paid for Beckham **14** False; Thierry Henry holds that record. Surprisingly, Owen has never scored 20 league goals in a season **15** True; Ruud Van Nistelrooy, James Beattie & Thierry Henry. Henry repeated the feat in 2005–06. **16** False; Wise is no stranger to red cards, but never for England **17** True; with Aberdeen and Manchester United **18** True; Forest lost the only final they reached under his guidance, in 1991 **19** False; he won the FA Cup with West Ham in 1964 **20** True; Rangers scored only once in 7½ hours

---

1 False; Feyenoord & PSV have also won the trophy **2** False; Keegan played for Hamburg in the Final, but they lost - he had moved on when they won the trophy **3** False; they won the Fairs Cup in 1969 **4** False; Hearts finished second in 2005-06 **5** False; we just made them up **6** True (1999-2001) **7** False; they were deducted 10 points, but were 14 points adrift of Rushden & Diamonds in 22nd **8** True; Cottee was player-manager at the time **9** False; they won the title in 1948-49 and again in 1949-50 **10** False; he won 2 caps **11** True; they racked up 142 (McLeish 77, Miller 65) **12** False; he played only for Preston **13** False; it was Trevor Sinclair **14** False; he started with Charlton Athletic **15** False; Sanchez was born in South London but won 3 caps for NI through his ancestry. **16** False; Magdeburg, Lokomotiv Leipzig and Carl Zeiss Jena all achieved this feat **17** True; with Aberdeen and Leeds United **18** True; they won the first leg 2-1, but were beaten 2-0 in Italy **19** True **20** False, although the inspiration was an English team - Notts County

1 True; and have suffered two 8-0 drubbings into the bargain **2** True; talk about winning the hard way **3** True; imagine the crowd's response today **4** True; along with many other splendidly named chaos from the Victorian era **5** False; West Brom beat Birmingham in 1931 **6** True; in 1934 when they beat Portsmouth 2-1 **7** False; he played in 1963 when United beat Leicester 3-1 **8** True **9** True; Liverpool won 2-1 against Nottingham Forest **10** False; they lost 9-0! **11** False; he won in 1993 and 1994 **12** False; he won the FA Cup with Ipswich in 1978 **13** False; he has over 30 caps for Ireland **14** False; they won the 1963 League Cup **15** True; Celestine Babayaro was the last to leave, in 2005 **16** False; but Paisley and Matt Busby were on the staff together **17** True; Jean Djorkaeff played in a far less successful side **18** True; he was 38 years old when he was picked in 1950 **19** True; and Crewe Alexandra **20** True; enterprising chap.

222 *Sun* Football Quiz - **Answers**

1 False; Shakhtor Donetsk won in 2002, 2005 and 2006 **2** False; he also has a genuine economics degree from Strasbourg University **3** True; Dynamo Berlin from the former East Germany, and Bayern Munich in the Final **4** False; they were in the second tier from 1958-1964 **5** False; they lost the ECWC Final in 1966 **6** False; none have – Liverpool have no ECWC, United have no UEFA Cup **7** True; in 1954 **8** True; Zidane's penalty was cancelled out by Materazzi's header **9** True; against Finland in October 2000 **10** True; they were 10th, 6th and 11th **11** True; The Royal Engineers in 1875 **12** True; He was playing for Swindon **13** False; it was another Arsenal legend, Ted Drake **14** True; just 6 league titles **15** True; it remains their only major trophy **16** True; England qualified both times **17** True; unsurprisingly he wasn't picked again by Michel **18** False; she was Milburn's cousin **19** False; it was Pizza Hut **20** True; 33 out of 181

1 San Marino **2** Agustin Delgado **3** Arsène Wenger (on Davor Suker) **4** Eric Cantona **5** David Platt **6** Toaster **7** Graham Taylor **8** Tony Adams **9** Mark Lawrenson **10** Tommy Docherty **11** Alex Ferguson to the 1999 Champions League victory **12** Ken Bates on Roman Abramovich **13** Chris Sutton; Glenn Hoddle **14** Peter Ridsdale; Leeds United **15** Bob Paisley, Liverpool manager, before Liverpool's first European Cup Final

1 Kevin Keegan **2** Tommy Smith **3** John Motson **4** Pele **5** George Best **6** Freddie Shepherd of Newcastle **7** Niall Quinn, on donating his £1m testimonial fund to charity **8** Kevin Keegan **9** Paul Gascoigne **10** Tommy Smith **11** Jock Stein on Bobby Moore **12** George Best on Paul Gascoigne **13** Princess Di & Sam Hamman **14** Glenn Hoddle; Eileen Drewery **15** Teddy Sheringham after England beat Argentina

1 Brian Clough **2** Jose Mourinho **3** Harry Redknapp **4** Brian Clough **5** Ian Holloway of QPR **6** Jesus Gil of Atletico Madrid **7** Kenneth Wolstenholme on Real Madrid's 7–3 victory over Eintracht Frankfurt in the 1960 European Cup Final **8** Bill Shankly **9** Gareth Southgate's, after he missed a crucial penalty at Euro 96 **10** Joey Barton **11** David Coleman; Raith Rovers play in Kirkcaldy **12** Ron Atkinson on Carlton Palmer **13** Malcolm Allison; Manchester City **14** Johnny Giles on his time with Don Revie's Leeds **15** Graham Taylor on the England job

1 Nigel Spink **2** Bobby Robson **3** John Gregory **4** Paul Walsh **5** Norwich City **6** Paul Walsh **7** Nick Pickering **8** John Gregory **9** 9 **10** John Barnes **11** Terry Butcher & Russell Osman **12** Trevor Francis; Sampdoria **13** Wayne Rooney; Everton **14** Nigel Spink; Aston Villa **15** Danny Thomas; Coventry City

1 Anton Johnson **2** Joe Mercer **3** Colin Lee **4** Gabor Kiraly **5** He lost a finger in a lawnmower 'incident' **6** Cricket's County Championship, with Worcestershire **7** Karl-Heinz Riedle **8** Alan Sunderland; Gary Bailey **9** Viv Anderson, George Berry, Chris Hughton **10** Swindon Town; Paul Bodin

1 Peter Beagrie **2** Kevin Francis **3** Vic Watson **4** Juan Carlos Lorenzo **5** 'Roy of The Rovers' **6** Doncaster Rovers **7** Owen Oyston **8** Bolton Wanderers; David Jack **9** Oleg Salenko; Cameroon **10** Kenny Jackett; Watford

1 Gary Megson **2** Leicester City **3** Arrigo Sacchi **4** Guy Roux **5** Steve Claridge **6** Scarborough **7** Motherwell **8** Milan; Guiseppe Meazza **9** Palermo & Messina (Sicily); Cagliari (Sardinia) **10** Rapid & Steaua Bucuresti

1 Paul Elliott **2** Dexter Blackstock **3** Paul Lambert (for Borussia Dortmund in 1997) **4** Nottingham Forest; Scotland **5** Graham Rix **6** Steve Nicol **7** Jorge Campos **8** Bradford Park Avenue (Bradford AFC will do); Cambridge United **9** Real Madrid; Olympique Marseille; SV Hamburg **10** York City; Lincoln City

1 Neville Southall **2** Mark Goodlad **3** Don Givens **4** Cambridge United **5** They were all scored during WWII **6** Junior Agogo **7** Charlie Buchan **8** Bristol Rovers; Reading **9** Latvia; Maris Verpakovskis **10** Alan Curtis; Robbie James

1 Millwall **2** Guy Butters **3** David Narey **4** Final of the Olympic Games football tournament **5** Johnny Carey **6** Hope Powell **7** Eddie Hapgood **8** Matthias Sammer; Borussia Dortmund **9** St Gallen, Hapoel Tel Aviv & Viking Stavanger **10** Kidderminster Harriers, Macclesfield Town, Stevenage Borough

224 **Sun** Football Quiz – **Answers**

1 Mark Palios **2** Alex Calvo-Garcia **3** Kuwait **4** Billy Meredith
5 Stephen Ireland **6** Syunsuke Nakamura **7** Kristine Lilly **8** Chris
Birchall (Port Vale) & Dennis Lawrence (Swansea) **9** Elgin City &
Peterhead **10** Pat Jennings; Alex Stepney

1 Tommy Tynan **2** Doncaster Rovers **3** Allan Clarke **4** Frank Swift
5 Eamonn Dunphy **6** Stockport County **7** The teams swapped ends,
as was the custom **8** 1986; none **9** Gordon Durie & 'Dixie' Deans
10 Hartlepool United, Sunderland

1 Woking **2** Gillingham **3** Eddie Hopkinson **4** Derek Dooley **5** Theo
Paphitis **6** Nicolas Anelka **7** Charles Alcock **8** Tony Popovic (Crystal
Palace) & Luke Wilkshire (Bristol City) **9** Bordeaux & St Etienne
10 Cardiff City & Reading

1 Norwich City **2** Martin Ling **3** Mark Atkins **4** Welsh Cup **5** Gordon
Watson **6** Neil Shipperley **7** Undertaker **8** Brazil; Gerry Hitchens **9** PSV
Eindhoven, Sporting Lisbon, FC Porto, Barcelona **10** Stern John;
Sunderland

1 West Ham United **2** Steve Cotterill **3** Mark Wright **4** He was Italy's
first black international **5** Ipswich Town **6** Jermaine Pennant **7** They all
have university degrees **8** Bob Crompton & Eddie Hapgood
9 Galatasaray & Benfica **10** Milene (Domingues); Ronaldo

1 Steve Moran **2** Jim Gannon **3** Ian Porterfield **4** Bob Hatton **5** Roy
Bentley **6** Peter Thompson **7** Jim Cumbes **8** Warren Feeney; Luton
Town **9** Clive Allen; Arsenal **10** Raich Carter; Hull City